# THE HOLLYWOOD STORY

## ROY PICKARD

CHARTWELL
BOOKS, INC.

**Photographic acknowledgments**

All photographs in this book are from The Kobal Collection, London, with the exception of the following: © The Walt Disney Company, Burbank, California/Kobal Collection, 69, 70/71, 140, 141, 142/143, 144/145; Roy Pickard, 67, 231; Frank Driggs, New York, 10, 14 bottom, 18, 19, 20, 23, 25, 32, 36, 38, 39, 40, 42, 50, 54, 57, 62, 76, 81, 82, 88, 90, 101, 105 bottom, 118, 137 bottom, 146, 168, 176, 177, 178 top, 187, 193 bottom, 204, 237; Roy Pickard, 14 top, 63, 66, 67, 79, 93 bottom, 102, 108, 111, 115 bottom, 119 top and bottom, 122, 124, 128, 133, 136, 150, 154, 156, 158, 159, 166 top, 167, 170, 186, 193 top, 195, 196 bottom, 205, 214, 222, 223, 230, 233, 239, 240, 244, 245; © Universal City Studios 251

Front cover: *There's No Business Like Show Business*. Stars, from left to right: Johnnie Ray, Mitzi Gaynor, Dan Dailey, Ethel Merman, Donald O'Connor, Marilyn Monroe. Twentieth Century-Fox/Sol C. Siegel, 1954 (Kobal Collection, London)

Titlespread: Filming of *Camille* with Greta Garbo, MGM 1936 (Frank Grimes, Kobal Collection, London)

Back cover: Christopher Reeve in *Superman*, Warner Bros./Alexander Salkind, 1978 (Kobal Collection, London)

For copyright reasons this edition is for sale only within the U.S.A.

This edition published 1986 by
Chartwell Books, Inc.
A division of Book Sales, Inc.
110 Enterprise Avenue
Secaucus, New Jersey 07094

Prepared by
The Hamlyn Publishing Group Limited
Bridge House, Twickenham, Middlesex TW1 3SB, England
London · New York · Sydney · Toronto

Copyright © 1986 The Hamlyn Publishing Group Limited
ISBN 1-55521-021-X

Printed in Italy

# CONTENTS

# Introduction

This book, I should emphasize, is not a catalogue or a reference book. It is a volume that tells a story – a story that rivals the most intriguing and colourful of the 20th century; the rise and fall and rise again of Hollywood.

It's a story that is made up of great films and legendary names. The great stars from Garbo and Gable, Bogart and Monroe to those superstars of the present, the producers, directors and the writers, and the ruthless moguls such as MGM boss Louis B. Mayer and Columbia's Harry Cohn are all here, rubbing shoulders as the Hollywood Story unfolds year by year, decade by decade, proceeding from the first faltering talkies at Warner Bros some 60 years ago to the modern cinema of Steven Spielberg and George Lucas. To encapsulate an entire history in just over 250 pages has not been an easy task but it has been a fascinating one and what follows on these pages will, I hope, provide at least a feeling and the flavour of the golden days of Hollywood as it was and as it is today.

I have concentrated mainly on the nine major studios that made Hollywood such a household name across the world: MGM, Paramount, Twentieth Century-Fox, Columbia, Warner Bros., Universal, RKO, United Artists and Walt Disney. Through their development I have traced the history of Hollywood from its golden years through the 1960s, when it underwent a change of image, and up until the present day. Whenever possible, I have personalized the story, and I have told it chronologically, highlighting in each chapter a Hollywood studio at a key moment, and interweaving from one chapter to the next the stories of the ruthless moguls and their stars.

The book is based, in part, on two trips I made to Hollywood in the 1980s to meet and interview many of the stars and directors who worked in Hollywood, and to see for myself the huge studios where so many of the great films were produced. Apart from RKO, they are all still operating, even though many of their giant sound stages are now occupied as much with television films and soap operas as they are with films for the big screen.

But the ghosts still linger. The writers' building in *Sunset Boulevard* can still be seen on the Paramount lot and the huge outdoor tank used by Cecil B. DeMille for his spectaculars still stands ready for action. Harry Cohn's office is still preserved as a kind of shrine at Columbia on Gower Street, the precise walkways at Disney including Dopey Drive are as neat as ever and there are reminders of the huge outdoor sets of *Hello Dolly* at Fox. And at Burbank the hills still overlook the sound stages of Warner Bros.

*The Hollywood Story* has, as they used to say in the movie colony, 'just about everything but the kitchen sink'. It has glamour, superstars, scandal, tragedy, vulgarity, power struggles, excitement and a cast of thousands. Until you can pay a visit to Hollywood and glimpse for yourself something of the wonders of MGM, Paramount, Universal and the rest, it is hoped that this book will provide you with many hours of pleasure and entertainment. So sit back and relax – the show starts now . . . .

*It all looks so simple on the big screen but this shot of a movie being made at Culver City indicates just how complicated a job putting a film together really is.*

# 1927

# Warner Bros.

## The Beginnings of Sound

'This 100 per cent talkie is 100 per cent crude!' On the face of it this *Variety* review for the first all-talking picture wasn't a very auspicious beginning for the modern cinema as we know it today, but that scathing notice was indeed how it all started, back on 7 July 1928.

The film that was so mercilessly hammered by *Variety* was called *Lights of New York*. It was only 57 minutes long and hardly boasted a cast of any great significance – Helene Costello, Cullen Landis and Gladys Brockwell featuring in the leading roles. But the fact that it *was* the first all-talkie made it

all-important as far as audiences were concerned. They ignored *Variety*'s warning and flocked to see the film in their thousands, not only in New York where it first opened at the Mark Strand Theater, but all over the United States.

The studio that produced it was Warner Bros. and it too was not overly concerned about the downbeat notice. It might well have been more worried had it been used to describe its first part-talkie, the Al Jolson musical *The Jazz Singer*, when it had premièred just nine months earlier on 6 October 1927. Had that particular film been taken

*Lights of New York (1928), a tale of gangsters and leggy showgirls and the first all-talkie produced by Warner Bros.*

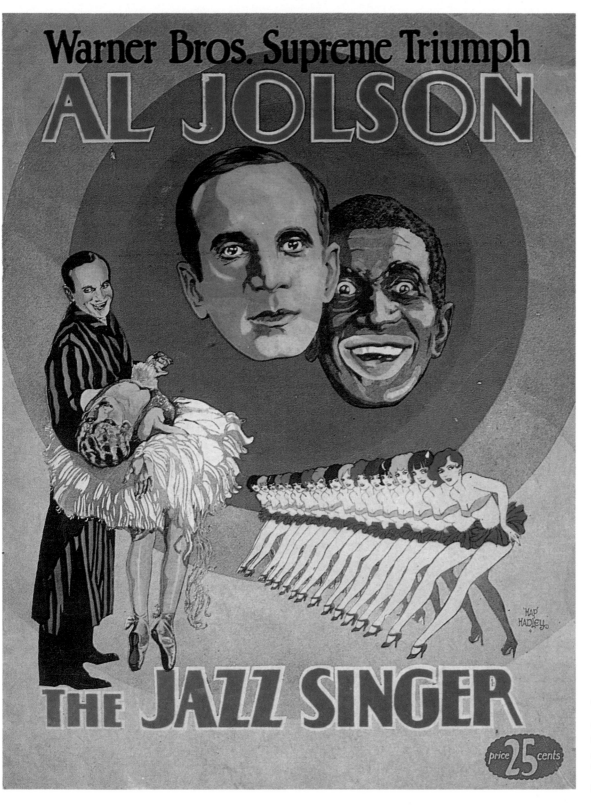

The Jazz Singer (*Warner Bros.*, 1927), *the movie that signalled the end of one era and the beginning of another. 'You ain't heard nothing yet,' said Jolson, and he was right.*

apart by the critics, the Warner studio might have foundered and movie history might have taken a very different course.

However, *The Jazz Singer* didn't flop. It was a resounding success, and by the summer of 1928, Warners realized that they were home and dry and had stolen a march on the other studios, most of whom had regarded Warners' painstaking two-year experiment with sound with a kind of amused tolerance, convinced that sound movies would be nothing more than an overnight gimmick. When *The Jazz Singer* and *Lights of New York* proved otherwise, they were caught on the hop and forced to rush their own 'talkies' into

production. And this time, it was the turn of the four Warner brothers – Harry, Albert, Jack and Sam, all of whom had been in movies since the first years of the century – to sit back and smile. They were suddenly the 'in' people of Hollywood and their studio became just as abruptly one of the most famous in the world.

Most film history books record the October première of *The Jazz Singer* as the real starting point of the modern movie, but although it did indeed demonstrate the possibilities of the spoken word and singing on film, it contained no more than 281 words of dialogue (five of them being the immortal

The 'talkie pioneers' – (left to right) writer Darryl F. Zanuck, music director Louis Silvers, composer Irving Berlin, director Lloyd Bacon, star Al Jolson and studio executives Jack and Albert Warner.

'You ain't heard nothing yet!') and just a handful of songs. For the rest of its running time, this schmaltzy tale of a cantor's son who decides on a Broadway career against his rabbi father's wishes was silent.

For the Warner Studio, *Lights of New York*, for all its crudity, was much more important. A story of two men who leave their upstate home to set up a barber shop in New York City and subsequently become involved with bootleggers, it was a mixture of crime, melodrama and backstage musical, entertainment forms that either by accident or design were to form the basis of the company's most successful movies of the Thirties. The film's prologue stated that 'This is a story of Main Street and Broadway – a story that could have been taken out of last night's newspapers.' The faltering dialogue that followed contained at least one line that was destined to be

repeated many times over the years, the declaration 'I'm gonna take him for a ride!'

In production as a two-reel silent at the time of *The Jazz Singer*, *Lights of New York* was gradually enlarged at the insistence of director Bryan Foy. It finished up as a seven-reeler with a budget of $75,000 – a lot of money for a piece of 'crudity' lasting less than an hour. The crudity paid off, however: *Lights of New York* earned Warner Bros. close to $2 million. The studio's claim in their advertisements that it would 'revolutionize the industry' was more than justified.

It took another two years for Warners to take up crime films seriously. In the interim, they turned their hands to just about every other form of entertainment they thought would show a profit. They were never slow in informing the public (and their Hollywood competitors) that they had scored another 'first'. For instance the 1929 *On with the Show*, with Sally O'Neil and Joe E. Brown, was advertised proudly as the first all-colour (i.e. two-colour) musical, while *The Terror* (1928), a little-known thriller about a maniacal killer who terrorizes the inhabitants of an old English inn, was hailed as the film with talking all the way through . . . even through the credits. The man called upon to read the latter was Conrad Nagel, who delivered his lines clad in tails, opera cape and domino mask!

However, it wasn't long before crime, crooks and the sudden burst of machine-gun fire, coupled with the staccato delivery of the gangsters themselves, became the studio's trademark. Stories snatched from contemporary headlines became the byword, strongly suggesting that *Lights of New York* might have had more influence than had at first appeared.

The man who did the snatching was not Jack L. Warner who headed the production side of things in Hollywood. Nor was it either of the two remaining Warner brothers Harry and Albert, Sam having died just before the première of *The Jazz Singer* in 1927. It was a young 28-year-old whiz-kid named Darryl F. Zanuck, who had joined Warners in 1923 as a staff screenwriter and story editor. His job was to outline stories and write titles for much of the studio's product, especially the silent films of Rin Tin Tin, the handsome German shepherd dog whose movies made enormous profits for Warners in the days immediately preceding sound.

The Rin Tin Tin films appeared at the rate of three or four a year, which meant that Zanuck was kept busy. He was a talented writer on whom Warners could rely to deliver the goods, and he was also fast. In fact, he delivered his scripts so quickly that he was forced by Warners to adopt pseudonyms lest people thought that Zanuck and not the Warners were really running the studio. Thus Zanuck featured on the credits as 'Melville Crossman', a name he used for 'class' pictures, as 'Gregory Rogers' for comedies and as 'Mark Canfield', which he reserved for the melodramas and the Rin Tin Tin films.

Zanuck's zest, energy and vigour paid dividends. He was just 27 when Jack Warner made him head of production at the studio, even though his youth was something that worried the studio chief. 'Well, you're in,' Warner told Zanuck in 1929, 'but even if you don't need glasses, get some window panes and grow a moustache. It'll give you a little age!'

Zanuck's stay at Warners lasted for four more years (1929-33), and it was during that period that the Warner style really evolved.

Social protest films (brought on by the early effects of the Depression) went hand in hand with the crime melodramas as the studio came of age. Action was the name of the game, and the tough stuff became Warners' bread and butter. Everything from top Edward G. Robinson and James Cagney vehicles to second-feature 'B' pictures had the same formula – action, snappy dialogue and stories pared to the bone.

Zanuck not only ensured that the films were put into production, he also searched for the stories and themes. Highly conscious of the importance of the writer's role in the newly arrived sound cinema, he delved avidly through novels, newspapers and magazine articles. His stumbling across an item in a

*Rin-Tin-Tin, arguably the most appealing Warner star of the 1920s. Between 1921 and 1930 he featured in nearly 30 movies for the studio.*

1929 issue of *Reader's Digest* led to the beginning of the famous Warners' gangster cycle of the Thirties. The article mentioned that 486 gangsters had been killed in the previous year. Zanuck realized that, with proper handling and some talented directors behind the camera, Warner Bros. could make both big money *and* good movies out of stories devoted to crime.

One novel in particular caught his eye – *Little Caesar* by W. R. Burnett. Syndicated in 82 American newspapers, it stood out from others of its kind and was written in a clipped Hemingway-like prose. Urged on by Mervyn LeRoy, a top director at the studio, Zanuck purchased the book, and the result was one of the first gangster classics of the screen. It was a brutal story of the rise and fall of a small-time hoodlum, based loosely on the career of Al Capone and starring Edward G. Robinson, whose last line in the movie – 'Mother of

God, is this the end of Rico?' – belongs with the most quoted last liners in all cinema.

Far from being a tough guy, in real life Edward G. Robinson was the mildest of men. It is not generally known that he was absolutely terrified when he was called upon to fire a gun, and LeRoy had to try and persuade him not to squeeze his eyes shut in fright when he was supposed to be looking tough. He didn't always succeed, but none the less, Robinson's performance remains a milestone in the history of gangster movies.

Robinson was the first of the studio's two tough guys of the early 1930s. James Cagney, who appeared in *Doorway to Hell* in 1930 and in 1931 as *The Public Enemy*, (*Enemies of the Public* in UK), was the other. Slight, fleet of foot and looking as if he would soon explode and land a right to the jaw, Cagney emerged as an even bigger star than Robinson. His film persona was also tough but he took it one

*Edward G. Robinson as Rico Bandello in Mervyn LeRoy's* Little Caesar *(1930), the first Warner gangster film of the 1930s.*

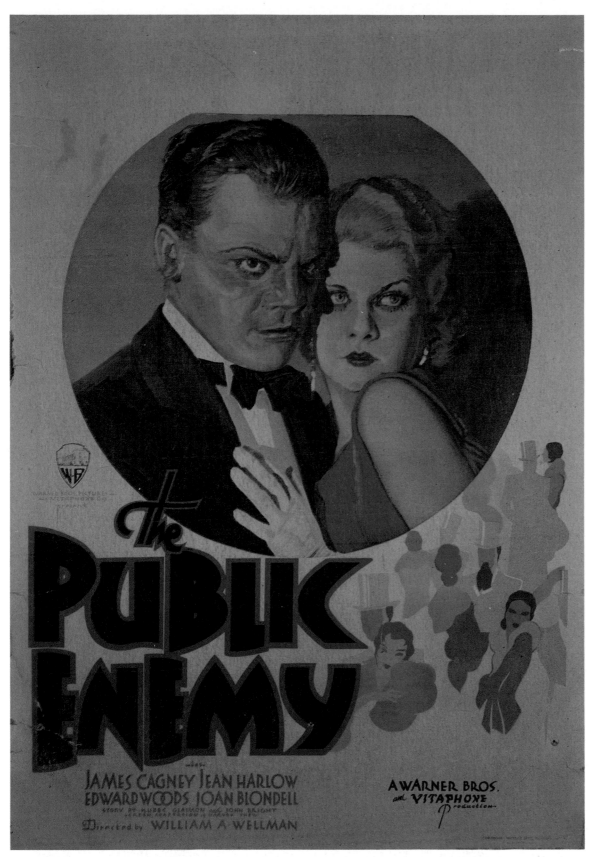

The Public Enemy (*Warner Bros., 1931*), *a movie 'snatched from the headlines', and the film that made James Cagney a star!*

stage further when he viciously shoved a grapefruit in the face of his screen girl-friend Mae Clarke. The film was *The Public Enemy* and the scene hit the headlines. Many people protested at its brutality, but the public loved it. The grapefruit incident was based on fact: a gangster named Hymie Weiss once hit his girl-friend in the face with an omelette!

In answer to criticism that Warners were starting an unhealthy trend with the gangster film, Zanuck – by then chief executive in charge of all productions for Warner Bros.

and First National, a once-powerful company that Warners had absorbed in 1929 – insisted that a written card be inserted at the beginning and end of *The Public Enemy*. This stated that James Cagney's gangster anti-hero, Tom Powers, and Robinson's Rico Bandello were problems that 'we, the public, must solve'.

It was an astute move, for the United States was by then in the grip of the worst economic Depression the world had ever seen, and crime, especially in Chicago, was rampant.

Warners fed on the crime and also on the social injustice the Depression produced notably when it filmed Mervyn LeRoy's *I Am a Fugitive from a Chain Gang* (1932) and exposed the injustices of the penal system in the American South. Paul Muni starred as an innocent man who is sentenced to imprisonment in the South, escapes and finishes his life as a fugitive from justice. His final line, in answer to the heroine's question of how he has survived, is 'I steal!' and then the screen fades into darkness. The great power of the film stemmed from the fact that it did not have a happy ending. Its release brought about such an outcry that reforms were made in the prison system in Georgia.

By 1932, Warners were producing some of the most challenging films in Hollywood. In the six years after the première of *The Jazz Singer*, they had lost their biggest moneymaking star of the Twenties, Rin Tin Tin (who had appeared in more than 20 films between 1923 and 1930, earning in excess of $5 million for his owner Leland Duncan), but they had gained Cagney, Robinson and Muni. Also entering the limelight was a young Bette Davis who, in the 1932 production *Cabin in the Cotton*, delivered one of her most famous lines: 'Ah'd love t' kiss ya, but ah jes washed mah hayuh.'

The nucleus was there for a star line-up that was eventually to compete with those of Metro-Golwyn-Mayer and Paramount. In 1931 and 1932, Warners were operating on perhaps three of their five cyclinders, but they were on the move. From being a studio that, in the early Twenties, had been struggling to keep solvent, it had finally broken into the big time and, just as important, it had achieved a certain style. Once Cagney and Robinson (and behind the scenes, Zanuck) arrived on the scene, cinema audiences throughout the world started to become aware of just what that famous trademark – the shield with accompanying fanfare – was beginning to represent.

*Girl gets grapefruit! James Cagney gives Mae Clarke the rough treatment in* The Public Enemy *(Warner Bros., 1931).*

*Victim Paul Muni in* I am a Fugitive from a Chain Gang *(1933), an early example of Warner's social protest movies.*

## Universal

### Gothic Horror: Karloff and Lugosi

If Warners discovered their true identity by developing the talkies, Universal tended to re-establish and improve on theirs. As Warners headed for crime, Universal plumped for horror!

Not that they discovered the commercial advantages of sound horror movies immediately. Between 1928 and 1930, they wavered uncertainly, producing just about every kind of film to cash in on the talkie boom. Their first all-talkie – a romantic drama entitled *Melody of Love* (1928) – was a very mediocre affair. It starred Walter Pidgeon and was shot in exactly seven days because the sound equipment loaned to the studio by Movietone had to be returned to its owners after a week. It was hardly of 'Grade A' calibre, and neither were the box-office returns.

Universal's early musicals were also disappointments. Harry Pollard's first version of *Show Boat* (1929), starring Laura La Plante and Joseph Schildkraut, was only part-talkie (it was filmed as a silent with the songs and dialogue added later); *Melody Lane* (1929), the studio's first all-sound musical, was a hackneyed weepie starring minstrel Eddie Leonard; and the $1 million version of the Phillip Dunning/George Abbott stage hit *Broadway* (1929), although elaborately presented and containing two-colour Technicolor sequences, lacked the then vital ingredient to make it a success – star names.

The studio's one major triumph of the period came right out of the blue when Lewis Milestone directed a screen version of Erich Maria Remarque's classic anti-war novel *All Quiet on the Western Front* (1930). In fact, it was so accomplished a film that it didn't really seem to belong in the Universal stable. A bleak, bitter cry against the horror of modern warfare, it followed the experiences of a group of German youths who volunteer to serve the Fatherland during the Great War only to find themselves disillusioned by the endless death and misery surrounding them in the trenches. By the film's close – a famous one in which the hero, Lew Ayres, is shot by a sniper while reaching for a butterfly – all have been killed and replaced by a new set of volunteers. Deservedly hailed as a great film, *All Quiet on the Western Front* did much for Universal's prestige and even managed to put the studio's name on the role of honour at Academy Awards' time by winning Oscars for best film of the year and best direction.

It was, however, an isolated quality success, and Universal, under the aegis of their benevolent boss, German-born 'Uncle' Carl Laemmle (a former book-keeper in a Wisconsin clothing store who had helped found Universal back in 1912), decided not to compete with other studios in the quality market. They also decided against a policy of building a roster of star names. Instead, they aimed their sights a little lower down the scale – at the horror market – and cut their cloth accordingly. In the Twenties, when the great Lon Chaney had appeared in the classics *The Hunchback of Notre Dame* (1923) and *The Phantom of the Opera* (1925), the genre had served them well, and as the Thirties got under way, the horror film was again to reward them, this time beyond their wildest dreams.

The first film they decided to put before the cameras was a version of Bram Stoker's

"ALL QUIET ON THE WESTERN FRONT"

*story by*
ERICH MARIA REMARQUE

with
LOUIS WOLHEIM · LEWIS AYRES
JOHN WRAY · RAYMOND GRIFFITH
A CARL LAEMMLE Jr. Production
Adaptation and Dialogue by Maxwell Anderson and George Abbott
A UNIVERSAL PICTURE

*Presented by*
CARL
LAEMMLE
*Directed by*
LEWIS
MILESTONE

*The winner of Universal's first Oscar for best picture – Lewis Milestone's devastating anti-war story of the First World War,* All Quiet on the Western Front *(1930).*

vampire novel *Dracula* (1931). It was an eerie tale about a mysterious count whose taste for human blood turns him into a blood-sucking fiend at night, and whose lonely Transylvanian castle became the stuff of which nightmares are made – just the kind of film, in fact, to kick off a brand new horror cycle. The story had been filmed once before (by the German director F. W. Murnau in 1922) but, because of copyright problems, under a different title – *Nosferatu the Vampire* – so to all commercial intents and purposes, Universal's 1931 *Dracula* was the first film version of the tale.

The Hungarian actor Bela Lugosi became the first to essay a sound portrait of the dreaded vampire count. He'd already played the role on the New York stage in a loose adaptation produced in 1927, so he was not exactly an original piece of casting. However, this in no way prepared Universal for the huge audience reaction to his sinister performance. He induced shudders whenever he appeared, and when he uttered the words 'I never drink . . . wine!' he brought to women not only a chill of horror but also a thrill of sexual excitement. Universal seemed to be well

aware of the sexual connotations of the story when they advertised it as 'the story of the strangest passion the world has ever known!'

*Dracula* made Lugosi a major star. So popular was he that he received as many fan letters as the great romantic screen idols of the time, 97 per cent of them from women. If he'd agreed to play the monster in Universal's *Frankenstein* (1931), he might well have remained a major star for many years. At first he was tempted by the role, but when he saw the make-up devised by Jack Pierce, he recoiled at the idea, stating that it made him look like some huge green Golem, and that under all the paint and putty, he would be unrecognizable. He was, he argued, now a star and he didn't want his features to be completely hidden throughout an entire movie.

It was a mistake he later regretted, for it brought to Universal an actor who was quickly to supersede him as the studio's number one horror attraction. He was an Englishman whose real name was William Pratt but who in Hollywood was known, rather more colourfully, as Boris Karloff. He had been around for years playing character

Dracula, *Universal's St. Valentine's Day release for 1931.*

*'The strangest passion the world has ever known!' Bela Lugosi and sleeping victim-to-be in* Dracula *(Universal, 1931).*

*The face that caused a thousand nightmares – Boris Karloff's monster in James Whale's* Frankenstein *(Universal, 1931).*

parts (nearly 70 at all the major studios), and by the time *Frankenstein* came along, he had almost certainly resigned himself to playing character parts for the rest of his life. But the fates were with him in 1931. When director James Whale saw the results of his screen test, he knew immediately that Karloff was the man for the part of Mary Shelley's grotesque monster – a creature put together by the obsessed Baron Frankenstein from parts of dead bodies stolen from churchyards and hospital dissecting rooms.

Karloff was both delighted and surprised that he had landed the part. He certainly had no idea that he and not Lugosi, who from the mid-1930s began a tragic slide into mediocre 'B' pictures, would become the king of horror and remain so for a quarter of a century. 'It was a fascinating role,' he said of the Frankenstein monster, which he played on three occasions for Universal – *Frankenstein* (1931), *The Bride of Frankenstein* (1935), *Son of*

*Frankenstein* (1939) – 'for the creature had no speech and hardly any intelligence, yet you had to convey the sense of the tragic. Half-a-dozen actors tested for the part but I was the lucky one. I say "lucky" because any one of them would have played the part as well as I did – and would also have reaped the benefits that came to me.'

He did, however, often baulk at the time-consuming and uncomfortable make-up he had to endure every day on set: 'Despite the fact that the picture made me, it was rather a horrible experience. The make-up was quite an ordeal. I had to arrive at the studio every morning at 5.30 and spend three-and-a-half hours in the make-up chair getting ready for the day's work. The make-up itself was quite painful, particularly the putty used on my eyes. There were many days when I thought I would never be able to hold out until the end of the day, but somehow or other I always did.'

*Frankenstein's mate: a screeching Elsa Lanchester in Whale's satirical sequel,* The Bride of Frankenstein *(Universal, 1935).*

*Frankenstein* cost Universal $250,000 to make and went on to gross $12 million. Within the space of just six months, the studio had produced two horror classics, created two household names in Lugosi and Karloff and, most important of all from their point of view, earned for themselves very healthy profits indeed. It wasn't too surprising, therefore, that the order went out from Laemmle for more of the same. Actors, directors, writers and cameraman were all assembled to develop and profit from a genre that had turned out to be a veritable goldmine.

And Universal were by no means slow in putting new horror movies into production. Just a year after appearing as Dracula, Lugosi was back in *Murders in the Rue Morgue*, this time as Dr. Mirakle, another 'Mr. Sinister', whose speciality was injecting gorilla blood into beautiful women in order to prove they were derived from – gorillas! Karloff's 1932 assignment, *The Mummy*, was somewhat different. Once again his features were hidden as he played the 3,700-year-old Egyptian priest

Imhotep who was walled up alive and accidentally brought back to life by an English archaeologist. His slow snapping of his bonds and the first opening of his eyes were the stuff of pure horror. 'He went for a little walk,' babbled the archaeologist, pointing insanely to the empty space in the tomb.

A year later, Universal asked director James Whale to follow his success with *Frankenstein* and his version of J. B. Priestley's *The Old Dark House* (1932), by filming what seemed, on the face of it, an impossible subject: H. G. Wells' novel *The Invisible Man*. Whale, however, overcame all the obstacles and succeeded brilliantly, not least in his very imaginative use of trick photography. And if Lugosi had earlier suffered doubts about appearing under monster make-up, British star Claude Rains had no such qualms about accepting the role of Wells' mad scientist, even though it meant that his performance amounted to not much more than a radio portrayal. In fact, Rains' debut remains one of the most unusual in all cinema. Heard but not seen until the final reel, he played Jack Griffin

*Universal's* The Mummy *(1932) starring Boris Karloff – seen here with Zita Johann – as a 3,700-year-old Egyptian priest brought back to life by an English archaeologist.*

*A doubtful Una O'Connor can't quite believe it but* The Invisible Man *(Universal, 1933) it is. Hiding beneath the overcoat? Claude Rains.*

as a man who thoroughly enjoys his powers of invisibility before developing an acute case of megalomania. 'We'll start with a few murders,' he says. 'Big men. Little men. Just to show we make no distinction.'

Universal's golden age of horror lasted for most of the Thirties. In their own way, pictures such as *The Black Cat* (1934), *The Raven* (1935) and *The Invisible Ray* (1936), all of which teamed Karloff with Lugosi, did as much as the comedies and musicals produced by other studios to stave off the misery of the bread queues. What they presented inside the theatres was just as frightening as what was going on outside them, but it was make-believe fright and it managed to keep the Depression blues at bay for at least 90 minutes or so.

Universal produced antidotes to their horror fare of course. In 1930, for instance, they produced the all-star two-colour Technicolor musical *King of Jazz*, the film in which Bing Crosby made his first screen appearance as one of 'The Rhythm Boys'. The studio also

filmed a series of distinguished soap operas, many of them directed with great skill by John Stahl, who guided several fine actresses through tear-stained scripts: Irene Dunne in *Back Street* (1932) and in a version of Lloyd C. Douglas's *Magnificent Obsession* (1935), Margaret Sullavan in *Only Yesterday* (1933) and Claudette Colbert in *Imitation of Life* (1934). At times audiences seemed to enjoy the tears almost as much as they did the terrifying goings-on of Karloff & Co.

However, in the Thirties there was no doubt that it was horror that kept Universal alive. Later in the decade, the studio would decline as the appeal of the horror film began to wane and they would struggle for many years before they would make it back into the major league. But while Boris Karloff and Bela Lugosi and director James Whale and cameraman Karl Freund were around, the genre was, for the first time, taken seriously by both the public and critics alike. Horror came of age at Universal in the early 1930s.

# 1931
# Paramount

*Herbert Marshall and Kay Francis pictured with director Ernst Lubitsch on the set of* Trouble in Paradise *(Paramount, 1932).*

According to the studio's own publicity machine, in the 1930s a Paramount Picture meant that it was 'the best show in town' – and so, quite often, it was. However, that slick public-relations catchphrase really gives no hint as to what a Paramount picture was really like during that period.

The Paramount style certainly had little to do with crime thrillers or horror shows. Only rarely did the studio visit the underworld or open up the magical box of tricks of the make-up artist. Instead, theirs was a magic of a different kind, a make-believe world of elegance and escape, one notable for the fact that it was peopled by several remarkably talented European artists, among them Marlene Dietrich, Maurice Chevalier, director Ernst Lubitsch, production designer Hans Dreier and screenwriter Ernest Vajda.

Paramount put in front of its audience a sleek type of living that most people were never likely to see in real life, a world that glittered with luxury and fun, an elegant world made up of exotic romances, shimmering costumes, cocktails and ultra-modern apartments. More often than not this elegance and sophistication would be based in Paris, on the Riviera or in Spain, but an imaginative sleight of hand by Hans Dreier could quickly turn the Paramount backlot into any exotic corner of Europe if so desired. When he was asked whether he had been in Europe lately, ace Paramount director Ernst Lubitsch nodded and then added as an afterthought: 'But you know, I think I prefer Paris, Paramount, to Paris, France.'

And so too did the audiences who each week paid out their money at the box office to see a Paramount picture. They enjoyed not only the Paramount style but also the Lubitsch style, reflected in a series of witty, deft comedies that poked fun at people's weaknesses, vanity and illusions.

Maurice Chevalier and Jeanette MacDonald – *The Love Parade* (1929) and *One*

*Hour with You* (1932) – were just two of the many stars who worked for Lubitsch at Paramount in the Thirties. Others included Herbert Marshall, Miriam Hopkins and Kay Francis, who all appeared for the director in *Trouble in Paradise* (1932), as well as Charles Laughton who featured in one famous sequence of the short-story compendium *If I Had a Million* (1932), and Fredric March and Gary Cooper who starred in Lubitsch's version of Noel Coward's *Design for Living* (1933).

At the other end of the scale, there were the films of that master of the epic, Cecil B. DeMille; of action director Henry Hathaway, who frequently teamed up with Gary Cooper, notably in *The Lives of a Bengal Lancer* (1935); and of ex-vaudeville comedian W. C. Fields, who featured in a number of comedies including *Million Dollar Legs* (1932) and *Tillie and Gus* (1933). The latter is the movie in which Fields supposedly spiked child star Baby LeRoy's orange juice with gin. And of course there were the zany Marx Brothers, who started their film careers at the studio in such comedy escapades as *Animal Crackers* (1930), *Monkey Business* (1931) and *Duck Soup* (1933). In each one, the cigar-smoking Groucho excelled with the insults. Said he about the forever formidable Margaret Dumont: 'Remember, men, we're fighting for this woman's honour, which is probably more than she ever did.'

But it was a Paramount *partnership* that fascinated the public more than anything else – that between star Marlene Dietrich and director Josef Von Sternberg.

Von Sternberg first directed Dietrich in Germany in 1930 in the celebrated *The Blue Angel*. The film told the story of a middle-aged college professor (Emil Jannings) who becomes infatuated with, and is then completely destroyed by, a heartless cabaret singer. It was a harsh, sad and finally tragic movie and demanded a very special kind of actress for the role of the destructive Lola-Lola. Von Sternberg believed he had found her in the then relatively unknown Dietrich. Jannings, then one of the world's major stars, was unhappy with the choice and argued against her getting the part, but Von Sternberg insisted and was proved right. From the moment she first appeared on screen, Dietrich completely dominated the film.

Reclining on a barrel, a silk top hat perched nonchalantly on her head, her right leg pulled up seductively towards her breasts by two sensuous arms, she looked at the audience and sang the now famous melancholy refrain, 'Falling in love again, never wanted to. What am I to do? Can't help it.' High heels, suspendered stockings and a flash of white thigh produced an effect of almost overwhelming sensuality. Not only did Jannings' professor (and Von Sternberg himself) fall for her charms, but so did most of the movie going public.

The Lola-Lola performance in *The Blue Angel* was Dietrich's passport to America

*Irresistible! Emil Jannings succumbs to the seductive charms of Marlene Dietrich in* The Blue Angel *(Paramount, 1930).*

EMIL JANNINGS
in "The Blue Angel"

WITH
MARLENE DIETRICH
DIRECTED BY
JOSEF VON STERNBERG
An ERICH POMMER Production
a Paramount Release
An UFA Picture

*Top billing for Emil Jannings, but the Dietrich legs have it in this poster for Josef Von Sternberg's 1930 production* The Blue Angel *(Paramount).*

where she carried on her partnership with Von Sternberg, a collaboration that became one of the most talked about in Hollywood. He was described as her Svengali; she refused to make films for any other director. Inevitably, there were rumours that the alliance was not just professional, that each of them, although married, was enjoying each other not only on screen but off it as well. The gossip-mongers crashed away at their typewriters,

and so intense did the rumours become that Von Sternberg's wife actually took out an action against Dietrich for alienating her husband's affections. Marlene, protesting her innocence, took up arms, fought and won.

Together, director and star made six films for Paramount, starting with *Morocco* in 1930 and ending with *The Devil Is a Woman* in 1935. Dietrich's striking beauty – the lips suggestive and slightly parted, the cheeks hollow, the eyes cool and unwavering – was extremely hypnotic, and her accent fascinating. Audiences couldn't keep their eyes off her. Broody, sensual and with a hint of mystery and cynicism, she was Paramount's answer to MGM's Garbo. Indeed, two of Dietrich's films – *Dishonored* (1931), in which she played a First World War streetwalker who becomes the notorious spy X27, and *The Scarlet Empress* (1934), in which she played Catherine the Great – were direct competitors to Garbo's *Mata Hari* and *Queen Christina*.

Dietrich's reign at the top at Paramount was, however, relatively short – no more than six years all told. She received an Oscar nomination for her first American role – as cabaret singer Amy Jolly in *Morocco* (1930) – and achieved a huge financial success with her third Hollywood film, *Shanghai Express* (1932), but after that, things began to slide. The reason for this remains obscure. It may have been that one Hollywood mystery woman (i.e. Garbo) was enough for any one decade. More probably it was because of the arrival at the studio of a young lady with an hour-glass figure and a very earthy sense of humour. Her name was Mae West, and she flaunted her appeal in such an obvious way that she left no doubt as to her intentions as far as sexual matters were concerned.

The arrival of Mae West at Paramount in 1932 quite literally 'saved' the studio, which had been edging towards bankruptcy because

*An Oscar-nominated Marlene Dietrich with legionnaire Gary Cooper in* Morocco *(Paramount, 1930).*

of the effects of the Depression. Dietrich's films were splendid-looking affairs, but apart from the early productions, they didn't make a profit. Mae West's did: they cost little and made a lot. Her first starring film, *She Done Him Wrong* (1933, a version of her stage play *Diamond Lil*), was shot in just 18 days at a cost of $200,000. Within just three months of its release, it had grossed more than *$2 million*, a huge amount at the height of the Depression.

Mae West's films were accused of being crude and vulgar, and they caused offence in any number of quarters. The Legion of Decency wanted to have her banned; the public did not. She wrote many of her lines herself and in any one of her films she could be counted on to come up with at least a dozen ripe, or over-ripe, wisecracks. Her supply of sexual innuendo, witticisms and *double entendres* seemed to be inexhaustible. In the 1934 *Belle of the Nineties*, for instance,

*The gal who saved a studio! Box-office star Mae West in* She Done Him Wrong *(Paramount, 1933).*

in which she played a saloon entertainer in love with two men, she wisecracked: 'A man in the house is worth two in the street.' And in the same film, she added for good measure: 'There are no good girls gone wrong, there are just bad girls found out.' In *Klondike Annie* (1936), she reasoned that 'Some men are all right in their place – if only they knew the right places,' and in *Go West, Young Man* (1936), she maintained that 'A thrill a day keeps the chill away.'

Like Dietrich, whose golden period at Paramount only ran from 1930 to 1935, Mae West's reign at the studio was also relatively short – 1932 to 1939 – but while she was there she proved to be a goldmine for Paramount's co-founder Adolph Zukor. She used sex to get laughs, and she got laughs from audiences all over the world. Even her billing outside movie houses was not without its humour: for *I'm No Angel* (1933), she was billed as 'a lady lion tamer who lost her reputation and never missed it!'

Sex had always been a key box-office ingredient of the movies, of course, even in the silent days, but very few used it as successfully as Paramount in the Thirties. Lubitsch handled sex in a subtle and sophisticated manner. Von Sternberg and Dietrich made it seem sultry and mysterious. Mae West turned it into something bawdy and enjoyable.

As for DeMille? Well, although he tended to trade in the more spectacular side of things in such films as *The Sign of the Cross* (1932) and *Cleopatra* (1934), he was by no means unaware of the potency of sex on the screen. Back in 1919, he had persuaded Gloria Swanson to take a nude (but discreet) dip in an ornate bath in *Male and Female*, and from that moment on did his best to include a bathtub scene in every one of his movies. Even in *The Sign of the Cross*, he didn't disappoint his audience, revealing as he did that Claudette Colbert had a more than shapely anatomy by having her bathe in a sunken pool of asses' milk. It was something that Miss Colbert found luxurious at first, but which quickly turned into an ordeal as the milk curdled into foul-smelling cheese after just two days' of shooting. None the less the sight of Miss Colbert, her lovely shoulders just visible above the massive expanse of white milk, proved to be as erotic an image as any conjured up by the Hollywood films of the Thirties.

The image of Paramount itself began to change as the decade drew ever closer to the 1940s. Sex was never far from the surface, but gradually that snow-capped mountain ringed with stars came to represent a somewhat different type of entertainment to that which

had been presented so successfully earlier in the decade. DeMille remained (as he was to for the rest of his career), but those who had helped mould the distinctive Paramount style of the early 1930s slowly began to leave the studio. The Marx Brothers left for pastures new at MGM, as did Lubitsch. Dietrich left the lot and also Mae West and W. C. Fields, Maurice Chevalier and Jeanette MacDonald.

In their stead came a new breed of stars headed by the crooning Bing Crosby and the wisecracking Bob Hope, and backed by such up-and-coming newcomers as Ray Milland, Dorothy Lamour, Fred MacMurray and Paulette Goddard. They, together with writer-director Billy Wilder and stars Alan Ladd and Veronica Lake, were to remould the Paramount image in the Forties. A Paramount picture would, once again, be hailed as 'the best show in town', but it would be a very different type of picture to that which followed that famous mountain trademark in the early Thirties.

*Cecil B. DeMille's 1932 epic* The Sign of the Cross. *Rome burns but that seems of minor significance compared with the other events highlighted by Paramount!*

# 1932
# Metro-Goldwyn-Mayer

## Mayer, Thalberg and
## 'More Stars Than There Are In Heaven'

Paramount might have claimed that their films were invariably the best shows in town, but in the early Thirties, the handsome productions of Metro-Goldwyn-Mayer were nearly always the most star-studded films on view. The studio's president, Nicholas Schenck, summed up the MGM philosophy in one succinct sentence: 'There's nothing wrong with this business that a star worth $10,000 a week won't cure.' The studio's publicity machine went even further, claiming that the studio had on its payroll 'more stars than there are in heaven!'

This was a slight exaggeration, but the Hollywood hyperbole put the message across with some style and other studio executives certainly weren't going to ask MGM to authenticate their claim. They could see with their own eyes that the studio had a star for just about every role: Greta Garbo for the women of mystery, Jean Harlow for the dumb blondes, Clark Gable for the rugged heroes, Joan Crawford for the sexy dames, Norma Shearer for the ladylike roles, and so on right across the Culver City lot. The other studios could only look on with envy as MGM paraded its stars through a roster of comedies and dramas and sophisticated entertainments that, in style and presentation at least, were second to none.

Never was the studio's star power more convincingly demonstrated than in 1932, when MGM released its film version of Vicki Baum's bestseller *Grand Hotel*. The film's plot was nothing out of the ordinary – it concentrated on the lives of some guests staying at a luxury Berlin hotel – but the star line-up most certainly was. Heading the list were John

Barrymore as a roguish, impoverished baron, his brother Lionel Barrymore as a bookkeeper suffering from an incurable disease and determined to enjoy one last fling, and Wallace Beery as a Prussian business tycoon. Following close behind were Joan Crawford as Beery's ambitious stenographer, Lewis Stone as a war-scarred physician and Jean Hersholt as the all-seeing hotel porter. And topping them all was Greta Garbo as a famous but ageing ballerina. It was in this film that she spoke the immortal words: 'I want to be alone.'

*Grand Hotel* marked the first occasion that any Hollywood studio had paraded as many as seven stars above its title. Usually, a film boasting three stars was deemed to be pretty good value, but a film with seven was quite a dazzling event. No one was surprised when *Grand Hotel* was named best picture of the year at Oscar time. Neither were they surprised that it was MGM who became the first Hollywood studio to display two best picture Oscars in its front office, the first having been won three years earlier for the musical *The Broadway Melody*.

As if to prove that the all-star cast was no fluke, MGM repeated the process the following year when it brought together another six top stars (among them Jean Harlow, Marie Dressler, John and Lionel Barrymore and Wallace Beery) for its version of the George S. Kaufman/Edna Ferbert stage play *Dinner at Eight*. The movie delved into the private lives of some of the dinner guests attending a party thrown by social climber Billie Burke, but it was Harlow who stole the show. At the film's close, she said to Dressler: 'I was reading a

book the other day. It's about civilization or something . . . Do you know the guy said machinery is going to take the place of every profession!' 'Oh, my dear,' replied Dressler, pausing to give Harlow the once-over, 'That's something you'll *never* have to worry about!'

During the early and mid-1930s, MGM certainly didn't have to worry about its profits or indeed any of its films. Its regular target was 52 movies a year and 52 top movies at that. If it had any problems at all, it was in finding enough suitable story material to match up with its huge galaxy of stars. When hard-up for a convincing story line, studio boss Louis B. Mayer and his talented young lieutenant Irving G. Thalberg overcame the problem by linking two of their most attract-

ive stars into a team. When one of those teams looked as though it might provide an on-going sexual chemistry, the two stars were cast together several times over.

Guiding the stars through their films was a squad of professional directors – headed by Victor Fleming, Robert Z. Leonard, Jack Conway, Clarence Brown and W. S. Van Dyke – who worked with supreme efficiency. Few of them were stylists, but that mattered little as far as Mayer and Thalberg were concerned. What did matter was that each one of the directors could bring in on time, and with the minimum of fuss, an attractive and smartly tailored piece of movie entertainment.

MGM movies invariably had a kind of

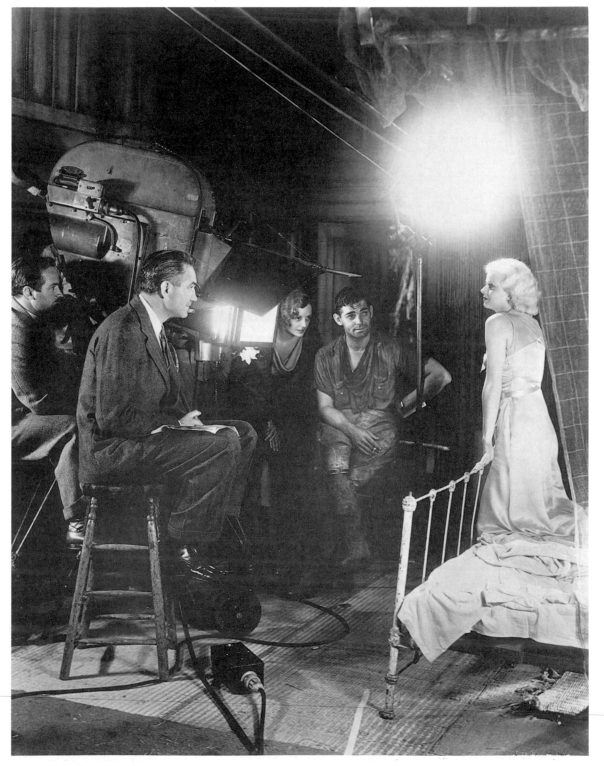

*Director Victor Fleming, Clark Gable and blonde bombshell Jean Harlow during the filming of* Red Dust *(MGM, 1932).*

 JOHNNY WEISSMULLER IN TARZAN AND HIS MATE

A Metro-Goldwyn-Mayer

Tarzan and His Mate
(1934), the second film in
MGM's long running 'Ape
Man' series. Johnny
Weismuller featured as
Tarzan, Maureen O'Sullivan
as Jane.

gloss and sheen about them. The stars were dressed in lavish gowns or elegant suits, photographed to perfection under shimmering lights and required to perform against a luxurious background of extravagant sets designed by Cedric Gibbons and his colleagues. One actor who experienced this deluxe treatment in 1931 was the 30-year-old Clark Gable. He was by no means a star at the beginning of the year, when he was sometimes only ninth on the cast list, but he most certainly was by the year's end when he co-starred with Joan Crawford in *Possessed* and Greta Garbo in *Susan Lennox: Her Fall and Rise*. In the 12 months of 1931, he served a vigorous and occasionally exhausting apprenticeship by appearing in some nine films for MGM. By 1932 he was established as one of the major stars in America.

By 1934, the handsome Robert Taylor had also joined the MGM payroll, Spencer Tracy had made his first picture at the studio and Johnny Weissmuller had become a permanent fixture as 'Tarzan the Ape Man'. William Powell and Myrna Loy had also joined up as the sophisticated sleuthing team, Nick and Nora Charles, enjoying cocktails and swapping one-liners as they investigated a complex series of murder cases in *The Thin Man* films. In 1935, the Marx Brothers increased MGM's star power even further by moving over from Paramount to appear in *A Night at the Opera*.

The men behind this energetic and never-ending search for stars were, of course, Mayer

and Thalberg. Both had been in at the birth of the studio in 1924 when the 38-year-old Mayer was made first vice-president and head of the studio and Thalberg, 14 years his junior, was named as vice-president in charge of production. Both were answerable to Nicholas Schenck, president of MGM's parent company Loew's Inc. in New York, but both ruled supreme on the Culver City lot and came in conflict with Schenck only when one of their pictures failed to make money, which wasn't often.

Thalberg was the most ambitious of the two – literate, thoughtful and quietly ruthless. He was the man who provided the studio with much of its class and much of its style. Mayer was exactly the opposite. A former scrap metal dealer, he enjoyed the power more than the pictures, and by the mid-Thirties, he was earning $1 million a year. His tastes, too, were very different to those of the cultured Thalberg: 'I like warm stories, sentimental entertainment,' he said. 'Sophisticates call that corn. All right, so it's corn. But what's wrong with good corn?'

Mayer also, rather surprisingly, had a touch of genius when it came to star-spotting. In the 1920s, he found a Swedish actress working in a German film studio. 'I think she's got something,' he said to his companions. 'Yeah, muscles,' they replied. 'So has Strangler Lewis!' Mayer ignored their doubts, signed her up, put her on a diet, gave her English lessons and starred her in such films as *Flesh*

A Night at the Opera
(MGM, 1935). Groucho,
Chico and Harpo Marx with
the long-suffering Margaret
Dumont, the regular butt of
their zany humour.

*and the Devil* (1927) and *Anna Christie* (1930). Later, after films such as *Mata Hari* (1931), *Queen Christina* (1933), *Anna Karenina* (1935) and *Camille* (1937), most people agreed that Greta Garbo did have 'a little something'.

By nature, Mayer was a violent vengeful man. He was heavily built and could easily lose control, once hurling a full ink bottle at a startled agent sitting across from him in his office. On another occasion, he literally threw himself across his desk, grabbed producer Walter Wanger by the lapels and began shaking him vigorously. He also laid out Sam Goldwyn with one punch at a Hollywood party, and even had a fist fight with Charlie Chaplin in a hotel corridor.

The main difference between Mayer and Thalberg, apart from the obvious ones of age and background, was that Mayer concerned himself mainly with profits while Thalberg lived, ate and slept movies. They were his life, 24 hours a day.

Married to the beautiful Norma Shearer, Thalberg was as able a lieutenant as any studio boss ever had, yet he was by no means a gambler. He always checked very carefully before purchasing a book or play for the studio. When he considered buying *Susan Lennox: Her Fall and Rise* for Greta Garbo, for example, he first consulted the three secretaries in his outer office because the novel had been out of print for ten years. When he discovered that all three women knew who Susan Lennox was, he bought the book.

Thalberg provided the public with films of artistry, taste and entertainment all rolled into one, and if at a preview he discovered that the public did not react as he had expected, he would take the film back to the studio for two weeks of retakes, when it would be reshaped, trimmed and sometimes given a happier ending. Hence the saying that, in the 1930s, MGM did not so much make films as remake them.

Thalberg had a consuming passion for getting things on screen his way, and at all costs. Never a well man, he suffered from a heart condition and was often so tired that he could hardly stand behind his desk when a film conference was due to begin. Yet he never once let up. He was acquainted with virtually every problem of every movie being shot on the lot, and when directors went to consult him about a difficult sequence, he would tell them within minutes just where they were going wrong.

The inevitable end result of Thalberg's overwork was a heart attack. It occurred in December 1932. He was stricken after a particularly rowdy Christmas party at the studio and ordered to take a year's sick leave in Europe. When Thalberg left for Europe Mayer wasn't entirely sorry. He had been worried for some time by Thalberg's growing influence at the studio and the all too frequent references to him being a 'boy genius' and the real power behind the throne at MGM. Mayer had become much too fond of his own all-powerful position to let anything jeopardize it. The possibility that MGM might, even before the end of the decade, emerge as something closer to Metro-Goldwyn-*Thalberg* had crossed his mind several times. But, with Thalberg out of the way and his son-in-law David O. Selznick safely installed at a temporary replacement, he found that he could breathe easily again and concentrate once more on his grosses – and of course his stars!

*The beautiful face of tragedy. Greta Garbo in Rouben Mamoulian's* Queen Christina *(MGM, 1933).*

# 1933
## RKO

### Astaire and Rogers and King Kong

The RKO studio, nestling between Columbia and the mighty Paramount on 780 Gower Street, Los Angeles, could hardly claim to be in the same league as MGM, and certainly couldn't boast more stars than there were in heaven. In fact, in 1933, it was difficult for it to put together more than half-a-dozen performers who could truly be called stars – and one of those was an ape! However, that ape, all 40 feet of it, plus a couple of young dancers, were enough to put the studio on a sound financial basis for the rest of the decade.

As it turned out, 1933 was a lucky year and a vital one for a company that had begun life in 1928, having grown out of one of those complicated mergers that Hollywood used to favour so much. The companies involved were FBO (Film Booking Office of America), which had begun life as the British company, Robertson-Cole; its purchaser, the Radio Corporation of America; and the Keith–Albee–Orpheum vaudeville circuit, which the corporation merged with FBO. What emerged from all this complicated and feverish business activity was the RKO studio. It was a complicated birth, but as usual, the Hollywood promotion men did their best to make it sound simpler as well as dynamic: 'The radio titan opens the curtains of the clouds and a new greater year dawns for the most spectacular show machine of all time!'

Not surprisingly, things didn't quite live up to such a spectacular billing, not for a bit anyway. In its first four years, the studio struggled along in the wake of MGM and Paramount and the emerging Warner Bros., enjoying only the occasional, isolated hit. The

musical version of the hit Ziegfeld show *Rio Rita* (1929), starring Bebe Daniels and John Boles, was one such success; *Hit the Deck*, released a year later and containing such hit numbers as 'Sometimes I'm Happy' and 'Hallelujah', was another. Most surprising of all was the studio's production of Edna Ferber's bestseller *Cimarron* (1931). In terms of size and scope, the film belonged more to one of the bigger studios, and many people shook their heads in disbelief when they learned that it had been produced at RKO. The last laugh, however, went to RKO. The movie earned an Academy Award for best picture, grossed an enormous $2.5 million at the box office and established Richard Dix and Irene Dunne as two of the most popular stars of the year.

*Cimarron* was a long saga, spanning some 60 years, telling of the rise of an Oklahoma town from its settlement to its development into a thriving city in the centre of one of the richest oilfields in the world. The spectacular highlight of the film was the famous real-life 'Cherokee Strip' landrush, when pioneers made a frenzied stampede in wagons, on horseback, on foot and even on bicycles to claim two million acres of free government land. Offscreen, on the night of 10 November 1931, the achievement of *Cimarron* was equally spectacular. When it won its Academy Award, it outstripped such fancied competitors as MGM's *Trader Horn*, Paramount's *Skippy* and Howard Hughes' much acclaimed adaptation of *The Front Page*. To this day, it remains the only western to have won the award for best picture.

However, the occasional hit and award-winning film from more than 50 movies

produced by the studio each year was not enough to make a secure economic base and, during its early years, RKO was anything but financially stable. In fact, financial crisis rather than financial success was more the order of the day in the early Thirties.

Help was at hand, however, for in 1933, everything changed. *King Kong* appeared on the screen although even he, immortal though he is nowadays, was not immediately seen as an automatic RKO saviour. When it was first suggested that a film be made of his adventures, the project was not looked upon favourably by the RKO executives who, after producer Merian C. Cooper told them the story, blinked and reached shakily for their whiskies. The tale they were told was of a giant 40-foot ape who is captured on a remote island off the African coast and then taken back to New York as a sideshow attraction. When he runs amok through the city streets, he is tracked to the Empire State Building, which he climbs to escape his tormentors. There he is finally gunned to death by buzzing planes and plunges to the streets below.

It wasn't the story that dismayed the RKO executives so much; it was more the cost of the venture. They argued that RKO was in no fit financial position to gamble on such an elaborate fantasy which, because of its vast number of special effects, would cost a fortune. Soap operas featuring Irene Dunne, Kay Francis and Ann Harding were acceptable and indeed earned the studio small profits. Even livelier, more realistic vehicles starring spunky newcomer Katharine Hepburn – *A Bill of Divorcement* (1932), *Morning Glory* (1933) – were within the studio's scope, as were occasional, small-scale comedies. But *King Kong*, based though it was on an original story by the hugely popular Edgar Wallace, seemed much too big a risk.

Producer Cooper realized that he had quite a fight on his hands. He enlisted the help of David O. Selznick (production head at the studio from November 1931 to December 1932) and together they decided to make a test reel of *King Kong* to show the powers-that-be just what they had in mind. This contained a sequence showing Kong shaking a tree tunk and tipping some luckless sailors

*The Oklahoma landrush! A spectacular highlight from RKO's epic western* Cimarron *(1931).*

into a chasm as well as Kong's subsequent battle with the allosaurus, a scene that had been photographed with a combination of Willis O'Brien's unique model animation and other special techniques. The plan worked. The whisky was once again brought out but this time with enthusiasm, and the project was given the go-ahead. The final cost was an over-budget $650,000 but the extra expense was worth it: *King Kong* eventually earned RKO over $4 million.

The appeal of *King Kong* lay not so much in the fact that it was a monster-cum-horror movie, but because audiences all over the world tended to side with Kong in his predicament. During the final scene, when the poor beast lay dead in the New York streets, the tears simply streamed down the faces of audiences as they listened to the film's final line: 'It wasn't the airplanes, it was beauty that killed the beast.'

The beauty referred to was played by Fay Wray, who was by then something of a dab hand at featuring (and screaming) in horror films. She attracted the amorous attentions of the giant ape quite early on in the movie, and spent much of the time being cuddled and stroked in his massive furry paw. The fact that she appeared to be sexually enjoying some of the furry fondling caused the censor

*The tallest and darkest leading man of the 1930s: the mighty* King Kong *(RKO, 1933)! His co-star: a terrified Fay Wray!*

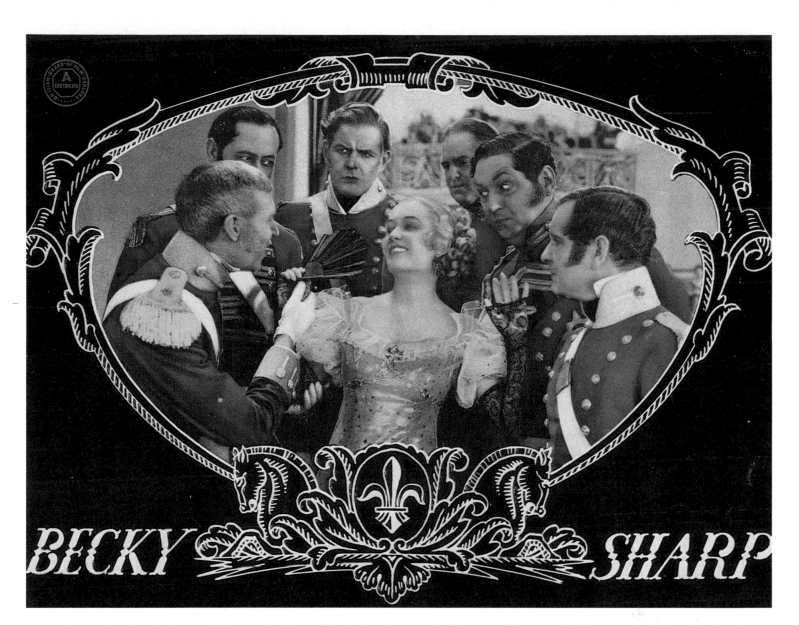

BECKY SHARP

more than a few headaches, which resulted in the deletion of several of the offending scenes.

In reality, Kong was quite small, just 18 inches high. He was not one but several models, all built of rubber and sponge and covered with shaggy lambskin. Articulated metal frames allowed movements of the limbs, mouth and eyes, and a 20-foot high bust of Kong's head and shoulders was used for close-ups. A mechanical hand and arm about 8 feet long was employed in the scenes in which Fay Wray was seen in Kong's grasp.

*King Kong* broke all records when it opened in New York at the city's two premier movie houses – the famed Roxy and the Radio City Music Hall, a 6,200-seater that had opened at the end of 1932 and was the largest cinema in the world.

The same Radio City Music Hall was also where a rather smaller-scale picture with normal-sized stars opened later in 1933. It was a musical and its title was *Flying Down to Rio*. Its stars were Dolores Del Rio and Gene Raymond, but it was not the leads that caught the eye of the public; it was a couple of dancers who featured in supporting roles –

Fred Astaire and Gingers Rogers. Their climactic speciality number 'The Carioca' was nominated for an Oscar as best song and turned them into stars more or less overnight.

Compared with the mighty Kong, Fred and Ginger were like miniature dolls, but when they danced 'The Carioca' their impact on audiences was almost as great. Whereas Kong's feet lumbered along, crushing all before them, Astaire's magical toes twinkled and flashed and provided a rhythmical magic the like of which had not been seen before.

If Merian C. Cooper, a genuine pioneer of the cinema who in late 1932 took over briefly as production head at the studio, had been allowed to have his way, *Flying Down to Rio* would have been the very first picture to have been shot in the new three-colour Technicolor process, and Fred and Ginger would have danced together in colour in their very first movie. However, RKO turned down the proposal, and another two years went by before Technicolor was used in a feature-length movie – *Becky Sharp*, a Rouben Mamoulian version of Thackeray's *Vanity Fair* starring Miriam Hopkins and released by

Becky Sharp, *the first three-colour Technicolor feature, released by RKO in 1935 and directed by Rouben Mamoulian.*

RKO, a notable first for the studio.

Fred and Ginger were therefore destined to remain in black and white throughout the decade. Not that it mattered: it was the music and dance that counted. In their very first film together as stars, *The Gay Divorcee* (1934), the formula of their films was immediately established: boy meets girl, boys falls out with girl, boy loses girl, boy wins girl. In between these four stages of the plot, the emphasis of which varied little from picture to picture, Fred and Ginger would dance their exquisite routines and audiences would be lulled into a simple make-believe world of musical elegance filled with the tunes of George Gershwin, Jerome Kern, Cole Porter and, most regularly of all, Irving Berlin. *Top Hat* (1935) was their most popular film together, but George Stevens' *Swing Time*, made in 1936, ran it a close second, as did *Roberta* (1935), *Follow the Fleet* (1936) and *Shall We Dance?* (1937). It didn't really matter which of their immaculately designed films was the most popular, since all earned handsome profits until the partnership drifted to a close in 1939. Ten years later they made one last film together *The Barkleys of Broadway*, at MGM, in colour.

As a result of the healthy grosses of the Astaire/Rogers musicals, RKO was able to expand its horizons in the Thirties, adding new sound stages to those already existing on its lot and moving into new areas of production. Katharine Hepburn was one star whose career was boosted by the new profitability of RKO. Cast in such films as *Morning Glory*, for which she won an Oscar as a stage-struck girl from Vermont, George Cukor's *Little Women* (1933) and George Stevens' version of Booth Tarkington's *Alice Adams* (1935), she had much to thank the RKO studio for. So did Bette Davis, whose performance as the sluttish waitress, Mildred Rogers, in *Of Human Bondage* (1934) – a film for which she was loaned from Warners – was described by *Life* magazine as probably the best ever recorded on the screen by an American actress. The little-known Victor McLaglen also got his big break at the studio in *The Informer* (1935). For his portrayal of Gypo Nolan, the pathetic giant who betrays his colleagues during the troubles in Dublin in the 1920s, he won an Oscar as the best actor. Director John Ford had shot the picture for just $200,000 in under three weeks.

*Opposite:* Top Hat *(RKO, 1935). Fred Astaire and Ginger Rogers at their peak.*

*Left: Katharine Hepburn and Fred MacMurray, stars of George Stevens' 1935 production,* Alice Adams *(RKO).*

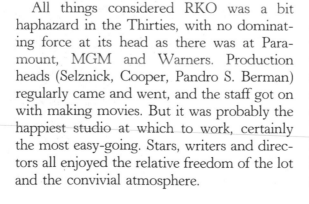

*John Ford's classic* The Informer *(1935), the RKO version of Liam O'Flaherty's story of betrayal and murder in Dublin during the Twenties.*

All things considered RKO was a bit haphazard in the Thirties, with no dominating force at its head as there was at Paramount, MGM and Warners. Production heads (Selznick, Cooper, Pandro S. Berman) regularly came and went, and the staff got on with making movies. But it was probably the happiest studio at which to work, certainly the most easy-going. Stars, writers and directors all enjoyed the relative freedom of the lot and the convivial atmosphere.

The studio had no particular image as such. The sight of its famous radio transmitter bleeping out from the top of the globe of the world didn't ensure that you were going to see a special type of movie, except in the case of the Astaire/Rogers musicals, but as the decade wore on, it did begin to signal quality. The profits (although healthy) may never have been great, but the enjoyment provided by many of the RKO pictures of the Thirties most certainly was.

# 1934
## Columbia

### Harry Cohn and the Comedies of Frank Capra

Just about the only thing that might have disturbed the happy-go-lucky conviviality of the RKO lot was the loud, cursing voice of Harry Cohn. Harry Cohn didn't work for RKO, of course; he was the boss of Columbia Pictures, but the lots of the two studios were so close that any innocent passer-by at RKO might well have heard Harry Cohn in full fury on one of his bad days – and Harry's bad days were regular and frequent.

But he did, on occasion, have some good ones, and one of those was when he said 'hello' for the first time to the young Sicilian-American director Frank Capra. His subsequent partnership with the talented young film-maker became one of the most unlikely ever to thrive in Hollywood, yet somehow, the two men managed between them to put Columbia on the map. They also managed to prove that studio moguls and creative artists could, if needs be, work together in harmony, even though it was often a fragile one.

It is doubtful whether either of the two men would have risen to the top had not fate thrown them together in the 1920s. Columbia, which Cohn had formed with his brother Jack and Joe Brandt back in 1924, would in all probability have remained a minor studio and Capra would have found work at other studios, where he would not have enjoyed the creative freedom he was allowed at Columbia. He would certainly not have risen in so short a time to become the most famous American director of the decade.

The 1934 film that Capra directed and which finally turned little Columbia into a force to be reckoned with was called *It Happened One Night*. It was a small-budget comedy starring Claudette Colbert as a runaway heiress, and Clark Gable (on loan from MGM) as the cynical, hard-boiled newspaperman who first pursues her and then ultimately woos her across America – a bright, escapist fairy tale, in fact. It was filmed in just four weeks for $300,000.

That $300,000 was not a lot of money but it turned out to be money well spent, for to the surprise of both Cohn and Capra, *It Happened One Night* turned out to be a sleeper. Not only did it make a small fortune

*His crudeness! Harry Cohn, the rough, tough, all-powerful boss of Columbia Pictures.*

*Reporter Clark Gable and runaway heiress Claudette Colbert on their way to their Oscars for their performances in Frank Capra's Academy Award-winning* It Happened One Night *(Columbia, 1934).*

for Columbia at the box office, it also became the very first picture to win all of the four major Academy Awards – best picture, best actor (Gable), best actress (Colbert) and best director (Capra). It also won a fifth award, for best screenplay, for its writer Robert Riskin.

For Frank Capra, the occasion was particularly satisfying. To him, the Oscar was akin to the Holy Grail: once you had won an Academy Award it meant that you had been acknowledged by your peers. It was also gratifying in another sense, for just the year before, he had suffered the ultimate in humiliation at the Academy Awards ceremony. He was up for the directing award for the Columbia comedy *Lady for a Day*, and when the master of ceremonies, homespun American comedian Will Rogers, announced: 'Come up and get it, Frank,' he was on his way, threading carefully through the tables at the banquet and acknowledging the cheers. It wasn't until he was halfway to the stage that he realized the spotlight was not on him but on Frank Lloyd who was accepting the award for *Cavalcade*. Capra described the return to his table as 'the longest crawl in history'.

When, on the night of 27 February 1935 at Hollywood's Biltmore Hotel, Capra at last earned his much-coveted prize, he didn't gloat exactly but he did gaze with admiration and pride at the gold statuette that stood before

him on the table. One man who did gloat, however, was Harry Cohn. An ex-song plugger, a coarse hustler and a general all-round bully, he couldn't help but smirk at the envious faces of those around him. Louis B. Mayer was there; so too was Thalberg, and Jack Warner and just about anyone else of importance in Hollywood. Just ten years before, when Columbia studio had been turning out cheap melodramas and 'B' westerns, those same people had sneered at and derided Columbia. Previously known as the CBC Company, the studio had been scornfully nicknamed as the 'Corned Beef and Cabbage outfit' by the top brass in Hollywood. 'Forget that,' said Cohn to himself on Oscar night in 1935. 'We are now serving up caviar!'

Frank Capra was 37 years old that famous February night. He had first joined Columbia (as a comedy gag man and director) back in 1927. He had not been employed because of any far-sighted judgement on Cohn's part; rather, he had been hired because the Columbia boss needed another director to work on the potboilers he was turning out so rapidly, and Capra's name was at the head of an alphabetical list of unemployed directors. When Capra was introduced to Cohn for the first time, he couldn't get a word in edgeways for Cohn, as always, was fixing up a deal on the telephone. When the executive Sam

Briskin tried to introduce the young fledgling director, Cohn waved him away impatiently. 'For Chrissake, Sam, will you get your ass outa here. I'm busy. Put him to work!'

That's exactly what Briskin did. In 1928 the young Capra delivered for the studio not once but seven times. Most of his films were quickies, but among them was a sea movie (originally begun by another director) called *Submarine*. Cohn had been dissatisfied with it during the early stages of shooting and Capra agreed to inherit it – provided he could reshoot the entire film in his own style. Budgeted at $250,000 *Submarine* later proved to be the studio's biggest moneymaker of the Twenties. Delighted with his protégé, Harry Cohn tore up Capra's one-year $500-a-week contract and replaced it with a new one – three years at $1,500 a week. The new contract signalled that the Cohn/Capra partnership had begun in earnest, a partnership that was to last throughout the Depression.

Most Hollywood films reflected the Depression in one form or another, or else, as in the case of the movies coming from MGM and Paramount, it was ignored altogether and audiences were asked to do likewise. Warners were interested in the crime and violence as well as the social problems that the era spawned, but at Columbia Capra preferred to be more optimistic. In his films, most of them

sharply written by Robert Riskin, he liked to delve into the hearts and minds of average people, and he tried to bring about a new kind of hope with his upbeat stories. More than those of any other director, his films reflected Franklin Roosevelt's famous philosophy: 'The only thing we have to fear is fear itself.'

A typical Frank Capra/Robert Riskin villain could be an unscrupulous banker, a Wall Street gambler or a corrupt politician, but a Capra/Riskin hero was always the same – honest, idealistic, frequently down but never out. Capra's films carried the message that, if people believed in each other and joined in a fight against injustice, everything would come right. In some cases, the message seemed to smack of that dirty word 'socialism', but Capra usually kept any political comment at bay by stressing the honesty of the individual, rather than any collective veracity.

Time and again Capra repeated his themes in his films. In *Mr. Deeds Goes to Town* (1936), Gary Cooper gives away his $20 million inheritance to dispossessed farmers because he discovers that the people advising him are a bunch of crooks. Again, in *Mr. Smith Goes to Washington* (1939), James Stewart, as an honest young politician, successfully defeats corruption in the US Senate.

In all his major films, Capra stressed his basic belief in the goodness of common

*'Here's to you, Frank!' The cast of* Lady for a Day *(Columbia, 1933) toast Frank Capra (next to camera) during the shooting of the picture. Capra, May Robson (sixth from the left along the wall), writer Robert Riskin and the film itself were all nominated for Academy Awards.*

people. Many critics considered his pictures too naïve and no more than fairly tales with a modern message to keep up morale during the dark days of unemployment. However, Capra's wasn't a bad philosophy and, fairy stories or not, his films struck a nerve and continued to hit the financial jackpot throughout the decade. Even when Capra departed from his usual Depression comedies and opted for a film version of James Hilton's bestselling *Lost Horizon* (1937), he could do no wrong. The story of an idyllic community hidden away high in the Himalayas, where people live without fear amid the luxury of

Shangri-La, not unnaturally appealed to audiences who felt the threat of war creeping uncomfortably closer year by year. Ronald Colman as the English diplomat who is chosen to succeed the 200-year-old lama was infinitely preferable to the all-too-real and less idyllic Adolf Hitler.

No other period in Hollywood history quite compares with that of Columbia during the Thirties, for at no other time did a studio head and a director work so closely and so successfully together. Capra's contribution to the partnership has always been well documented and rightly so since he made the

*Frank Capra, pictured on set with two of Hollywood's all-time greats, Cary Grant and James Stewart.*

GARY
COOPER

in

Mr. Deeds
Goes to Town

with JEAN ARTHUR

a FRANK CAPRA PRODU[CTION]

films, but Cohn's should not be overlooked. For many, he was the most despised studio boss in Hollywood, a vulgarian who was given to such outbursts as 'I don't get ulcers, I give them!' and 'if you've got talent, I'll kiss your ass; if you haven't got talent, I'll kick it!' Yet he was as shrewd as he was crude, knowing instinctively whether a movie was good or not, and he appreciated talent, especially that of writers who, despite their often vicious asides about their crude-talking boss, often found that they had a grudging respect for him. And few would quarrel with Cohn's method of testing whether a picture would or would not go down well with the public. 'When I'm alone in a projection room,' said Cohn, 'I have a foolproof device for judging whether a picture is good or bad. If my fanny squirms, it's bad; if it doesn't, it's good. It's as simple as that.'

In the Thirties scriptwriters such as Jo Swerling, Sidney Buchman, Norman Krasna and Charles MacArthur and Ben Hecht all worked on the Columbia lot on Gower Street, as did such directors as Frank Borzage,

Howard Hawks and John Ford, and between them, they came up with some excellent pictures. Borzage filmed *Man's Castle* (1933), a Depression tale starring Spencer Tracy and Loretta Young as two down-and-outs living in a shanty town on the outskirts of New York; Howard Hawks created the madcap comedy *Twentieth Century* (1934), which revolved around a series of love-hate battles between John Barrymore and Carole Lombard on the New York to Chicago super train; and John Ford came up with *The Whole Town's Talking* (*Passport to Fame* in UK, 1935) in which Edward G. Robinson featured in a dual role, that of a mild little clerk and a look-alike murderer being hunted by the police. There were also a number of successful Grace Moore musical vehicles – *One Night of Love* (1934), *Love Me Forever* (1935) and *The King Steps Out* (1936).

But dominating everything was Capra. After winning his first Oscar in 1934, he won again in 1936 for *Mr. Deeds Goes to Town* and for a third time in 1938 for *You Can't Take It With You.* His three awards in just five years

*Frank Capra's Mr. Deeds Goes to Town (Columbia, 1936), starring Gary Cooper as the tuba-playing country boy Longfellow Deeds who inherits a fortune and then gives it all away to help the country's economy.*

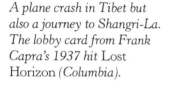

*A plane crash in Tibet but also a journey to Shangri-La. The lobby card from Frank Capra's 1937 hit* Lost Horizon *(Columbia).*

*Zany comedy from Howard Hawks. Carole Lombard (centre) and John Barrymore (right) in* Twentieth Century *(Columbia, 1934).*

made him the only director in Hollywood history to achieve a hat trick in so short a period.

When Capra eventually left Columbia his departure coincided with the end of the Thirties and, although it wasn't immediately apparent, his time as a major director was already over – the Second World War saw to that. Like novelist Scott Fitzgerald, who had made the Jazz Age Twenties so much his own and then had to struggle to adapt to a new era, Capra found himself unable to adapt to the new order of things. He joined the army to supervise and part-direct the superb series

of *Why We Fight* documentaries, and he also made a couple of movies for Warners – *Meet John Doe* (1941) and *Arsenic and Old Lace* (also made in 1941 but not released until 1944). But once the war was over, he found that his type of movie was over too.

Columbia and Harry Cohn, however, kept right on going. The Columbia trademark – the woman on a pedestal, with one hand holding high a glowing torch, the other clutching her Grecian gown, had in the Thirties already heralded greatness. In the Forties, more was to come, although this time the emphasis would be on glamour and the musical.

# Twentieth Century-Fox

## The Birth of a New Studio:
## Darryl F. Zanuck and Shirley Temple

The logo of the new Twentieth Century-Fox studio was much more dramatic than the elegant and silent Columbia lady. In 1935 when, for the first time, audiences heard the dramatic drum roll and the exhilarating fanfare and saw the searchlights beam high on to a futuristic skyline made up of huge letters spelling the studio's name, they sat up and took notice. Darryl F. Zanuck, once of Warners and the Rin Tin Tin pictures and now the production boss of the new outfit, made sure of that. Fox was a new studio and Zanuck wanted no silent ladies with torches, or mountains, or growling lions to herald his pictures. He wanted something that heralded the future – and he wanted something dramatic.

There were many in Hollywood who doubted the wisdom of starting a new studio at such a time. There were, they argued, enough studios to go round already and, 1935, right in the middle of the Depression, was no time to start up another, especially as the new-look Twentieth Century-Fox was really no more than a combination of the once giant, but subsequently ailing, Fox studio of the silent era and Joseph Schenck's two-year-old Twentieth Century Pictures, which had been run by Zanuck after he left Warner Bros. in 1933. It was, however, Zanuck's name that caused a few to have second thoughts. Many reckoned that if anyone could make a new studio work and also compete with the other majors it was Zanuck.

Those already employed at the Fox Studio very quickly discovered that Zanuck was no ordinary mogul. Not for him an inner sanctum where he could make decisions and sit

*Darryl F. Zanuck, dynamic production head of Twentieth Century-Fox, formed in 1935.*

back and count the profits. Instead, he had a creative interest in everything. His years at Warners stood him in good stead, having given him experience in just about every aspect of movie-making, and he put it to good use. Zanuck knew how to construct a story, how to write a story and how to edit and produce a story – ideal qualifications for someone taking on such a colossal gamble at such an uncertain time.

From the start, he attacked the job with the zest of three men. He knew that, financially, the new company was unsteady and that only by pruning the staff of the existing Fox studio could he make the necessary economies to start afresh. All those who did not figure immediately in his future plans were allowed to go, and only those he felt would be of use to him – notably director Henry King who was to prove a Fox stalwart in the years that lay ahead – were retained.

Zanuck knew only too well that his main enemy was time. A film company, like any other company, needs profits in order to operate successfully, and the only way that Zanuck could make those profits was by producing hit pictures as quickly as possible. He also knew that, in order to survive for any length of time, he had to bring together a nucleus of top moneymaking stars that would eventually be able to compete with those of MGM, Paramount and Warners.

His first venture was a disaster. A Lawrence Tibbett vehicle called *Metropolitan* (1935), it told a backstage story of a baritone's coming of age and flopped badly. The critics mauled it and the public stayed away. When a second film, *Thanks a Million* (1935), a corny little tale of a crooner (Dick Powell) who runs for governor, also received a cool reception at a preview, Zanuck's confidence took a knock. He hadn't expected instant success, but equally he hadn't expected to begin with a couple of flops. Determined that *Thanks a Million* would not go the same way as *Metropolitan*, he took the movie back to the studio and personally cut a reel out of it. That made all the difference and, in its tightened form, *Thanks a Million* was a hit. The new Twentieth Century-Fox studio was on its way.

For Zanuck, the middle and late Thirties were important years. It was an exhausting time but it was also exciting, for it was a period of searching for and grooming new stars. These weren't slow in arriving. In 1936, Zanuck signed the handsome young Tyrone Power and, more or less immediately, turned him into a top box-office attraction in the historical drama *Lloyd's of London* (1936). The same year former dance-band singer, blonde Alice Faye, also made her mark in the musical *King of Burlesque*. So too did Loretta Young, who was usually employed to play comedy roles, but in 1936 found herself cast in the company's first Technicolor production, *Ramona*, a film version of Helen Hunt Jackson's romantic novel of Indian life. Her co-star in the picture was Don Ameche, an actor with a wide and engaging smile who served as a kind of jack-of-all-trades at the studio. In 1986 he received an Academy Award as best supporting actor for his role in *Cocoon*.

*George Sanders, Madeleine Carroll and Tyrone Power in a scene from an early Fox hit,* Lloyds of London *(1936).*

*Shirley Temple, America's top box-office star between 1935 and 1938, pictured in a 1936 hit,* Captain January *(Twentieth Century-Fox).*

However, not a single one of these stars would have got their start at Fox had it not been for a little seven-year-old by the name of Shirley Temple. She and she alone kept the studio afloat while the Fox star team was being assembled.

The fact that she was under contract to Twentieth Century-Fox had, for a change, nothing to do with Zanuck. He had inherited her when the merger of Fox and Twentieth Century had taken place, but he knew a good thing when he saw one. His hope had been that the talented little child star and the homespun American comedian Will Rogers would, between them, see Fox through during the formative years of the studio. They probably would have done had not Rogers

been tragically killed in an air-crash in the very year the new studio was born. His death meant that Zanuck had to rely even more heavily on the talents of the child prodigy on his books.

Had Shirley Temple been a few years older – say, ten or eleven – Zanuck would have been in trouble, for the one big problem with child stars is that they grow up. Luckily for him, she was just the right age to allow him breathing space. He had something like five years to make use of Shirley Temple and he made the most of them.

The films that really turned her into a 'hot property' for Zanuck were both released in 1935: *Curly Top*, which was already in production when the studio was formed and in which she sang 'Animal Crackers in My Soup'; and *The Littlest Rebel*, in which she sang yet another hit song, 'Polly Wolly Doodle'. So heavily did Zanuck rely on her that he took the precaution of insuring her for $25,000. It was a wise move. From 1935 to 1938, between the ages of seven and ten, she was unstoppable, topping the *Motion Picture Herald* poll four times in a row. Try as they might, the big stars at the other major studios couldn't shift her from the number one spot. It was hers and hers alone.

A Shirley Temple film could fill to the brim a 2,000-seat movie house during a Saturday afternoon matinée and do almost equally as well in the evening, even though there were fewer children in the audience. Her pictures each made a $1 million, sometimes $1.5 million, during their first runs alone, which was some going in the Depression. The figures look even more impressive when one recalls that a child could get into a movie theatre in the Thirties for just 15 cents.

The other plus factor about the Shirley Temple movies was that they were cheap to produce. Shirley didn't need an expensive co-star (not until the final stages of her career anyway), the stories were simple and the films were always brought in on time. Her salary, however, was phenomenal for the time: at the beginning of 1936, she was on a revised contract of $4,000 a week for all 52 weeks of the year, plus a bonus of $20,000 a picture. That kind of money lasted for most of her Fox career. She appeared in nearly 20 pictures for the studio, among them her own favourite *Wee Willie Winkie* (1937), *Heidi* (1937), *Rebecca of Sunnybrook Farm* (1938) and *Susannah of the Mounties* (1939), in which she was orphaned in an Indian massacre. When *The Bluebird*, an expensive Technicolor version of the Maeterlinck fantasy, flopped in 1940, it was the first Shirley Temple movie to do so.

The beauty of the situation was, as far as Zanuck was concerned, that he knew he could rely on making millions in profits out of the

*Shirley Temple and Bill Robinson hoofing it in* The Littlest Rebel *(Twentieth Century-Fox, 1935).*

Rudyard Kipling's
WEE WILLIE WINKIE

STARRING Shirley
TEMPLE
AND Victor McLAGLEN

WITH C. Aubrey June Michael Cesar
SMITH LANG WHALEN ROMERO
Constance COLLIER Douglas SCOTT Directed by JOHN FORD
Associate Producer Gene Markey

A 20th Century PICTURE
Darryl F. Zanuck IN CHARGE OF PRODUCTION

*Shirley Temple's favourite of all her movies: John Ford's version of Kipling's* Wee Willie Winkie *(Twentieth Century-Fox, 1937).*

Shirley Temple pictures and, because of those profits, expand into producing bigger and more prestigious movies. One such lavish production was the Irving Berlin musical *Alexander's Ragtime Band* (1938), which starred Alice Faye, Tyrone Power and Don Ameche. It was a story about the ups and downs of a mythical dance band during the 1920s and 1930s but, as in all such films, the story counted for nothing and the music for everything, and in *Alexander's Ragtime Band*, the public weren't disappointed: there were no fewer than 30 Berlin numbers on offer. Zanuck wasn't too unhappy at Oscar time either, when the film earned six Academy Award nominations including one for the best picture. The cigar-chewing mogul noticed with satisfaction that the Hollywood colony was beginning to take his fledgling studio seriously.

The same year, Faye, Power and Ameche teamed up again in a rather different kind of film – *In Old Chicago*, an expensive family saga centring on the great Chicago fire of 1871. Alice Brady won an Oscar for best supporting actress for her portrait of a widowed mother trying to bring up three children, while Alice Faye sang 'Carry Me Back to Old Virginny' and revealed a most handsome pair of legs that, in one scene, were decorated with jewelled stockings valued at $1,500!

But nothing could compare with the great Chicago fire itself. Zanuck, determined to get his own back on MGM, who had destroyed San Francisco so successfully some two years earlier in a film of the same name starring Spencer Tracy, Jeanette MacDonald and Clark Gable, wasn't slow in coming forward with statistics including the most important one of all – the fire that lasted for 20 minutes on screen cost the studio $150,000 to

stage and burned for three days on the Fox back lot!

However, stars rather than songs, plots and special effects were the key to the success of Fox in its formative years, and once he had them on his books, Zanuck was never slow to mix 'em up as much as possible. He had seen how Louis B. Mayer had made that work at MGM, so he determined to do the same at Fox. Hence Tyrone Power appeared on five occasions with Loretta Young and three times with Alice Faye; Alice Faye appeared in six movies with Don Ameche; and so on.

There was no real 'feel', no distinctive style to any of the Fox movies of the late Thirties, but thanks to an expert group of screenwriters – Nunnally Johnson, Lamar Trotti, Philip Dunne – that style was to emerge early in the Forties. So was a new blonde singing star who was to break into movies in 1940 and prove to be as successful for the studio as Shirley Temple had been in the Thirties. She didn't have curls and she didn't have dimples, but she did have what many regarded as the best legs in the business. Her name? Betty Grable.

*Three of the top Fox stars of the 1930s – Alice Faye, Tyrone Power* (on fiddle) *and Don Ameche* (on piano) *in the Irving Berlin musical* Alexander's Ragtime Band *(Twentieth Century-Fox, 1938).*

# 1936
## Warner Bros.

### Trouble With the Stars: Bette Davis and Errol Flynn

Zanuck's departure for pastures new had, of course, left Jack L. Warner in a bit of a spot. Warner had been reluctant to let the young Zanuck go, especially as it had been Zanuck who had been mainly responsible for forging the well-established Warner style, one based firmly on a continual production of crime and social protest movies. Before his departure, Zanuck had even set the studio firmly on the musical trail with the memorable backstage musical *42nd Street* (1933), starring Warner Baxter and Ruby Keeler. With his success at Twentieth Century-Fox, Warner must have wished more than once that he had made even more strenuous efforts to keep Zanuck on the Burbank lot.

None the less, Warner was lucky for he found a more than able replacement in Hal B. Wallis. Like Zanuck, Wallis had been at the Warner studio since the 1920s, first as assistant to the head of publicity (he succeeded to that position the following year) and later as studio manager and production executive, so he knew all about the set-up and the Warner style.

Wallis was less of a showy character than all the rest. He didn't smoke large cigars like Zanuck, he didn't stamp and shout like Harry Cohn and he wasn't ruthless like Mayer. Rather, he was efficient, talented and quietly professional, and together with Jack Warner, he ensured that the Warner image of tough guys, tough cops and tough uncompromising movies was kept alive and allowed to flourish in the Thirties. He made sure that Cagney and Robinson were allowed to continue in the styles that had made them famous, although at the same time permitting them the oc-

casional breaks into musicals and comedies. He started Paul Muni on a new career in a series of distinguished biographies, including the studio's first best picture Oscar winner, *The Life of Emile Zola* (1937). And he was also astute enough to realize that Busby Berkeley's talent for forming geometric patterns with the white fleshy limbs of what seemed like hundreds of scantily clad girls not only served to set an audience's feet tapping but also provided a sexual feast for the eye.

*Paul Muni as the crusading French novelist in William Dieterle's Oscar-winning* The Life of Emile Zola *(Warner Bros., 1937).*

Jezebel (*Warner Bros.,
1938*), one of Bette Davis's
first major roles after her
much-publicized row with
studio boss Jack Warner.

Dick Powell, Ruby Keeler and Joan Blondell were ostensibly the stars of such Berkeley pictures as *Dames* (1934), *Gold Diggers of 1935* and *Stage Struck* (1936). However, the real stars were the Berkeley girls themselves, sometimes holding violins that glowed in the dark, sometimes plunging into waterfalls and sometimes being reflected a hundred times in mirrors.

Yet despite all this, Jack Warner had his problems, and most of these came from two of his most popular stars – Bette Davis and Errol Flynn. In 1936, it was Miss Davis who threw a grenade into the works when she baulked openly at the star contract system – and she did it in such a way that it made headlines and embarrassed the Hollywood moguls who all operated the system.

Under the contract system, stars had to sign contracts that lasted for seven years and, during that time, the studio could cast them in whatever vehicle they chose. Looked at in

one way, the system guaranteed employment, and this could mean a lot to the lesser stars and character actors who weren't too bothered about what they appeared in as long as they had work. However, looked at from a top star's point of view, the contract amounted to a kind of slavery; he or she had to appear in the movies chosen for them; otherwise they were put on suspension. If they were suspended for six months, that often meant no pay, and the six months were then added to the original seven years. In theory (and sometimes in practice), a star who continually refused to appear in studio-chosen movies and went on suspension could be forced to remain at the same studio for years.

The breaking point for Bette Davis came when she was set to star in the Warner studio's first all-Technicolor production, *God's Country and the Woman* (1936). Her co-star was George Brent, but she had no quarrels on that score for Brent was one of her favourite

*Busby Berkeley at his most
extravagant: the 'By a
Waterfall' number from*
Footlight Parade *(Warner
Bros., 1933).*

A WILLIAM WYLER PRODUCTION

A WARNER BROS. PICTURE

*Bette*
DAVIS

JEZEBEL

*with*

HENRY FONDA    GEORGE BRENT

MARGARET LINDSAY    DONALD CRISP    FAY BAINTER

RICHARD CROMWELL    HENRY O'NEIL    SPRING BYINGTON    JOHN LITEL

A WILLIAM WYLER PRODUCTION

SCREEN PLAY BY CLEMENTS RIPLEY, ABEM FINKEL & JOHN HUSTON FROM THE PLAY BY OWEN DAVIS, SR. MUSIC BY MAX STEINER

A WARNER BROS. PICTURE

55

*Triumph on Oscar night! Bette Davis, winner of the best actress award for* Jezebel *(Warner Bros., 1938) shares the acting honours with Spencer Tracy, named best actor of the year for his performance in MGM's* Boys' Town *(1938).*

Warners realized that they had to win the case at all costs for the entire studio machine in Hollywood was run on the contract system. Jack Warner stressed the seriousness of the situation when he commented: 'If Bette were to win, all the studio owners and executives in Hollywood would get trampled in the stampede.'

Warners didn't lose. Bette Davis might have been morally within her rights, but the seven-year contract, whatever its rights or wrongs, was proved to be a legal document. She therefore had no option but to return to Hollywood and take her medicine. However, although she had lost in the courts, she had also gained something of a victory, albeit a minor one. Jack Warner aware that, because of all the publicity, he dare not give one of the American cinema's foremost actresses any more films like *God's Country and the Woman*, welcomed her back and told her to forget all about the legal business. He then set his writers the task of providing scripts that had enough depth for an actress who, when given the right material, could act just about anyone else off the screen.

What followed was a series of roles that established Bette Davis as the premier screen actress in Hollywood. In *Jezebel* (1938), directed by William Wyler, she won her second Academy Award for her portrait of a spoiled Southern belle; in the tearjerker *Dark Victory* (1939), she died slowly and tragically from an incurable illness and had audiences the world over in tears; and in *The Private Lives of Elizabeth and Essex* (1939), she even shaved her eyebrows and the front of her scalp in order to bring more authenticity to her portrayal of the strong-willed English queen.

Although Bette Davis didn't manage to break the Hollywood contract system (Olivia de Havilland eventually fought it and won when she found a loophole in the law in 1943), she did send a few shock waves through the Hollywood corridors of power.

One Warner star who didn't really care too much one way or another about the system was the handsome Errol Flynn. He had come to the fore at the Warner studio in 1935 when the studio decided to add swashbucklers to their list of genre movies, starting with *Captain Blood*. The original star chosen to play the role of Rafael Sabatini's swordfighting doctor was the English actor Robert Donat, but Donat fell ill and Flynn stepped in at the last minute.

Jack Warner's problems with Flynn were very different from the kind he had experienced with Bette Davis. For all her outspokenness, Davis was a dedicated and deter-

leading men. Her quarrel was with the subject – a lumberjack story set in the great outdoors!

Already an actress of some distinction – she had earned great praise for her Mildred Rogers in *Of Human Bondage* (1934) at RKO, and had won an Oscar just the year after for her performance in *Dangerous* (1935) – Miss Davis decided that, if she were to continue her development as a serious actress, pictures such as *God's Country and the Woman* weren't likely to help her cause.

Instead of going on suspension, she walked out of the studio and, in September 1936, she took off for England, having accepted an offer to make a film there. Warners retaliated with an injunction, holding her to her contract, to which, according to the studio, she was legally bound until 1942. She sued the studio and in the English courts she stated that Jack Warner was working her 14 hours a day and that she was not receiving roles worthy of her abilities. Therefore, she maintained, she was entitled to look for roles elsewhere.

mined actress who would go to any lengths to give a great performance. Not so Errol Flynn. He viewed acting as nothing more than a lighthearted game, something he was lucky to participate in and get paid for. He spent freely and became known as one of the hellraisers of Hollywood.

Even in 1936 he was living life faster than anyone else. He drank heavily, he kept late hours and smoked up to 100 cigarettes a day. In addition Flynn was notorious for his philanderings and romantic escapades, but Jack Warner, with whom Flynn was never the best of friends, deliberately turned a blind eye to them. As long as Flynn turned up on time on the set and finished a movie on schedule, that was all he was interested in.

Not that actually starting a day's shooting was terribly easy for Flynn. The worst part of the day for him, especially after a hectic night out, was the 6.30 a.m. make-up call, when he was prepared by Percy Westmore. At times, Westmore's job wasn't all that easy, for Flynn's strikingly handsome face was often haggard and his eyes bleary.

In 1936, of course, none of the high living showed for very long on Flynn's features. He was only 27 and young enough to get away with all his outrageous activities without any marked effects on his looks. During that year, in *The Charge of the Light Brigade* he led the 600 into the Valley of Death at a cost to Warners of $1.2 million. The following year, he continued to swash and buckle in *The Prince and the Pauper*, and in 1938 he starred in his most famous swashbuckler of all, *The Adventures of Robin Hood.*

Never was an actor more perfectly cast.

*Swashbuckler supreme! Errol Flynn as* Captain Blood *(Warner Bros., 1935).*

*Errol Flynn and Olivia de Havilland, the romantic leads in* The Adventures of Robin Hood *(Warner Bros., 1938).*

Flynn leapt around the steps of Nottingham Castle with style and dash, crossing swords in a memorable duel with Basil Rathbone and wooing the lovely, dewy-eyed Maid Marian of Olivia de Havilland, all to the rousing strains of the music of Erich Wolfgang Korngold (which received an Academy Award). It was entertainment of the highest class. The superior Technicolor, the vigorously staged action sequences and the talented supporting cast (especially the outstanding Claude Rains as a sly Prince John and Alan Hale as a burly Little John) ensured that *The Adventures of Robin Hood* was one of the best of its kind ever filmed.

Even though the melodramas of Bette Davis and the swashbucklers of Errol Flynn brought a new dimension to Warners in the Thirties, the studio never lost faith in the kind of films that had earned them their reputation in the early years of the decade. Cagney still socked 'em in the jaw in such movies as *G-Men* (1935), *Angels with Dirty Faces* (1938) and the classic *The Roaring Twenties* (1939). So too did Edward G. Robinson in *Bullets or Ballots* (1936) and *Kid Galahad* (1937). Even Humphrey Bogart joined the club with a memorable performance as gangster Duke

Mantee in *The Petrified Forest* (1936). Social realism was also never far away. For example, *They Won't Forget*, made by Mervyn LeRoy in 1937, was inspired by a real-life murder case in the Deep South and emerged as one of the most outspoken condemnations of prejudice and bigotry ever shown on the screen.

By 1939, the salary call at Warners had James Cagney in the number one spot earning $12,500 a week. Paul Muni was at number two with $11,500, then came Edward G. Robinson on $8,000, with Claude Rains (arguably the best actor on the lot), George Raft and Errol Flynn all on $6,000. The top female star, Bette Davis, was on $5,000 a week.

For the last few years of the Thirties, the famous Warner shield stood mainly for a snarl and a quick right hook from Cagney; a leer from Bogart; lithe athleticism from Flynn; quiet adoration from De Havilland; intensity from Davis; and what seemed like a million milky white thighs cavorting in Busby Berkeley musical routines. It was a bit of a mixture, but if Jack Warner had been asked in 1930 whether he would have settled for such a line-up by the end of the decade, he would almost certainly have replied with a 'Yes!'

The Private Lives of
Elizabeth and Essex
*(Warner Bros., 1939), the
film that teamed the two
Warner rebels, Bette Davis
and Errol Flynn.*

# 1937

## United Artists

'Yes!' was also the key word being bandied about in the corridors of power at United Artists in 1937. Mary Pickford, Douglas Fairbanks and Charlie Chaplin were debating whether to use it and accept a financial offer from independent producer Sam Goldwyn for control of the company. Compared with the cut and thrust in the boardroom at UA, Jack Warner's battles with Bette Davis paled into insignificance.

To discover just how this turn of events came about, we need to go back to the year 1919, when a handful of top Hollywood stars and directors, dissatisfied with the dominance of the major Hollywood studios, decided to strike out on their own. Their idea was to form a company in which *they* would be the major shareholders, *they* would choose their movies and, because it was *their* money that was financing the pictures, *they* would make the profits. Had she been around 20 years earlier, Bette Davis, after her experiences at Warners in 1936, would almost certainly have sympathized with their aims.

The four founders were Mary Pickford, Douglas Fairbanks, Charlie Chaplin and D. W. Griffith. They called their company United Artists and promoted it rather ambitiously as 'The Tiffany's of the Industry'. There would be no big studio as such, no mighty complex as at Universal, Fox and Paramount. The four partners would just hire sound stages around Hollywood when a United Artists picture was ready for filming, thus cutting down overheads and allowing a certain flexibility when putting movies into production.

It was an idea that sounded fine on paper and also in theory. In order to make it work,

however, each of the four founder members had to deliver three pictures a year, but for a variety of reasons, the plan didn't work out as they had hoped. Chaplin was still bound by an earlier contract to First National and couldn't deliver his first United Artists picture until 1923; Pickford and Fairbanks, after an initial burst of frenzied activity, got married and enjoyed a long and expensive honeymoon in Europe; and the great D. W. Griffith, although proving that he was still capable of brilliant things – *Broken Blossoms* (1919) and *Orphans of the Storm* (1922) – quickly faded into a shadow of his former self and finally sold his shares in the company in 1927. Only the swashbucklers of Fairbanks – *The Three Musketeers* (1921), *Robin Hood* (1922) – and the films of 'America's Sweetheart' the beloved Pickford – *Pollyanna* (1920), *Little Lord Fauntleroy* (1921) – proved to be reliable moneymakers.

The net result was that by the early Twenties, Pickford, Fairbanks & Co. were forced to bring in additional product in order to ease the ever-worsening situation. Most of the early independent 'extras' were second- and third-rate programmers that did nothing to help foster the company's once proud 'Tiffany' boast, and it looked for a time as though the courageous experiment of United Artists might well flounder before it really got under way. However in 1925 help arrived when two more big names threw in their lot with the company. Gloria Swanson (then a top box-office attraction) signed a six-picture deal, and independent producer Sam Goldwyn agreed to distribute his movies under the United Artists banner. Most

expected that it would be the Swanson films that made the money, but instead the opposite happened. Swanson's films did little to help the company's flagging fortunes, and it was the Goldwyn films that became the company's mainstay.

In fact, the signing of Goldwyn was to prove the key to the fortunes of United Artists in the years that lay ahead. Between 1925 and 1937 he produced and released over 40 pictures through the company – a huge output compared with the number of films produced by the founders. After Goldwyn's arrival, for instance, Pickford made only seven more pictures and then, in 1933, retired; Fairbanks, too, only added just another seven action films until his swashbuckling energies ran out; and Chaplin was the worst offender of all, making only four films – *The Gold Rush* (1925), *The Circus* (1928), *City Lights* (1931) and *Modern Times* (1936) in all of 11 years. Admittedly, each of his films, all of them

featuring his beloved tramp figure, was a masterpiece of humour and pathos, but the time it took him to shoot each one constituted a crippling financial setback for a company that needed quality product at a fast rate. Compared to Chaplin, Goldwyn was a gold-mine! In the late Twenties and early Thirties, his offerings were regular and plentiful, and included the classic tearjerker *Stella Dallas* (1925), *Bulldog Drummond* (1929), *Arrowsmith* (1931), *Street Scene* (1931) and, for light relief, a whole string of Eddie Cantor musi-cals.

All this meant that, by 1937, Sam Goldwyn was dominant within United Art-ists, and he had gathered about him some of the most popular stars in the business. Hand-some, debonair Englishman Ronald Colman was his top attraction, and Gary Cooper was another high on the list, as were Miriam Hopkins, Fredric March, Merle Oberon, Joel McCrea and Kay Francis. To make sure that

*Pioneer days at United Artists!* Left to right: *Al Jolson, Douglas Fairbanks, Mary Pickford, Ronald Colman, Sam Goldwyn and Eddie Cantor.*

they and others who appeared in his films received the best guidance, Goldwyn signed the young and talented William Wyler, whom many in Hollywood felt was the best up-and-coming director in the business. The shrewd Goldwyn latched on to this quicker than anyone else, and signed him to a lucrative contract before any of the major studios became aware of his potential.

Goldwyn's films were usually sombre and serious in mood and subject, although the producer occasionally pandered to the lighter side of things as in the Eddie Cantor musicals, which first introduced the famous Goldwyn Girls and from whose ranks emerged such stars as Lucille Ball, Betty Grable, Virginia Mayo and Vera-Ellen. Primarily, however Goldwyn strove for perfection in the serious market.

He frequently drove everyone who worked for him crazy, maintaining that 'usually, when people are happy making a picture it is a flop.' His famous Goldwynisms – phrases that murdered the English language – belong to Hollywood folklore even though most of them can be credited not to him personally but to his team of publicity writers. 'In two words – impossible!' was one of his best-known remarks; 'Start with an earthquake and work up to a climax' was another. Others included: 'Anyone who visits a psychiatrist needs his head examined'; 'Tell me, how did you love the picture?'; 'We've all passed a lot of water since then'; 'Write music like Wagner, only louder'; and 'Let's bring this picture up-to-date with some snappy 19th-century dialogue!'

Goldwynisms were also aimed at directors: 'The trouble with directors is that they're always biting the hand that lays the golden egg,' he grumbled. In fact, he was particularly sensitive about directors. When a journalist once brought up the subject of 'William Wyler's *Wuthering Heights*', Goldwyn snapped back: 'I made *Wuthering Heights*. Wyler only directed it!'

Although many people admired Sam Goldwyn, few really liked or knew him well. When F. Scott Fitzgerald was working on a rewrite of *Raffles*, he was as baffled as everyone else. He commented: 'I like Sam Goldwyn. You always know where you stand with him – nowhere!'

Not so the paying public. It knew exactly where it stood with Sam Goldwyn, that the three words 'Samuel Goldwyn Presents'

*Charlie Chaplin in* Modern Times *(United Artists, 1936), a sociological satire on the perils of the machine age.*

*Jon Hall and Dorothy Lamour battling against the odds in Sam Goldwyn's 1937 spectacular* The Hurricane *(United Artists).*

heralded a film of style, taste and intelligence, and one that was always impeccably acted and directed. In 1937, it was presented with not one Sam Goldwyn entertainment but three: a remake of *Stella Dallas* starring Barbara Stanwyck, John Ford's spectacular *The Hurricane* and Wyler's *Dead End*, a one-set version of Sidney Kingsley's Depression play about the youngsters who fought for survival in the slums of New York's Lower East Side.

What the public at large was not aware of, however, were the dramatic events that were going on behind the scenes in the United Artists' boardroom. Matters came to a head in December 1937, when Goldwyn made a bid for control of United Artists and found himself involved in a tense confrontation with Pickford, Fairbanks and Chaplin. In a fierce boardroom battle, Goldwyn claimed that they were not putting any creative effort into the company and that his pictures and his pictures alone had kept United Artists afloat during the Thirties.

His offer to each of the three partners was $500,000 for their shares in the company. This was turned down. Chaplin, Pickford and Fairbanks came back with a counter-offer, telling the wily old independent that, if he could come back with $2 million for each of them, they *might* be prepared to listen. They wanted too much. Although Goldwyn

attracted the help of Hungarian producer Alexander Korda, who released his British-made productions through United Artists, he could only raise two-thirds of the necessary amount. He had lost.

Quite how things would have turned out if Goldwyn had gained control of United Artists remains one of the great imponderables of Hollywood. A direct result of his defeat was that, after filming his triumphant version of *Wuthering Heights* (1939) – with Laurence Olivier as Heathcliff and Merle Oberon as the doomed Cathy – he left United Artists to distribute his pictures through RKO. At least he had the satisfaction of seeing *Wuthering Heights* acclaimed across the world and even being named at best picture of 1939 (ahead of *Gone with the Wind*) by the New York Film Critics.

The departure of Goldwyn left a massive hole in United Artists' production schedules, and the producer's absence from the scene was to be keenly felt in the decade ahead. However, for the rest of the Thirties, they were lucky. Other independent producers had joined up to work for the company, and for a time at least, United Artists prospered.

Walter Wanger was one producer who helped to contribute to this prosperity. He persuaded the beautiful Hedy Lamarr to lure Charles Boyer to his doom in *Algiers* (1938), and also sent director John Ford off to

STAGECOACH

A WALTER WANGER production · directed by JOHN FOR[
with CLAIRE TREVOR · JOHN WAYNE · Andy Devine · John Carradi[
Thomas Mitchell · Louise Platt · George Bancroft · Donald Me[
Berton Churchill · Tim Holt                Released thru United Arti[

*Producer Walter Wanger's contribution to 1939 screen entertainment: John Ford's classic western* Stagecoach *(United Artists) starring John Wayne as the Ringo Kid.*

Monument Valley to shoot his classic *Stagecoach* (1939), a film that brought stardom (after more than 70 low-budget features) to John Wayne as the outlaw, the Ringo Kid, and a new lease of life to the western. Alexander Korda – *The Drum* (*Drums* in the US, 1938), *The Four Feathers* (1939), *The Thief of Bagdad* (1940) – was another producer whose films had the mark of quality as well as commercial appeal.

Most of all, however, it was the pictures of producer David O. Selznick that brought a touch of class to the company. In 1937, he had, like Goldwyn, three films on view, which were as varied as they were uniformly excellent. The funniest was *Nothing Sacred*, a screwball comedy about a small-town girl who is wrongly told that she is terminally ill. She is then given the time of her life by a New York newspaper that hopes to gain publicity by reporting on her last weeks. Carole Lombard played the girl, and Fredric March the reporter who snarls at his dyspeptic editor Walter Connolly: 'The hand of God reaching down into the mire couldn't elevate you to

depths of degradation.' Repartee of a different kind was provided by Douglas Fairbanks, Jr. and honest Englishman Ronald Colman as they duelled in a Ruritanian castle in *The Prisoner of Zenda*, and by Fredric March and Janet Gaynor in *A Star Is Born*. This was a bitter inward look at Hollywood, with March as an alcoholic movie actor on the way down and Gaynor as the young girl he discovers and turns into a star.

Selznick was equally successful in 1938 with his Technicolor version of *The Adventures of Tom Sawyer*, and in 1939 when he produced the worldwide success, *Intermezzo (Escape to Happiness* in UK), the story of the love affair between a renowned but married violinist (Leslie Howard) and his young protégée (Ingrid Bergman).

It was 1940 that saw Selznick's greatest success at United Artists, for it was then that he produced the film that won the company its very first best picture Oscar. The film was *Rebecca*, a version of the Daphne du Maurier bestseller about a timid young girl (Joan Fontaine) who finds life with her moody

Joan Fontaine and Laurence Olivier in Hitchcock's first American film, Rebecca (United Artists, 1940).

One of the best duels ever put on film: Douglas Fairbanks Jr. and Ronald Colman in the climax to David Selznick's 1937 version of The Prisoner of Zenda (United Artists).

upper-class husband (Laurence Olivier) more than she bargained for, and comes face to face not only with a dark secret in his past but also a pretty sinister apparition in the present – the forbidding housekeeper Mrs. Danvers (Judith Anderson). The film was the first of Alfred Hitchcock's distinguished Hollywood career, and opened with nine of the most famous words in contemporary fiction: 'Last night I dreamt I went to Manderley again.'

Words of a different kind, those uttered by Charlie Chaplin in *The Great Dictator* (1940), also made people sit up and take notice. They marked the end of one era and the beginning of another. Chaplin, having disowned his little tramp in 1936 after *Modern Times*, now also disowned the silent medium, and 13 years after the first talkie, spoke for the first time on screen. His first words were a mumbled 'Yes, sir' as he obeyed the order to fire in the opening war sequence of the film.

*The Great Dictator* was a satire on the evils of fascism. Chaplin, featured in the dual role of a Hitler-like dictator and a little Jewish barber, with Paulette Goddard as an impoverished girl of the ghetto and Jack Oakie as a Mussolini-style tyrant called Napaloni. The opening title read: 'This is a story of the period between two world wars – an interim in which insanity cut loose, liberty took a nose-dive and humanity was kicked around somewhat!'

These sentiments were more than applicable to United Artists itself. Its story, too, had been one that had developed between the wars. Liberty, in the form of the hopes and aspirations of its four founder members, had 'taken a nose-dive', and in the Forties, with Goldwyn and Selznick departing for pastures new, they too were to be 'kicked around somewhat'. But at least in the last three years of the decade, and thanks to such films as *Dead End*, *A Star Is Born*, *Wuthering Heights*, *Stagecoach* and *Rebecca*, they achieved a high standard of excellence and proved that independence, provided it was accompanied by skill, business acumen and a large slice of luck, could work – even in a Hollywood jungle dominated by ruthless tycoons.

*An historic moment in movie history: Charlie Chaplin about to utter his first words on film (a mumbled 'Yes sir!') in* The Great Dictator *(United Artists, 1940).*

# 1938
## Walt Disney

### The First Cartoon Features:
### *Snow White and the Seven Dwarfs*

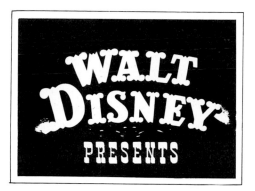

Another man for whom the word 'independence' was all-important during his long career was Walt Disney. He too liked to go his own way and be in charge of the making of a film from its beginning to its end. Only in his case, the situation was slightly different. Whereas all the other Hollywood studios dealt in live-action movies, be they westerns, horror films, thrillers or musicals, Disney dealt in only one kind of film – the cartoon.

Although the cartoon wasn't actually frowned upon, it wasn't held in very high esteem by the other Hollywood moguls. They agreed that a seven-minute cartoon supporting one of their main features was an amusing and novel idea, but that was as far as it went. They never once believed that the cartoon would ever amount to anything more than that, and they certainly didn't believe that, one day, a full-length animated feature would arrive on the market ('too costly', they had always argued) and rival the box-office takings of their own well-tailored features. But in 1938, they were jolted out of their complacency. Walt Disney produced *Snow White and the Seven Dwarfs* and Hollywood was never quite the same again.

The world première of *Snow White* actually took place during the last days of 1937, on 21 December at the Carthay Circle Theater in Hollywood. Just about every major star turned out to see what Disney had to offer: Charlie Chaplin, Marlene Dietrich, Charles Laughton, Mary Pickford, Cary Grant and many others. Most were curious to see just how it would feel to sit through an 83-minute cartoon, and whether they could manage it without getting restless or bored.

Disney himself was in a state of high nervous tension – understandably, for he knew that his entire future rested on the success of this one film. He had been making animated shorts since 1923 when he first arrived in Hollywood, and even in those early

*Walt Disney pictured in Hollywood in the early Thirties.*

days, he had hoped that one day he would fulfil his dream and complete a feature-length cartoon. When he at last premièred *Snow White*, he had been in Hollywood for over 14 years. Failure would have meant not only the end of his plans to produce a long series of cartoon features but also, quite possibly, the end of his career in Hollywood.

He need not have worried. *Snow White* did not fail. It was acclaimed the world over as a work of genius – colourful, imaginative, entertaining!

Disney first considered *Snow White* as a serious possibility in the early Thirties. Initially, he kept his plans to himself, content to watch as his gallery of cartoon characters made a name for themselves across the world – the wide-smiling Mickey Mouse, who had first appeared in *Steamboat Willie* back in 1928, the twittering Minnie Mouse, the short-tempered and irascible Donald Duck, the simple-minded bloodhound Pluto, Goofy and all the rest. Then in 1934 he announced to his wife and his alarmed brother Roy (who was in charge of finance at the company) that, if the studio were to survive and expand, they would have to go into feature cartoon production. He also announced that he was about to gamble $500,000 on a full-length feature cartoon based on the Grimm fairy tale of 'Snow White'.

At any other Hollywood studio, this budget would have been sizeable but easily manageable. At the Disney studio, it was an astronomical figure, for the company's profits were not large and depended on the turnover of the short cartoons of Mickey Mouse and Donald Duck and the slightly more ambitious *Silly Symphonies* – cartoon shorts adapted from musical themes and folk tales.

These were relatively cheap to produce and Disney had streamlined his operation so that they could be released quickly and efficiently. The production of *Snow White*, on the other hand, was a very different matter. Roy Disney estimated that it would take at least two years, possibly three, to complete, and even if things went well, it would almost certainly mean frequent and unenviable cap-in-hand trips to the bank for extra loans.

Thus Walt Disney was in a very different position from all the other moguls in Hollywood during the Thirties. His project (and his finances) could collapse at any moment, all of his artists would be thrown out of work and that would be the end as far as the Disney studio was concerned. The gamble he was taking was enormous.

Luckily, Disney had gathered around him a dedicated team of animators who were so enthusiastic about the project that they were prepared to work at all hours, sometimes round the clock and in their own time, to see *Snow White* finished and premièred. Eventually, as many as 730 artists worked on the picture – including 32 animators, 102 assistants, 176 in-betweeners (the artists who filled in the bits of action between the animator's drawings), 20 lay-out men, 25 background artists and 65 special-effects animators. At least 2 million drawings went into the 83 minutes of film. As many of the Disney employees were later to recall, they, as well as their ambitious boss, sensed that they were in on a piece of movie history, and they wanted to be part of the team that produced the very first feature-length cartoon.

They made it, but it was a close run thing in the end. There were, as Roy Disney had predicted, several trips to the bank. The most important was when production had just passed the halfway mark and Disney simply ran out of money. He had spent the first $500,000 and another million on top of that, and he still needed more. Otherwise, the film would come to a halt. The bank was the only answer, but it wasn't prepared to carry on financing Disney for ever. They began to demand collateral, and they asked politely if they could see what Disney had already filmed.

At first Disney refused. It was *his* project, he told his brother Roy, and no one would see it until it was finished. Roy, always the level-headed business partner, pleaded: 'Walt, you've got to show them what you've done on the picture so far. If you don't, we won't get the loan. And that will be the end of *Snow White*!' In the end, financial survival won out over Disney's obstinacy. He assembled all the completed sections of the film, linked them together with pencil sketches and a rough layout and then presented a makeshift 'première' to banker Joe Rosenburg. The time he chose was a quiet Saturday afternoon at The Disney studios on Hyperion Avenue. Only the two of them attended. Disney did all the talking; the banker just sat and watched the bits of celluloid linked by Disney's makeshift work.

When the preview was over, Rosenburg put on his hat and coat and prepared to leave. Disney later recalled: 'He showed not the slightest reaction to what he had viewed. After the lights came on, he walked out of the projection room, remarked that it was a nice day – and yawned! Then he turned to me and said: 'Walt, that picture will make a pot of money.'

The banker was right, of course. Throughout the world in 1938, children and adults thrilled to something completely new – a

cartoon feature about the young Snow White's adventures with the dwarfs in the forest and her frightening encounters with a wicked queen who could, within seconds and with the help of a magic potion or two, turn herself into the most hideous old witch imaginable. Until then, audiences had come to believe that, with the development of the three-colour Technicolor process in 1935, the cinema had reached the limit of new things it could offer the public. Disney's *Snow White and the Seven Dwarfs* proved that the medium still had a few surprises in store.

*Snow White* earned rave reviews from every quarter, and in its first year, it earned $4.2 million in the United States and Canada alone. It ran for an unprecedented five weeks at the Radio City Music Hall in New York, and in Paris it ran continuously for 31 weeks. It was eventually dubbed into ten languages around the world.

On the night of 23 February 1939, Disney received his just reward. During the Academy Awards' ceremony, he was presented (by Shirley Temple who urged him not to be nervous) with eight special Oscars for *Snow White* – one big one and seven little ones!

Most men would have been content to rest on their laurels after such a triumphant success, but not Walt Disney. He moved his studios from Hyperion Avenue to Burbank and plunged ahead with three new feature cartoon projects. One was *Pinocchio*, the story of a wooden puppet that turns into a real boy. Another was *Bambi*, Felix Salten's story about the life of a deer, from his early days as a baby fawn to when he reigns supreme as King of the Forest. The third was *Fantasia*, the most ambitious of the three films, comprising eight widely different pieces of classical music – ranging from Beethoven to Bach, Mussorgsky to Stravinsky – each animated in a different style and form. This time, however, the luck that had been with Disney during the making of *Snow White* deserted him. All three films ran into production problems that raised their costs way above their original budgets.

Disney was later criticized for trying to expand too fast, but he had no alternative. He had to produce more animated features as quickly as possible simply in order to survive. He knew that the box-office returns of *Snow White*, although gratifying, would not sustain the studio for ever and that unless he got

Snow White and the Seven Dwarfs, *the first full-length feature cartoon (© 1937 The Walt Disney Company).*

more films on the animation boards without delay he was back to square one. Whereas other studios, even the smaller outfits such as Columbia and RKO, could turn round a 'quickie' in a matter of months, sometimes even weeks, Disney could not. Cartoon features were all he could turn his hand to, and they could take anything from 18 months to over three years to produce. Disney reasoned that, if he could get three films going at once, he would stand a chance of making larger profits and put the company on a sound financial basis. Roy Disney later commented on the mood at the studio after *Snow White*: 'Success was hard to take,' he said. 'We thought we could do two animation films a year. And we couldn't.'

Production hiccups on his three new features weren't the only problems facing Disney. Storm clouds were gathering in Europe and the jackboots of Hitler's armies were soon on the march. From humanity's point of view, the result was horrendous. From Disney's, the result was equally catastrophic; the occupation of Europe meant that the market for his films had been halved. Combined with the delays in producing his three features, especially *Bambi* (1942) which, because it consisted of a cast of animal characters, took the longest to get off the drawing boards, the limitations of the market crippled Disney. By 1940 he was once more in debt to the bank, this time to the tune of $4.5 million. *Pinocchio* (1940) had cost over

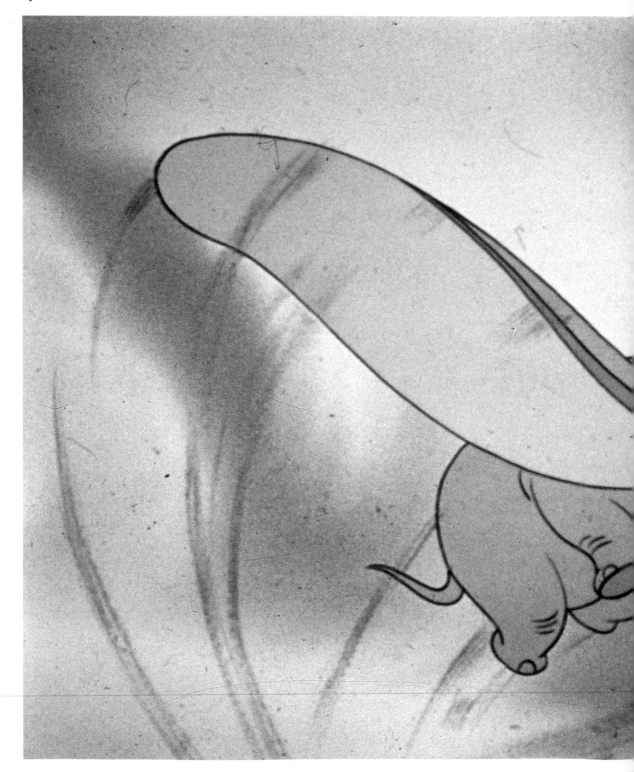

$2.5 million, *Fantasia* (1940) more than $2.25 million, and *Bambi* would not be ready for another two years.

Disney didn't need a crystal ball to tell him that he would need something approaching a miracle if he was to show a return on his two costly 1940 films. That miracle did not occur. Despite critical acclaim, both flopped, and with their failure went Disney's last chance of keeping his head above water in the years to come. In just a year's time, the United States too would be entering the war and the audiences that had so eagerly greeted *Snow White and the Seven Dwarfs* were then much more eager to be entertained by lavish musicals and pin-up girls and movies that waved the flag for the war effort. Cartoon characters didn't seem to fit into the general scheme of things.

Only *Dumbo* (1941) – the story of the baby elephant with ears so big he could fly, and which was made quickly simply to provide cashflow for Disney – showed a profit. Disney survived the war years by becoming less ambitious, cutting his cloth to fit the needs of his wartime audience. He continued to produce the Mickey Mouse and Donald Duck shorts and made a series of information and training films for the armed services. While there were many at the studio who felt that the war had crippled for ever the boldest experiments in animation the world had ever seen, Disney, as he had so often done in the past, was to prove them wrong.

*An elephant with ears so big he can fly! The baby Dumbo (© 1941 The Walt Disney Company).*

# 1939
## Metro-Goldwyn-Mayer

### Mickey Rooney, Judy Garland and
### *Gone With The Wind*

MGM's claim to be the top Hollywood studio still held good in 1939. 'Make It Good . . . Make It Big . . . Give It Class!' remained their motto and a studio of 'Stars, Stars and Yet More Stars' still summed them up pretty well. Just about the only type of stars they did't have under contract were those of the animated variety coming from Disney.

However, even in the world of the cartoon MGM was beginning to make a challenge for supremacy. In the late Thirties, two animal characters were under development by William Hanna and Joseph Barbera under the guidance of producer Fred Quimby. One was a cat, the other a mouse, and while they weren't yet known as 'Tom and Jerry', they were clearly the prototypes for the ever-feuding twosome who were to prove so popular in the Forties and whose madcap escapades were to earn MGM no fewer than seven Academy Awards. In their first film together, the Oscar-nominated *Puss Gets the Boot* (1940), Tom was known as 'Jasper' and the mischievous Jerry as 'Dat Mouse'. A year later, they were rechristened Tom and Jerry and began their adventures proper in *The Midnight Snack* and *The Night Before Christmas*.

All things considered, life had worked out pretty well for L. B. Mayer since the mid-1930s. As he had suspected, Irving Thalberg had not remained in contention for very long after his return to the studio at the end of 1933. Still a stick man, he had continued for another three years, but found that David Selznick had made the most of his opportunities as his replacement and produced several pictures that were up to Thalberg's

standards, including *Anna Karenina* (1935) with Garbo and the two highly praised Dickens adaptations: *David Copperfield* and *A Tale of Two Cities* (both 1935). The result was that, when Thalberg returned, the MGM set-up had changed considerably, and instead of supervising over 50 pictures a year, Thalberg was in charge of only a select few. When ill health, in the form of pneumonia, struck him down once more, he did not recover, dying in September 1936, aged 37.

By dying young, Thalberg became something of a legend and the subject of many discussions about 'what-might-have-happened-at-MGM' had he enjoyed a normal lifespan. Mayer could live quite easily with such speculation. Much more important to him was that, by dying young, Thalberg had left him in sole command. Selznick had left the studio in 1935 to form his own independent company, so there was no one left to argue with or influence any of his decisions. He had the field, or rather the entire MGM studio, to himself.

On the day of Thalberg's funeral, Mayer put on a tear-stained performance of which many of the stars under his command would have been proud. After the service, he waited silently in the car that would take him away from the gloomy scene. His companion was MGM executive Eddie Mannix. As the car moved off, Mayer looked across to Mannix and smiled. 'Isn't God good to me?' he said.

He was indeed. The fates had been kind to Mayer, and by 1939 he was busily at work changing the image of the studio, moving it away from the classical approach of Thalberg and towards a more wholesome All-American

*W. C. Fields as Mr. Micawber and a young Freddie Bartholomew as David Copperfield (MGM, 1935), directed by George Cukor.*

style made up of patriotism, sentiment and schmaltz.

The stars, of course, remained, for it didn't really matter what kind of movie they appeared in just as long as they did appear – and regularly. Thus Clark Gable still seduced with an effortless and reckless smile; Spencer Tracy – a double Oscar winner for *Captains Courageous* (1937) and *Boys' Town* (1938), and star of King Vidor's *Northwest Passage* (1940) – ran him a close second for the title 'King of the Lot'; Norma Shearer was still all sweetness and light; Joan Crawford remained

deadly and dangerous and dressed to kill; and William Powell and Myrna Loy still wisecracked their way through *The Thin Man* films. In Lubitsch's *Ninotchka* (1939), Greta Garbo even laughed for the first time on screen when she played the Soviet commissar in Paris bewitched by the debonair Melvyn Douglas. The only star missing from the still glamorous line-up was the vivacious Jean Harlow. In 1937, aged just 26, she had died of cerebral oedema after collapsing on the set of *Saratoga* with a kidney disorder. Harlow's mother, a woman of strong religious beliefs,

at first refused to let doctors attend her daughter, but when she relented, it proved to be too late.

As always, Mayer's search for new faces met with some success. Lana Turner smouldered sexily in several movies; the red-headed Greer Garson achieved immediate fame as the young wife of schoolmaster Robert Donat in *Goodbye Mr. Chips* (1939); and the seductive Hedy Lamarr also joined the ranks, usually typecast as a woman of mystery.

The area in which MGM changed most in 1939 was that of the musical. It had always been a musical studio of course, but during the Thirties its reputation had suffered because of the success of the Astaire/Rogers musicals at RKO and the leggy chorus-line spectaculars of Busby Berkeley at Warners. MGM's main contributions had been the long and highly popular series of lightweight operettas starring Nelson Eddy and Jeanette

MacDonald, the Oscar-winning *The Great Ziegfeld* (1936), which was more of a biography with musical sequences than a genuine musical, and the extravagant and none-too-successful (financially) musicals of the tap-dancing Eleanor Powell – *Born to Dance* (1936) and *Rosalie* (1937). However, in 1939, thanks to a young producer by the name of Arthur Freed and the talents of the young Mickey Rooney and Judy Garland, things changed.

Mickey Rooney first became popular when he appeared in the Andy Hardy series, films put into production by Mayer as examples of how a clean-cut American boy belonging to an upper middle-class family (his father was a judge) was supposed to live and behave. The films weren't meant to become a series but they became so popular that Rooney finished up making more than one a year for ten years. By 1939 the early films in the series had

helped him push Shirley Temple off the top spot as America's number one movie star.

Judy Garland began her career rather more sedately. Her first big moment in the movies occurred when she sang 'Dear Mr. Gable (You Made Me Love You)' to a photograph of Clark Gable in *Broadway Melody of 1938* (1937). Just 15 years old, she stole the show with this one scene and, later the same year, was awarded her first top billing opposite Mickey Rooney in a little picture called *Thoroughbreds Don't Cry*. In 1939, she became a star throughout the world when she played Dorothy in *The Wizard of Oz* and followed the yellow brick road into a magical Technicolored fairyland, accompanied by Ray Bolger's Scarecrow, Jack Haley's Tin Woodman and Bert Lahr's Cowardly Lion – and also by a Harold Arlen/E. Y. Harburg score that included 'Over the Rainbow'.

Freed's subsequent teaming of Mickey

Rooney and Judy Garland proved to be as inspired as that of Nelson Eddy and Jeanette MacDonald. The Garland/Rooney pictures were bright and shiny and modern, and included songs by Rodgers and Hart and George Gershwin. They bounced along with such energy and pace that any disbelief in their plotlines was temporarily suspended. Basically they were little more than 'putting-on-a-show' musicals, set in wholesome American neighbourhoods where every little house was scrubbed and clean, every garden was neat and tidy and everyone's morals and motivations were beyond reproach. Boasting a song every ten minutes or so, they were climaxed by huge production numbers staged by Busby Berkeley who had, at long last, been lured away from his beloved line of chorus girls at Warners. The finales of *Babes in Arms* (1939), *Strike Up the Band* (1940) and *Babes on Broadway* (1941) were so spectacular that

*'Greta Garbo laughs!' said the billboards. But not in this scene. Melvyn Douglas is the one checking out the facts, Garbo is the rather suspicious Russian. A scene from Ernst Lubitsch's 1939 comedy* Ninotchka *(MGM).*

*Judy Garland and Ray Bolger on the yellow brick road. A scene from MGM's 1939 musical fantasy, The Wizard of Oz.*

*Judy Garland and Mickey Rooney in* Strike Up the Band *(MGM, 1941).*

there was no way they could have been staged by kids from the neighbourhood, but that didn't really matter. The more removed they were from reality, the better the audiences liked it. And as long as Rooney and Garland were on hand to deliver the numbers, there was no cause for complaint.

However, although Rooney and Garland sang their hearts out and Garbo laughed and all the other stars did their bit at MGM in 1939, they were still no more than 'also-rans' when compared with the stars who featured in the picture that everyone knew was going to be the hit of the year – *Gone with the Wind.*

Even before it went before the cameras, everyone was discussing the film. Who, for instance was going to play the handsome blockade runner, Rhett Butler? That one was easily settled, and although Errol Flynn, Ronald Colman and even Basil Rathbone were all mentioned as possibilities, there was never any real doubt that the role would go to Clark Gable. Author Margaret Mitchell even confessed that she had written the book with Gable in mind. No one complained either

about the casting of Leslie Howard as Ashley Wilkes or Olivia de Havilland as his cousin Melanie. The real problem lay with who was going to play Scarlett O'Hara, the southern belle around whom Margaret Mitchell's massive romance about the Old South during and after the Civil War revolved.

At first, producer David O. Selznick was confident. It seemed that every actress in Hollywood wanted to play Scarlett, from Bette Davis to Katharine Hepburn, and it was just a case of whittling away until the right girl was found. But gradually he found that first one star and then another was unsuitable for the role and then he began to get worried. Tests with such actresses as Paulette Goddard, Lana Turner, Susan Hayward, Joan Fontaine and Jean Arthur came to nothing. So did hundreds of others. All were found wanting.

In the end Selznick actually began shooting *Gone with the Wind* without the role of Scarlett being cast. Legend has it that on the night the cameras first began turning on the burning of Atlanta, Selznick's brother Myron

brought the young Vivien Leigh to the set and touched Selznick gently on the arm. Selznick thrilled at last that his epic production was under way, turned to see the face of the beautiful young English actress. 'David,' said Myron, 'I would like you to meet your Scarlett O'Hara!'

*Gone with the Wind* quickly established itself as the biggest moneymaker of all time, holding the record for a quarter of a century until it was eventually displaced by *The Sound of Music* in 1965. It took over five months to film (140 shooting days were officially recorded on the shooting schedule) and featured 59 leading and supporting actors. A close examination of that arduous schedule reveals just how much of a strain the role was for the 26-year-old Vivien Leigh. Of the 140 days, she worked no fewer than 125, compared with Gable's 71, de Havilland's 59 and Leslie Howard's 32. The directors suffered almost as much as the stars: George Cukor began the

film but was sacked after a few days; Victor Fleming, who directed most of the main story of Rhett and Scarlett, contributed over 55 per cent of the film before collapsing from a heart attack; and Sam Wood finished the picture. Production designer William Cameron Menzies and second-unit director B. Reeves Eason also shot key scenes in the movie. The final running time of the film (after a first rough-cut of 5 hours) was 3 hours and 42 minutes, and the final cost was $3,957,000. The result at the end of the day? Nine Academy Awards and, against all the odds, a great film.

Actually *Gone with the Wind* wasn't really an MGM film at all. It was an independent production made by David O. Selznick and it was Selznick's money that went into the picture. Louis B. Mayer, however, as sharp as ever, had cleverly acquired the distribution rights in theatres across the world, which meant that he could make almost as much money from the film as Selznick himself. The

Gone with the Wind (*Selznick/MGM, 1939*). Left to right: *Harry Davenport, Clark Gable, Leslie Howard, Vivien Leigh and Olivia de Havilland.*

reason he was able to pull off the deal was because he had Clark Gable under contract and, without Gable, *Gone with the Wind* would not have gone ahead. The public let their views be known on that score long before a camera turned.

*Gone with the Wind* brought to an end a decade that many were glad to see pass into history. The Depression had made it a decade to endure rather than to enjoy. The Hollywood studios, through their stars and movies, had helped make it more bearable, with glamour and great stories and music raising many a spirit in the dark days. The studios were to provide a similar service in the decade that lay ahead, one which, as Britain declared war on Germany on 3 September 1939, was to prove just as dangerous, just as dark.

*Vivien Leigh gets the Gable treatment in Victor Fleming's* Gone with the Wind *(Selznick/MGM, 1939).*

# 1940
# Twentieth Century-Fox

## Pin-up Girl: Betty Grable

Fox's immediate answer to the question of keeping up morale in wartime was Betty Grable, a young blonde who had been around Hollywood for years without anyone taking too much notice of her. Her big break came about because of a huge stroke of luck. Alice Faye, who had been set to co-star with Don Ameche in *Down Argentine Way* (1940), was suddenly struck with appendicitis and Grable was rushed in as a replacement. Without that lucky break, it's quite possible that audiences' eyes would never have feasted on those famous legs nor would they have enjoyed the warm, sexy personality that was Grable. And that, without question, would have made the Second World War just that much harder to bear for thousands, indeed millions of servicemen across the world.

Mind you, Grable needed all the luck that was going in 1940. She had appeared in more than 30 films over a period of ten years before she was eventually signed by Zanuck. In her early days, she had even struggled along as a Goldwyn girl, and had even felt like quitting the movies. But when Faye fell ill, she was for once in the right place at the right time, and after *Down Argentine Way*, she never looked back.

As far as Zanuck was concerned Betty Grable was an 'overnight success'. The public's reaction to her was immediate, especially that of the male members of audiences. In modern parlance, she was a superstar, for between 1942 and 1951, she was never once out of the list of Top Ten moneymaking stars in the United States. Zanuck must have wondered, more than once, just what he had done to deserve such luck: just as Shirley Temple was growing into awkward ado-

lescence, along came a brand-new money-maker, seemingly right out of the blue. And like so many other top female stars at the studio, she was a blonde.

Betty Grable's appeal lay in the fact that she wasn't only a sex symbol, she was also very much the girl next door. She was pert, bouncy and vibrant, her blonde hair, peaches-and-cream complexion and warm, friendly personality all combined to make her something very special to the American male. Whenever she appeared in a musical, which was on average twice a year, Zanuck knew that he could sit back and count the dollars. Not one of her pictures was of any consequence, all were absurd trifles, but once the musical numbers took over from the clichéd plots, things always brightened up considerably. The songs were invariably tuneful, zippy and lavishly staged. All were bathed in the richest of Technicolor and all displayed the stunning Grable legs to their very best advantage.

Grable was Zanuck's insurance policy. What is more, she happened at just the right time, not only for Fox but for the United States as a whole. When, after the bombing of Pearl Harbor on 7 December 1941, thousands of young GIs began to be shipped out overseas, many of them never to return, she came to represent something they could all identify with – the 'All-American Pin-up Girl'. During the Second World War, it was estimated that three million servicemen requested pin-up photographs of the blonde Fox star. Especially popular was the photo in which, according to one critic, 'she was squeezed, perhaps sewn, into a white bathing

*Betty Grable – Twentieth Century-Fox's top box-office star throughout the 1940s.*

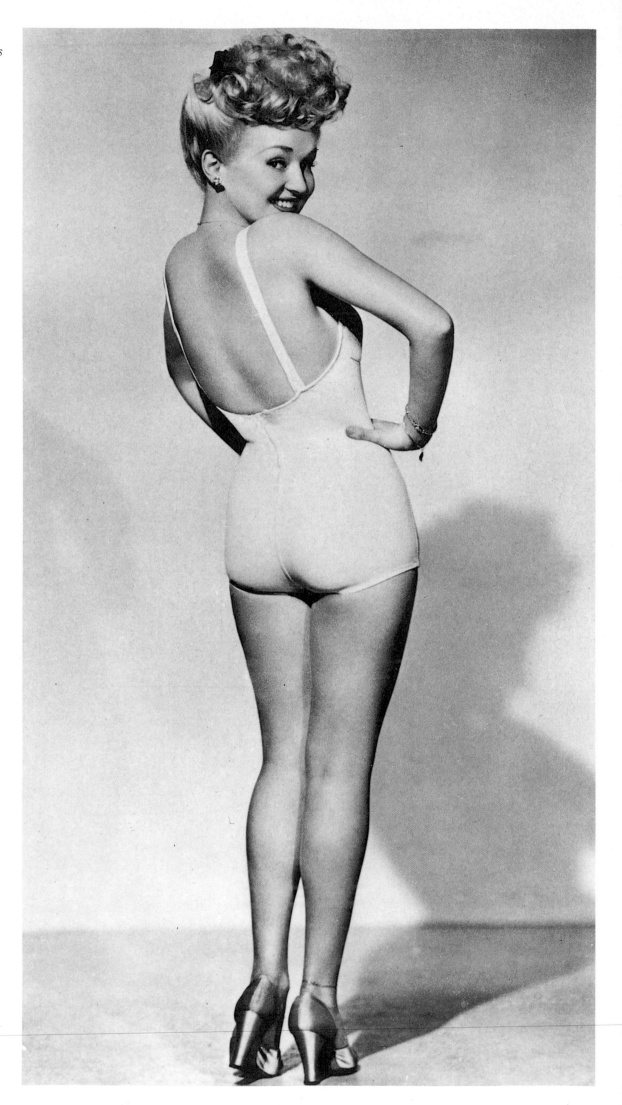

*Betty Grable plus white bathing suit! The most famous pin-up photograph of the Second World War.*

suit and peeked saucily over her shoulder.'
The studio publicity department made sure
they never ran out of that particular picture,
and in fact they stocked it in five sizes,
ranging from the very small 'over-the-heart'
size to an enormous display print, ideal for
posting in lockers, barracks and similar
places.

The movies that helped foster such ex-
treme adoration included *Tin Pan Alley*
(1940), in which, together with Alice Faye,
she performed 'The Sheik of Araby' in sheer
pantaloons and sequinned bra; *Moon over
Miami* (1941), in which she was one of three
girls seeking millionaire husbands; and *Coney
Island* (1943), in which she sang 'Cuddle Up a
Little Closer' and was fought over by rival
saloon proprietors George Montgomery and
Cesar Romero. She had no such problems in
real life: on 5 July 1943 (and much to the
chagrin of millions of males across the world),
she married jazz trumpeter Harry James in a
Las Vegas hotel room. The marriage lasted
for 22 years.

The Betty Grable musicals of the early
Forties represented the commercial side of
Twentieth Century-Fox, as did those of Alice
Faye and Glenn Miller. In addition, there
were the Tyrone Power swashbucklers – *The
Mark of Zorro* (1940) and *The Black Swan*
(1942) – and Laird Cregar's foray into Gothic
horror *The Lodger* (1944), a bloodcurdling tale
of Jack the Ripper. However, there was also a
more serious side to the studio and, in the
early Forties, Zanuck was anxious to exploit it
and earn, both for himself and for Fox,
something that was still missing from the
shelves in his office – an Oscar. The studio
had won Oscars, of course, but never the one
for best picture and that was something that
niggled at Zanuck. It was also something he
was determined to put to rights.

Many thought that he should have
achieved his ambition in 1940 when he
personally produced one of the enduring
masterpieces of the American cinema, John
Ford's version of the John Steinbeck novel *The
Grapes of Wrath*. Few great books are turned

*Betty Grable at the height of
her popularity in the
Technicolor musical* Coney
Island *(Twentieth Century-
Fox, 1943).*

*Right: Masked avenger Tyrone Power in the Rouben Mamoulian swashbuckler* The Mark of Zorro *(Twentieth Century-Fox, 1940). On the wrong end of the blade: J. Edward Bromberg!*

*Opposite: One of Hollywood's greatest sets. The Welsh mining village designed by Richard Day and Nathan Juran for John Ford's* How Green Was My Valley? *(Twentieth Century-Fox, 1941).*

*Below: A Fox masterpiece; John Ford's version of John Steinbeck's Depression novel* The Grapes of Wrath *(1940).*

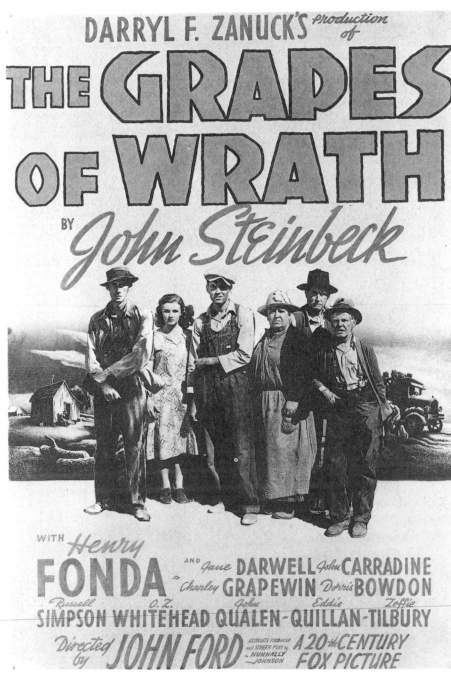

DARRYL F. ZANUCK'S *production of*

# THE GRAPES OF WRATH

BY *John Steinbeck*

WITH *Henry* **FONDA** AND *Jane* **DARWELL** *John* **CARRADINE** *Charley* **GRAPEWIN** *Dorris* **BOWDON** *Russell* **SIMPSON** *O.Z.* **WHITEHEAD** *John* **QUALEN** *Eddie* **QUILLAN** *Zeffie* **TILBURY** *Directed by* **JOHN FORD** *Associate Producer and Screen Play by NUNNALLY JOHNSON* A 20th CENTURY FOX PICTURE

into equally great films, but *The Grapes of Wrath*, beautifully crafted by Ford, was an exception. A story of a family of Oakies who, during the Depression, are forced to leave their homes in the Oklahoma dustbowl and seek new lives in California, it earned praise from all the major critics and Oscars for Ford as best director and Jane Darwell as best supporting actress, but it missed out on the major prize, best picture.

As it turned out, Zanuck didn't have too long to wait for his best picture Academy Award. It came his way just a year after he had missed out with *The Grapes of Wrath*. The film was *How Green Was My Valley?* (1941), a version of Richard Llewellyn's moving tale of life in a Welsh mining village at the turn of the century, with stars Walter Pidgeon, Maureen O'Hara and a young Roddy McDowall. It won five Academy Awards in all, including one for Zanuck and another for John Ford, the director who had served him so faithfully for so many years.

One that got away (financially) but which is held in almost as high regard as *The Grapes of Wrath* was *The Ox-Bow Incident* (*Strange Incident* in UK), made by maverick director William Wellman in 1943. A harsh, uncompromising western, it focuses on a lynch mob that hangs three men for cattle rustling and then discovers too late that the men are innocent after all. Henry Fonda (who as a boy had witnessed a terrifying lynching in real life), Dana Andrews and Anthony Quinn headed the strong cast. When Wellman first showed Zanuck the finished film, which ran for only 75 minutes, the latter waited for a long time before he passed comment. After

*Betty Grable and Dick Haymes in the 1945 musical hit* Diamond Horseshoe *(Twentieth Century-Fox).*

several minutes, he turned to Wellman and said: 'Bill, I don't think it will ever make a dime, but it's something I want my studio to have. I want to have my name on it.'

There were other pictures in the early Forties with which Zanuck was glad to be associated. For instance, Otto Preminger's classic thriller *Laura* (1944) earned plaudits for the seductive Gene Tierney and acclaim for Clifton Webb, a dancing star of the Twenties who made a sensational comeback as the murdering columnist Waldo Lydecker. Then there was *The Song of Bernadette* (1943), which turned Jennifer Jones into a major star as Marie Bernarde Soubirous, the Maid of Lourdes, and which, although not highly rated critically, none the less earned $5 million at the box office. Zanuck wasn't even sorry to have on his payroll the outrageous Brazilian dancing star Carmen Miranda who literally went bananas in the 'Lady in the Tutti-Frutti Hat' sequence in *The Gang's All Here* (1943).

His one major disappointment was the failure of his long and painstaking biography *Wilson* (1944), an account of the political career or President Woodrow Wilson. It was a serious miscalculation. In 1944, while they were busily engaged in fighting and trying to win the current conflict, audiences were just not interested in learning about a president who, in 1917, had tried to prevent the United States from entering the First World War. *Wilson*, which starred Alexander Knox, lost money and went down as one of the great failures of Zanuck's career. However, it was an isolated failure, for 90 per cent of the Fox movies were either critical successes or box-office hits, and that wasn't a bad basis on which to build a still young Hollywood studio.

By 1945, Grable was still top of the tree, just as she had been in 1941 and throughout the war. The directors who worked with her – Walter Lang, Irving Cummings, Henry Koster – weren't the great ones but they realized her worth. Many felt that she should have been awarded her own special Oscar for services rendered to the Fox studio. Henry Koster, who worked with her later in her career once remarked: 'A girl like Grable who has been carrying the box office for years ought to have some special recognition. Her money-earning musicals have made possible many Oscar-earning films. Maybe there should be a small credit line engraved on each Oscar: "Betty Grable helped pay for this." '

Betty herself said of her talent: 'I'm strictly a song-and-dance girl. I can act enough to get by. But let's face it, that's the limit of my talents. It's not that an acting role scares me. If I have a good enough director, he can usually pull me through the tight places. But I feel more secure if they let me do a few numbers. I'm no Bette Davis nor am I out to prove anything with histrionics. I just want to make pictures that people will like.'

That she succeeded and people did like the pictures she made can best be gauged from the astonishing grosses of her films as a top Fox star. She made 28 films all told, and between them they earned in the region of $100 million!

*Henry Fonda tries to stop a hanging, without success, in William Wellman's powerful* The Ox-Bow Incident *(Twentieth Century-Fox, 1943).*

# 1941
## RKO

### Orson Welles and *Citizen Kane*

*Orson Welles as* Citizen Kane (RKO, 1941), *regarded by many critics as the greatest film ever made.*

Orson Welles, although rather more talented than Betty Grable, was never able to command such undying admiration at the box office. As far as the movies were concerned, he was always the darling of the critics but never, sadly, of the public. Yet when he first arrived in Los Angeles in July 1939, great things were expected of him. He had, after all, scared America half to death just a few months before (on 30 October 1938) with an on-the-spot radio version of H. G. Wells' *War of the Worlds*, so many were interested to see what he would make of Hollywood – and, indeed, what Hollywood would make of him.

Before he actually got there, there was much talk about which studio would be the first to employ the 24-year-old *wunderkind*. Harry Cohn's Columbia, maybe; Cohn was always prepared to take a gamble. Or perhaps Zanuck at Fox – he and Welles would almost certainly have found something that would have worked to their mutual advantage. That, in the end, the studio turned out to be RKO came as no surprise, however. The artistic freedom at the studio had been enjoyed by many in the Thirties, and with no all-powerful mogul in charge, RKO was able to give Welles exactly what he wanted – a contract that stated that he could produce, direct, write and act in a minimum of one film a year. The fact that he got his way amazed many of those in Hollywood. Admittedly, RKO were almost back to square one after the break-up of the Astaire/Rogers dancing team, but a contract such as the one they offered Welles was surely asking for trouble. It certainly created a degree of hostility on the RKO lot. Mark Robson, a director who was to work on the RKO horror films of producer Val Lewton, commented: 'Welles came to RKO with a free-wheeling contract and was given what in those days was a great deal of money to make films. It caused RKO ruptures with several directors who were upset by the freedom given to Orson that they did not have. There were great jealousies around.'

*Orson Welles and Dorothy Comingore – plus jigsaw puzzle – in Welles' 1941 production* Citizen Kane *(RKO).*

However, despite the *carte blanche* contract, Welles found that he had trouble getting started. During the months of August and September, he sat and studied two films for hours on end – the expressionist German silent classic *The Cabinet of Dr. Caligari* and John Ford's western *Stagecoach*. Once he had learned as much as he could from those two movies, he announced that his first film would be *Heart of Darkness*, a million-dollar version of the novel by Joseph Conrad. But that idea quickly fell through and Welles next opted for something less ambitious, a detective thriller called *The Smiler with The Knife*. When that too came to nothing and Welles, after many months, was still without a project, many in Hollywood began to smirk about the boy wonder who wasn't able to come up with anything, and they wondered aloud whether Welles would indeed make a movie after all.

At the very moment the gossip mongers were in full cry, Welles was, at the third attempt, at last at work. He called his movie *Citizen Kane*. He cast himself in the leading role and produced, directed and co-wrote

*Orson Welles at work on set directing* The Magnificent Ambersons *(RKO, 1942).*

(with Herman J. Mankiewicz) the entire production. In the other parts, he cast members of his Mercury Company who had been with him earlier in the theatre and on radio – Joseph Cotten, Ruth Warrick, Agnes Moorehead, Everett Sloane and Paul Stewart – all making their film debuts in the picture.

The movie was based loosely on the life of newspaper magnate, William Randolph Hearst. Its story begins after the tycoon's death (when he utters the single dying word 'Rosebud') and centres on the efforts of a reporter to uncover the meaning of that word as he interviews people Kane had known in his lifetime. The secret of 'Rosebud' is revealed only in the very last shot, being the name on a sledge that Kane had owned in childhood. The meaning of the final shot was

felt by many to be ambiguous, but Welles later stated that it was meant to symbolize Kane's loss of innocence, before he became corrupted by power.

It wasn't so much the story of *Citizen Kane* that made it so extraordinary. Rather, it was the *way* in which it was made, with its expressionistic deep-focus photography (by Gregg Toland), its audacious use of flashbacks, sets closed in by ceilings, bizarre camera angles and its complex plot involving five narrators.

In Hollywood, no one had ever seen anything quite like it before, and those at RKO viewed it with trepidation. If they had hoped to make money out of Welles, they knew then and there that they had made an error. *Kane* was too complex, too experimental, too good even, to make much impact with the public.

Many actors who worked on the film later admitted that they had little idea that they were working on a picture that was destined to be hailed as the greatest film ever made.

It was the technicians rather than the actors who were aware of what was happening. Robert Wise, the editor of *Citizen Kane* and himself the Oscar-winning director of *West Side Story* and *The Sound of Music*, was in no doubt that he was involved with something special: 'I saw a lot of the shooting and, of course, a lot of marvellous rushes coming in. And we knew we were getting something quite out of the ordinary. I mean you couldn't look at the dailies and see those magnificent shots and great performances and not know that it was something quite special, that Orson was really producing quality material.'

As far as newspaper magnate William Randolph Hearst was concerned, the quality of the material was the last thing on his mind. He believed firmly that the film was a biographical account of his own life, but the fact that it contained nothing libellous drove

him to fury. He immediately forbade his newspapers to carry advertisements for or even mention the film, threatened to sue and even offered RKO a sum of money to burn the film's negative. RKO fought back every inch of the way and premièred the film in New York on 1 May 1941. The critics (as had been expected) were euphoric, the public (again as the studio had expected) were indifferent. At Oscar time, when many felt that the film should have walked off with all the major awards, it earned just one – for best original screenplay, shared by Welles with his co-writer Herman J. Mankiewicz. There was even hissing when the Welles' name was read out. He had been called a draft dodger and a communist, and the fact that he should even win one award was an unpopular decision.

After *Kane*, Welles' position at RKO became more precarious, and when his next film – an eventually mutilated version of Booth Tarkington's *The Magnificent Ambersons* (1942), about the decline of a wealthy Midwestern family during the early years of the 20th century – proved to be another box-office flop, his days at the studio quickly

The Magnificent Ambersons *(RKO, 1942), Orson Welles' follow-up to* Citizen Kane*. Left to right: Richard Bennett, Joseph Cotten, Dolores Costello, Tim Holt, Agnes Moorehead and Ray Collins.*

became numbered. He made one more film – the thriller *Journey into Fear* (1943) in which he starred, produced, co-wrote (with Joseph Cotten) but directed only his own scenes – before leaving RKO to freelance as an actor and, when he was allowed, as a director. He was never again to achieve the cinematic excellence he realized with *Citizen Kane*, and the rest of his film career was all downhill. It was a sad waste of an extraordinary talent, and the decline of Orson Welles was to prove one of the great tragedies of Hollywood.

That RKO should have come out ahead during the Orson Welles era was, in retrospect, surprising, but despite all the problems, they still managed to emerge from those

turbulent years in the black. The year 1941 itself wasn't too good, just $500,000 in profits, but in 1942 that had edged up to $750,000, and by 1943 the figure had jumped dramatically to $7 million. In 1944 and 1945, RKO still managed to average between $5 million and $6 million in annual profits.

It was a remarkable success story for a studio without stars and only a handful of outstanding films. Those movies were of undoubted quality: Hitchcock directed *Suspicion* (1941) in which he cast Cary Grant as a happy-go-lucky cad whose wife (played by an Oscar-winning Joan Fontaine) believes he is trying to kill her. William Dieterle filmed *All that Money Can Buy* (1941), a version of

*Poisoned milk? Joan Fontaine can't be sure but who'd refuse Cary Grant? A scene from Alfred Hitchcock's* Suspicion *(RKO, 1941).*

*Dick Powell, the first actor to portray Chandler's private eye Philip Marlowe, in a scene from* Murder My Sweet *(Farewell My Lovely in UK, RKO, 1944). Under cross-examination: Esther Howard.*

*Tom Conway (left), star of RKO's popular 'B' movie series,* The Falcon, *in the early 1940s.*

Stephen Vincent Benét's *The Devil and Daniel Webster*, a Faustian tale about a New England farmer who sells his soul for a pot of gold. Ginger Rogers cast off her dancing shoes to win an Academy Award as *Kitty Foyle* (1940), a girl from the wrong side of the tracks who has to choose between a rich married socialite and an industrious young doctor. Former Warner singing idol Dick Powell also changed his image by starring as Raymond Chandler's private-eye Philip Marlowe in *Murder My Sweet* (*Farewell My Lovely* in UK, 1944).

Another plus factor as far as the studio was concerned was that they distributed the films of both Walt Disney and Sam Goldwyn, who, in 1939, had severed his connections with United Artists and opted to release his movies through the RKO outlets instead.

Goldwyn's films of the early Forties were frequently memorable, none more so than Howard Hawks' fast-moving comedy *Ball of Fire* (1941), which starred Gary Cooper as one of seven professors writing an encyclopaedia who finds that burlesque dancer Barbara Stanwyck offers him rather more pleasure than books, and William Wyler's *The Little Foxes* (1941), which presented Bette Davis with one of her greatest and bitchiest roles, that of the scheming Southern vixen Regina Giddens, who lets her husband, played by Herbert Marshall, die of a heart attack without moving a muscle to help him.

RKO also got quite a lot of mileage out of the horror films of Val Lewton, an intelligent and very literate producer whose films were refreshingly subtle in their approach. Lewton's first horror film for RKO, *Cat People* (1942), had, on the face of it, a story that was laughable – that of a Balkan-born girl who has the ability to change into an outsize homicidal cat. What was not so laughable was what was up on the screen and the question that usually arose with Lewton's films was 'What *was* up there?'

In *Cat People*, for instance, audiences witnessed a young girl being pursued by something through Central Park at night. But what *was* that something? They couldn't see clearly for Lewton never showed them. Similarly, later in the film, when the girl is trapped in a dark, deserted swimming pool and the only sounds are those of lapping water and the breathing of the stalking cat, Lewton never actually showed the cat. He left everything to the imagination, and that was always much worse than anything he could possibly show on the screen.

Lewton played similar tricks with his audiences throughout a whole series of movies in the early and mid-Forties. In *I Walked with a Zombie* (1943), he transferred the *Jane Eyre* story to the West Indies and conjured up a hauntingly eerie walk through the cane fields at night, every step of the way accompanied by the constant beating of voodoo drums. In *The Seventh Victim* (1943), he dealt subtly with devil worship in contemporary New York, and in *Bedlam* (1946), he had that master of the horror movie, Boris Karloff, bricked up alive by the inmates of an asylum. *The Leopard Man* (1943), *Curse of the Cat People* (1944) and *The Body Snatcher* (1945) were other Lewton productions in similar vein. They cost virtually nothing to produce – in fact, the first film in the series was brought in for as little as $130,000 – but all of them showed a handsome profit and began the careers of three talented directors: Robert Wise, Jacques Tourneur and Mark Robson.

Just as it had been in the Thirties, the RKO studio was run in the Forties by a succession of production heads – George J. Schaefer, Charles Koerner, William Dozier – whose names have long since been forgotten and who didn't even enjoy much fame when they were actually at the studio. The fact that they were little known and had very little influence on how RKO developed almost certainly worked to the studio's advantage. The studio just carried on, stumbling along in its own unpredictable and appealing way. It was to prove to be something of an irony, therefore, that when the studio was eventually taken over by a major figure – namely, Howard Hughes in 1948 – it began, not to make money, but to lose it more steadily than at any time since its formative years in the early Thirties.

*I Walked with a Zombie (1943), an early Val Lewton horror movie and one of several popular films of its kind made at RKO during the 1940s.*

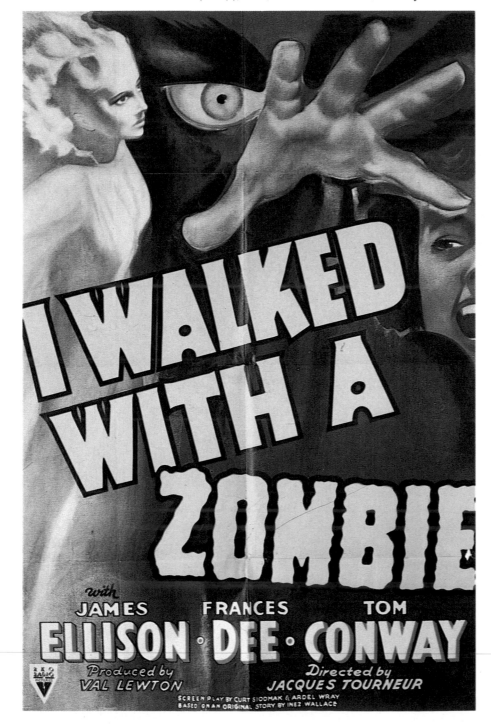

# 1942
## Columbia

### The Rita Hayworth Years and the Musical

In 1942, Harry Cohn was still as crude and foul-mouthed as he had been at Columbia in the Thirties when he had first tasted success at his little studio on Gower Street. However, although Harry hadn't changed one iota since the great days with Frank Capra, his studio most certainly had – and it had changed out of necessity.

When Capra left in 1939, Cohn had found himself in a similar quandary to that facing the production heads of RKO, when Astaire and Rogers left. He found that, profitable though it was to enjoy a steady stream of hit movies from one source (i.e. Capra), once that source had dried up, a studio could be in trouble if it didn't have adequate reserves of talent in the acting and directing fields. In the early Forties, Cohn found himself to be just that little bit short on reserves.

He had two major problems on his hands, both of which he had to solve quickly. The first was to find a director who could do for the studio what Capra had done for it in the Thirties. The other was to try and find someone on the company payroll – male or female, it didn't matter which – who might be groomed into a moneymaking star for the company. He expected to succeed in finding a new director but held out little hope of discovering a star. As things turned out, the reverse happened. He missed out on the director but found the most glamorous star imaginable – Rita Hayworth.

The two directors Cohn brought in to temporarily help out with the comedy situation were both men of considerable stature – Howard Hawks and George Stevens. Between them, they contributed a classic trio of films

that were so tasteful and sophisticated that people marvelled at how so crude a tycoon as Harry Cohn could initiate such stylish entertainments. The secret was, of course, that 'King Cohn' knew how to appreciate class. He recognized style when he saw it, and was quick to stamp a Columbia label on a class product when he could. The Hawks/Stevens comedies showed that appreciation. All were clean, fast and witty.

Hawks' 1940 Columbia comedy was *His Girl Friday*, an ingenious and fast-talking reworking of the 1931 hit *The Front Page*. Hawks recast it with Cary Grant as the newspaper editor Walter Burns, and Rosalind Russell (in a role originally played by a man)

*Editor Cary Grant and irate reporter Rosalind Russell in Howard Hawks' fast-moving newspaper comedy His Girl Friday (Columbia, 1940).*

as reporter Hildy Johnson who, covering an execution, suddenly finds herself in the possession of a once-in-a-lifetime scoop.

George Stevens' contributions were *The More the Merrier* (1943), with Joel McCrea and Jean Arthur involved in romance amid the housing shortage in wartime Washington, and *The Talk of the Town* (1942), with Cary Grant as a wrongly accused arsonist hiding out in the house of eminent law professor Ronald Colman and arguing that the law should have a human as well as a legal side. The latter film was elegantly played and had a theme that, on occasion, even bore a passing resemblance to one of Capra's.

While all this frenetic comedy activity was taking place, the young Rita Hayworth was steadily working her way up the Columbia ladder. It would be more accurate to say 'slowly' rather than 'steadily' for she had been at the studio since 1936, when she appeared (under her real name of Rita Cansino) in her first Columbia picture, *Meet Nero Wolfe*, a detective thriller starring Edward Arnold.

It wasn't until three years and 12 movies later that she first made an impression, as the wife of shattered pilot Richard Barthelmess in Hawks' *Only Angels Have Wings* (1939), but for once Harry Cohn was slow to react to the situation. He could see that her long auburn tresses, brown eyes and peaches-and-cream

*Above: Caught in the act! Jean Arthur on the trail of Charles Coburn in George Stevens' 1943 comedy* The More the Merrier *(Columbia).*

*Right: Cary Grant, Jean Arthur and Ronald Colman in* Talk of the Town *(Columbia, 1942).*

*Opposite: Rita Hayworth, Columbia's beautiful dancing star of the 1940s.*

Phil Silvers, Rita Hayworth and Gene Kelly having a ball in Columbia's 1944 Technicolor musical Cover Girl.

complexion made her a natural, but because she was basically a musical star (she was a superb dancer), she seemed to be at the wrong studio, for Columbia – apart from the Grace Moore vehicles – didn't go in for musicals. Columbia had only six or seven sound stages, hardly enough to warrant embarking on a large-scale musical programme, and in any case, musicals meant large-scale production numbers, increased staff and higher costs and that was something Cohn felt he could not handle. The New York office always kept a close watch on the Columbia purse strings (Capra's departure from the studio had been because he had not been allowed to make a film on the life of Chopin in colour!) and musicals were definitely not on the schedule.

Harry Cohn therefore took the easy way out and loaned Rita to other studios. In that way, he could make money during her loan-out periods and also check on how she

developed as a box-office star. She developed much quicker than he had ever imagined. As she starred opposite Tyrone Power in Blood and Sand for Fox and James Cagney in Strawberry Blonde for Warners, the public suddenly sat up and took notice, and when Life magazine published a spread showing her sprawled on a double bed, wearing only a black lace-and-satin négligé, Cohn knew that his worries for the future were over. On the spread, Rita's hair was russet-coloured and shoulder length, her legs were slim and long, her smile warm and beckoning. The caption beneath the photograph read: 'the goddess of love of the 20th century!'

Cohn needed no more convincing. Musicals might be expensive, but from that moment on they and not comedies were going to be the order of the day. Capra seemed suddenly to belong to the past, Hayworth to an appealing and very profitable future.

Cohn astutely cast her with Fred Astaire in her first two Columbia musicals, *You'll Never Get Rich* (1941) and *You Were Never Lovelier* (1942). Rita matched the master step for step, especially in the latter movie, and with her long hair falling seductively over her shoulders, she proved that she was as good a dancer as Ginger Rogers ever was. The dance duets were quite breathtaking: 'I'm Old-Fashioned' and 'Dearly Beloved' provided the romance, the jive number 'The Shorty George' the verve and snap. The only thing missing was Technicolor.

That arrived in the next big ones, *Cover Girl* (1944), in which Rita danced with another musical genius, Gene Kelly, who was then in the early stages of his career, and *Tonight and Every Night* (1945), in which she co-starred with Jane Blair in a story about an English revue that carried on throughout the London Blitz.

Her most famous film, *Gilda* (1946), in which she co-starred with Glenn Ford, was not a musical but contained probably the most famous dance routine Rita ever performed on the screen. Its title was 'Put the Blame on Mame, Boys' and it caused a sensation. Performed in a South American casino, it was as exciting as a strip-tease yet

there was no way it could be censored for all Rita removed was a black glove. It was the *way* she removed it that mattered: every moment, every gesture caused a sharp intake of breath and raised a vital question among cinema audiences: would the shimmering black evening gown she was wearing stand up under the strain? The moral code of Hollywood at the time, embodied in the Hays Office, saw to it that it did – but only just. For a few moments in *Gilda*, the temperature of the audience went soaring and the screen seemed to be white hot with torrid sex.

Harry Cohn was lucky with Rita Hayworth in more ways than one. If one of her pictures was not doing well (a rare event, incidentally), he could always rely on her private life to help out with the publicity. Two of her five marriages belong with the most famous in movie history, and both occurred during Rita's reign as the Columbia 'love goddess' of the Forties. In 1943, she married Orson Welles, and in 1949 she wed Prince Aly Khan, but neither marriage lasted any great length. The Hayworth/Welles affair was nicknamed 'Beauty and the Brain' and lasted until 1947. It frequently had its stormy moments. Rumour has it that, on one occasion, Rita was wakened at dead of night by her husband and

*Rita Hayworth sings 'Put the Blame on Mame' in the 1946 film noir, Gilda (Columbia).*

You Were Never Lovelier
(Columbia, 1942), the second
of the two musicals Rita
Hayworth made with Fred
Astaire at the studio during
the war years.

photo-flashed by two photographers at her bedside. Welles was quoted as saying that he had done it out of pride – to prove that Rita looked lovely at any hour of the day or night.

Whatever its difficulties, the Welles/Hayworth marriage did not affect Rita's career, for she went on making hit movies for Columbia just as she had always done. It was her marriage to Aly Khan that ruined her future

at the studio, for in order to get married, Rita had to walk out on her contract. It was a mistake. The marriage lasted only 16 months, and by the time she returned in 1951, Rita was 33 years old and found it difficult to re-establish herself at the top. The break – short though it had been – was disastrous, not only in personal terms but also from a career point of view. Harry Cohn, who had grown genuinely fond of Rita, was despondent at the turn of events, but by the late Forties, he was already looking once again in new directions and preparing for what was to emerge as Columbia 'Mark 3'.

However, for six golden years – 1941 to 1947 – Columbia, Cohn and Hayworth had shared a partnership that has gone down in film history as one of the most affectionately remembered of all time. It was not as artistically rewarding as the Capra partnership, but in the public mind at least, it was infinitely more exciting. Hayworth produced the goods for the studio and kept it buoyant. Her dancing was flamboyant, sexual, tantalizing – tossing back her hair with a nonchalant flick of the head, she attacked a number with an energy that set the pulses racing.

Cohn built his whole strategy around Rita in the Forties and he was wise to do so, for servicemen put her on almost as high a pedestal as Betty Grable. Even the Germans and the Japanese had her photograph pinned up in their barrack rooms. Cohn did manage to bring on other stars during the period: Glenn Ford, Rita's co-star in *Gilda*, was one, William Holden, who had made his debut in *Golden Boy* (1939) and appeared in several Columbia westerns of the Forties, was another. Cornel Wilde in *A Song to Remember* (1945) and Larry Parks, who came out of nowhere to act the part of Al Jolson and mime to his recordings in *The Jolson Story* (1946), also owed their start to the Columbia boss. But in the end, it was all down to Hayworth, just as in the Thirties it had all been down to Capra. And it was all down to Cohn too, of course. He was still a holy terror at his studio on Gower Street, but holy terror or not, he knew his business – and Columbia business in wartime and postwar America was very big business indeed.

*Moody . . . sultry . . . inviting . . . Rita Hayworth as* Gilda *(Columbia, 1946).*

# 1943
## Warner Bros.

Here's Looking At You Kid: Bogart and *Casablanca*

Bogart! If ever a male star dominated a studio during the Forties, it was Humphrey Bogart at Warner Bros. He wasn't, of course, a newcomer to the lot; in fact, he had made no fewer than 40 movies during the Thirties. Yet, despite his obvious talent for essaying characters on the shady side of the tracks (for example bootleggers and gangsters), he had always found it difficult to escape the shadows cast by Cagney and Robinson, especially the former. Towards the end of the decade, he could usually be found around third or fourth on the cast list but that was his limit, and major stardom seemed to elude

him. As Bogart himself so succinctly put it: 'I've always been the guy behind the guy behind the gun!'

By 1943, however, things had changed and very much for the better. Bogey had become a star of the first magnitude, he had won his first Oscar nomination and he had appeared in a film that, although no one realized it at the time, was destined to become an enduring American classic – *Casablanca*. Once the film went into general release, Bogart became a superstar and he remained a superstar for the rest of his career.

*Casablanca* (1943) was the film that consolidated Bogart's position at the top, but the movies that had first earned him his place among the top moneymaking stars of Hollywood had both been made two years earlier. One was a crime thriller in the traditional gangster mould, the other a detective story adapted from a Dashiell Hammett novel that had already been filmed twice before by the studio, and on both occasions unsuccessfully. On the face of it, the projects seemed to be little different from those that Bogart had been associated with many items before. However, it just so happened that the gangster film had a little bit more depth than usual, and the private-eye movie marked the debut of the talented young director John Huston. And as far as Bogart's career was concerned, that made all the difference.

The gangster film was *High Sierra* (1941). It was directed by the always efficient Raoul Walsh and recounted the final days in the life of the fugitive Roy Earle, the last of the Dillinger gang, who becomes emotionally involved with a crippled girl and meets his

High Sierra (*Warner Bros., 1941*). *Ida Lupino tends the dying gangster Roy Earle (Humphrey Bogart), the last of the Dillinger mob.*

*Humphrey Bogart – the dominant star at the Warner studio throughout the 1940s.*

death in a dramatic shoot-out in the mountains. It was a tough, fast-paced and well-made movie that, in its central relationship between the doomed Bogart and the young crippled girl he befriends, contained a degree of pathos and elements of genuine tragedy not usually associated with a Warner crime movie.

A few months after the release of *High Sierra*, Bogart improved on his new-found status even further when he played Hammett's private-eye Sam Spade in John Huston's *The Maltese Falcon* (1941). When he read the script, he discovered that it was a beauty, an almost perfect adaptation of the original novel. His role as the laconic Spade called for him to be tight-lipped, unsentimental and unsmiling, which he managed with no trouble at all. And somehow he also managed to sort out the complicated plot (revolving round a bizarre gang of crooks in search of a priceless statuette) and put paid to the machinations of beautiful *femme fatale* Mary Astor.

Cagney had been tough with his women in the Thirties, and Bogart showed them the same disregard in *The Maltese Falcon*. 'When you're slapped, you'll take it and like it,' he snarled at Astor during the course of the film.

*Humphrey Bogart as Dashiell Hammett's private eye, Sam Spade, in John Huston's 1941 version of* The Maltese Falcon *(Warner Bros.). The man behind the gun: a nervous Peter Lorre.*

In the end, he turns her over to the cops with a wry detachment and tells her, almost as an afterthought, that he'll wait for her. Then he adds, matter-of-factly, 'Unless, of course, they hang you. Then I'll always remember you.'

This was a new and assured Bogart and the public warmed to him. He had fine scripts to work with (W. R. Burnett and John Huston wrote *High Sierra*, and Huston worked solo on *The Maltese Falcon*) and he proved worthy of those scripts, emerging as an actor in complete control of his material. That control was demonstrated even more effectively in 1943 in *Casablanca*. Bogart's role was that of the cynical Rick Blaine, owner of the Café Americain and living out the war in a world-weary self-imposed exile in North Africa. On the surface, he is hard, jaded and unfeeling, interested only in looking after himself, but

beneath the surface he is as soft and vulnerable as the next man, especially when his lost love Ingrid Bergman emerges from his past and jolts him back to reality and into remembering his life as it used to be.

By the film's close, Dooley Wilson had sung 'As Time Goes By', Bogart had shot the Nazi chief Conrad Veidt, Bergman and her husband Paul Henreid were off on a plane to freedom and Bogey was walking off into the mist, arm in arm with French police captain Claude Rains. Along the way, he managed to deliver two of the most famous lines in the movies, both of them to Bergman: 'The problems of three people don't amount to a hill of beans in this crazy world,' he philosophizes at the film's close, and, as he gently turns up the chin of a tear-stained Bergman, 'Here's looking at you, kid.'

All of this is romantic and melodramatic nonsense, of course, and certainly was regarded as such when producer Hal Wallis first came across the script early in 1943. It was based on an unpublished play called *Everybody Comes to Rick's*, and there were so many characters in it that it resembled MGM's *Grand Hotel*, with intrigue and murder as added ingredients. Doubts were expressed at the Warner head-office, and even Wallis hesitated for quite a while before deciding to take a chance with the picture.

What eventually persuaded him to take the gamble was the 1938 film *Algiers*, which had starred Charles Boyer and Hedy Lamarr and had been a big success at the box office. Wallis reckoned that, if he changed the title of his project to *Casablanca*, he might have a reasonable chance of success, and if he added a number of the Warner top stars who were available on the lot, so much the better.

The really intriguing thing about *Casablanca* is that not a single member of the cast enjoyed making it. Bogart grumbled constantly about the script, which was unfinished when shooting began and in a constant state of change from day to day. Ingrid Bergman had one eye on the screenplay, which refused to tell her whether she finished up with Bogart or Paul Henreid, and one eye on the finishing date, for she was anxious not to miss the start of her next picture, Paramount's *For Whom the Bell Tolls*. Art director Carl Jules Weyl was unhappy with the sets and had them rebuilt; and composer Max Steiner even grumbled about the use of the song 'As Time Goes By'!

What is more, no one found working with director Michael Curtiz an easy matter, even though he'd been a Warner director throughout the Thirties and knew, more than most,

Casablanca *(Warner Bros.), named best picture of 1943 by Hollywood's Oscar Academy.*

*They all went to Rick's place in* Casablanca *(Warner Bros., 1943). Seen here with Humphrey Bogart – Claude Rains, Paul Henreid and Ingrid Bergman.*

Yankee Doodle Dandy
(*Warner Bros., 1942*), the
musical biography of George
M. Cohan and the film that
earned James Cagney his best
actor Academy Award.

how to make a movie fast, efficiently and with style. His main problem was that he was a manic depressive *and* a workaholic: in his book, a lunch break was simply a waste of time. Worse, very few people could understand him. A Hungarian by birth, he had first arrived in Hollywood in 1926 and, although he had mastered the film medium with ease, he had failed lamentably to come to terms with the English language. When making a western, he would frequently refer to cowboys as 'boy cows'; when filming a thriller, he would often startle his actors with the warning 'This next scene will make your blood curl'; and when directing a love scene, he would instruct a young starlet: 'It is morning and a haystack and lots of sunlight – turn over on your stomach and look sex.' Perhaps the most famous of all his mangled phrases was 'Bring on the empty horses!' (later immortalized by David Niven) and 'The next time I send a dumb sonofabitch to do something, I go myself.'

Somehow his actors *did* manage to understand him and on the night of 2 March 1944, at Grauman's Chinese Theater, there were few on the Warner lot who begrudged Curtiz his Academy Award for his work on *Casablanca*. There were also few who would have denied the film the award for best picture and writers Jules J. and Philip G. Epstein and Howard Koch their Oscars for best screenplay. The Academy of Motion Picture Arts and Sciences has often been criticized for

getting things wrong at award time, but in 1944, when the awards for 1943 were handed out, it got things right.

As a studio, Warners, too, got most things right in the Forties. They didn't try anything new, but were content to rely on the trusted formulas that had served them so well in the previous decade. They were kept buoyant by five forms of mainstream entertainment: crime movies, musicals, biographies, 'women's' pictures and swashbucklers.

Bogart was on hand to help out with the crime movies; the musicals often took on a wartime patriotic slant – among them, Irving Berlin's *This Is the Army* (1943); and the biographies, instead of delving into the lives of such historical figures as Zola and Pasteur, as they had done in the past, concentrated instead on glamorizing the lives of composers and entertainers. Thus James Cagney earned himself an Academy Award for his portrait of George M. Cohan in *Yankee Doodle Dandy* (1942), Robert Alda appeared as George Gershwin in *Rhapsody in Blue* (1945) and Cary Grant as Cole Porter in *Night and Day* (1946).

Bette Davis was the star who perhaps enjoyed herself most of all, for she ran the whole gamut of emotion in a long series of well-crafted 'women's' pictures. In the Somerset Maugham adaptation *The Letter* (1940) she played the murdering planter's wife Leslie Crosbie; in *Mr. Skeffington* (1944) she featured as a selfish New York beauty married to blinded financier Claude Rains; and in *The Corn Is Green* (1945), she starred as Emlyn Williams' English schoolteacher who discovers a pupil of genius in the Welsh valleys.

Her most memorable film of the period was *Now Voyager* (1942). She appeared as the frumpish young spinster Charlotte Vale who emerges from Claude Rains' psychiatric clinic (looking decidedly more chic than when she went in) and becomes romantically involved with the soulful (and married) Paul Henreid. Like Bogart in *Casablanca*, she enjoyed two of the most famous cinematic moments of the Forties – having a cigarette lit for her by Mr Henreid (the much-copied trick was to light both cigarettes in the mouth at the same time); and at the film's close, saying: 'Oh Jerry, don't let's ask for the moon. We have the stars.'

Only the swashbuckler went out of fashion for a while. Errol Flynn's last wartime venture into swordplay and derring-do was in Michael Curtiz' splendid *The Sea Hawk* in 1940. Thereafter he exchanged his rapier for a machine-gun and worked his way through a long series of wartime action adventures, including *Desperate Journey* (1942), *Northern Pursuit* (1943) and *Objective Burma* (1945).

Jack Warner's main problem was that he relied just a bit too heavily on the established stars at his studio and didn't concern himself overmuch with searching for new performers. Lauren Bacall, who slunk seductively through the Bogart classics *To Have and Have Not* (1945) and *The Big Sleep* (1946), was certainly a worthwhile addition to the line-up, but she became famous more by her association with and her eventual marriage to Bogart than for any star appeal she possessed. Joan Crawford was Warner's one big acquisition. She moved over from MGM and began a new career for herself at Burbank at the age of 41. The films

*Bette Davis as Charlotte Vale in* Now Voyager *(Warner Bros., 1942).*

A slinky Lauren Bacall, a tough Bogart – and a corpse. A scene from Howard Hawks' 1946 thriller The Big Sleep (Warner Bros.), derived from the novel by Raymond Chandler.

The most famous couple in Hollywood in the late 1940s: Humphrey Bogart and Lauren Bacall pictured together at a Hollywood party.

in which she was most at home were polished, smartly written melodramas that allowed her to suffer in at least a dozen major scenes and always when she was dressed most fashionably. In 1945, she proved to Louis B. Mayer, who had let her go, that she was by no means finished as a major star by winning an Oscar for her portrayal of a long-suffering mother in *Mildred Pierce*.

There the new talent ended, and Warner had to take comfort from the fact that he did at least have Bogart. With his hat pulled low and his trenchcoat pulled up high behind his neck, Bogart had become, without anyone realizing it or understanding why, the cinema's first anti-hero, and a 43-year-old anti-hero at that. His appeal was to last long after his death and to attract succeeding generations, who turned him into a cult figure. Certainly at the box office, his name counted

for everything as far as Jack Warner was concerned. A quick check on the top money-making stars of the period reveals that the only Warner star to appear regularly (he was never out of the top ten in the 1940s) was Bogart. As novelist Raymond Chandler once said of him: 'All he has to do to dominate a scene is to enter it.'

Bogart continued to dominate scenes in Warner pictures throughout the Forties. It was only in 1948 – when he was enjoying one of his most notable successes as the gold prospector Dobbs in John Huston's *The Treasure of the Sierra Madre* – that a box-office successor at last appeared on the scene, and she wasn't at all like Bogart. She was much prettier for one thing, and she could sing. Her real name was Doris von Kappelhoff, although she was to become much better known as Doris Day.

# 1944
## Metro-Goldwyn-Mayer
### The Musicals of Arthur Freed

*Judy Garland and Margaret O'Brien in Vincente Minnelli's* Meet Me in St. Louis *(1944), the film that began the golden age of the musical at MGM.*

In 1944, it was not Doris Day but another top singing star who hit the headlines in Hollywood – Judy Garland. She made news because she featured as one of the stars of the Arthur Freed/Vincente Minnelli musical *Meet Me in St. Louis*, and it was this film that began what was to become known as the 'Golden Age of the Musical' at MGM, a period that was to last for 15 years.

*Meet Me in St. Louis* was essentially a nostalgic valentine to a past age, a story of family life in turn-of-the-century St. Louis where Mr. and Mrs. Smith live with their five children (including four rapidly growing daughters), a grandfather and, as in all good movie families, a maid! Its appeal lay in its charm, delicacy, warm sentiment and a near-perfect cast – Garland, Margaret O'Brien, Lucille Bremer, Leon Ames and Mary Astor. And adding to the general feeling of all-round cosiness were the songs of Hugh Martin and Ralph Blane: 'The Boy Next Door', 'The Trolley Song' and 'Have Yourself a Merry Little Christmas'.

Financially and artistically, it was Freed's breakthrough film. With *Meet Me in St. Louis*, everything he had planned and worked for during the previous five years at the studio came to fruition. Garland was there as one of his main stars. Fred Astaire had just joined up, as had Gene Kelly and Frank Sinatra. Singer Kathryn Grayson was at the studio as well as the husky-voiced June Allyson, Cyd Charisse and Lucille Bremer. Behind the cameras were directors Vincente Minnelli and George Sidney, dance director Charles Walters, associate producer and musical arranger Roger Edens and musical directors George

Stoll and Lennie Hayton. It was quite a line-up, one that was to be the envy of other studios for years to come.

Freed had assembled his team with both taste and vision. His aim was to take the musical to new heights and experiment with it as never before. He was a kind of musical Thalberg, a former songwriter who had both talent and imagination and who knew exactly where he was going with the film musical. Not everything he touched turned to gold, but Mayer could be reasonably confident that four out of every five Freed pictures would be a success and that was a good enough batting average for him.

Charles Walters, who began at MGM as a dance director and then graduated to full director status in 1947, said of Freed: 'Arthur Freed's great claim to fame was that he was able to surround himself with talent. He could spot it, know it, sign it and use it!' Walters also added: 'by the mid-Forties, L. B. Mayer had complete trust in Arthur and his judgement. Arthur would go to him and say, "I'm going to do this and I'm going to do that," and L. B. would simply say, "Ok, go ahead." There was never a question mark.'

From 1944 onwards, the name of Arthur Freed became synonymous with style and class and invention. In 1946 he gathered together a huge all-star cast for his tribute to the *Ziegfeld Follies*; a few months later, he sent Judy Garland out West as one of *The Harvey Girls* (1946) – a film that earned the studio an Academy Award for best song for 'On the Atchison, Topeka and Santa Fe'; and in 1948, he cast Garland and Gene Kelly in Minnelli's elaborate version of Cole Porter's Broadway

hit *The Pirate*. By the end of the decade, Astaire and Garland had teamed in *Easter Parade* (1948), Fred and Ginger had got back together again for *The Barkleys of Broadway* (1949) and Gene Kelly, Frank Sinatra and Jules Munshin had featured in the classic *On the Town* (1949), the story of three sailors and their adventures with three girls (Vera-Ellen, Ann Miller, Betty Garrett) during a 24-hour shore leave in New York.

Between 1944 and 1949, Arthur Freed had established himself as the all-time musical king of Hollywood. His films were bright and shiny and bouncy. They had a verve and edge and moved at a tremendous pace – and, most important of all, they made money. The basis for his success was, of course, teamwork. Within his own little unit, he established a nucleus of musical stars that he could swap around to his heart's content, just as Louis B.

Mayer was still doing with so much relish in the larger MGM universe outside Arthur Freed's Camelot.

During the Forties, Mayer found that his talent for teaming stars had in no way diminished and, if anything, it had increased. This was especially true of the Greer Garson/Walter Pidgeon team. They first appeared together in the 1941 weepie *Blossoms in the Dust*, the story of Edna Gladney, the founder of a Texas orphanage who devoted her life to welfare work for illegitimate children. However, the film that really established them as a team rather than two separate big name stars was the Academy Award-winning *Mrs. Miniver*, directed by William Wyler in 1942.

The film recounted the experiences of a supposedly typical English middle-class family in wartime, fighting tooth and nail against everything the Nazis could throw at

*Astaire and Rogers together again in* The Barkleys of Broadway *(MGM, 1949).*

*Opposite: The all-star musical* Ziegfeld Follies *(MGM, 1945). Cracking the whip: the glamorous Lucille Ball.*

113

*Frank Sinatra, Jules Munshin and Gene Kelly loose in New York in* On the Town *(MGM, 1949).*

them. It was made as a tribute to Britain, when she had her back to the wall and stood alone against Nazi Germany. It had a tear-a-minute in every other scene and won the hearts of both Americans and Britons, even though Mr. and Mrs. Clem Miniver could hardly be classified as ordinary, their lifestyle seeming to belong more to the aristocracy than to ordinary people. But it was the 'we will never give up' message that counted.

Greer Garson came across as warm and sincere, the kind of mother just about everyone would like to have, and the Canadian-born Walter Pidgeon emerged as a thoughtful pipe smoker with a likeable personality and a commonsense approach. Mayer sensed the box-office potential of the two stars and teamed them together in another six films, including *Madame Curie, The Youngest Profession* (both 1943) and *Mrs. Parkington* (1944).

Mayer was in his element with the Garson/Pidgeon movies. During the Second World War, sentiment, pathos and tears were the order of the day, and nothing could have fitted better into Mayer's scheme of things. He thrived on the huge emotional reactions the war produced, as was typified when he cast Garson opposite Ronald Colman in *Random Harvest* (1942), a story of a dance-hall girl who befriends a First World War amnesiac with romantic, tragic and then ultimately happy results.

A slightly more down-to-earth and certainly more adult team did, however, manage to emerge from the sentimental, make-believe world of L. B. Mayer – that of Spencer Tracy and Katharine Hepburn. They were first cast in George Stevens' brilliant battle-of-the-sexes comedy, *Woman of the Year* (1942), in which Tracy played a New York sports reporter, and

Hepburn featured as the intellectual political columnist Tess Harding working on the same paper. Love and then marriage interferes with their respective careers, and instead of getting along happily together, the two find themselves constantly at odds. In many ways, it was an early, tentative feminist film, and it was a theme that was to repeat itself regularly in the eight Tracy/Hepburn films that followed.

Most of them were made at MGM, and included Frank Capra's political satire *State of the Union* (*The World and His Wife* in UK, 1948), George Cukor's *Pat and Mike* (1952) and the same director's *Adam's Rib* (1949), in which lawyers Tracy and Hepburn found themselves involved in the same legal case – he acting for the male, she for the female – after a distraught wife has attempted to murder her husband and his mistress. Like *Woman of the Year*, the film was sharp and witty, and had much to say about the role of men and, particularly, women in contemporary society.

Mayer inevitably lost several of his top stars to the armed services. Robert Taylor, for instance, left for the Navy, and the 'King', Clark Gable, distraught after tragically losing his wife Carole Lombard in a plane crash, opted for service in the Army Air Corps. Mayer also lost (or let go) stars for other

reasons. Joan Crawford left partly because she felt she wasn't getting the roles she thought she deserved, but more importantly because Mayer didn't renew her contract, and Garbo also bade farewell.

Garbo left of her own accord. After making *Two-Faced Woman* in 1941, she retired at the peak of her career, when she was just 36, having been an MGM star for 15 years in 25 films. Early in her career, she had commented: 'Being in the newspapers is awfully silly to me. It's all right for important people who have something to contribute to talk. But I have nothing to contribute.' In the Forties, there were many who disagreed, but Garbo remained true to her decision. Despite innumerable attempts to lure her back to the screen, she refused them all.

Mayer found replacements for many of the stars who had left the scene. Van Johnson, Robert Walker and comedian Red Skelton were quickly groomed to be the new white hopes on the MGM lot. Lana Turner continued to grow into a major star, especially when she appeared as the murderous Cora Smith in *The Postman Always Rings Twice* (1946) and the equally deadly Milady De Winter in *The Three Musketeers* (1948). However, Mayer's real triumphs of the decade were in discovering Elizabeth Taylor, an 11-year-old child star, and an animal star called Lassie!

Mayer figured that if Greer Garson and Walter Pidgeon could cause wartime audiences to shed tears aplenty, then so too could animals. He also figured that animals plus

*Garbo's farewell:* Two-Faced Woman *(MGM, 1941).*

children in an atmosphere full to overflowing with loneliness and sadness must surely equate with box-office gold. Mayer's commercial instincts proved him right, and animals and children became an essential part of the MGM line-up in the mid-Forties. Thus in 1943, Elizabeth Taylor appeared with Roddy McDowall and the beautiful collie Lassie in *Lassie Come Home* and, a year later, she teamed with Mickey Rooney and a horse in *National Velvet*. Louis B. Mayer simply sat back and smiled contentedly. MGM and the handkerchief trade cleaned up!

Easily Mayer's most unusual attraction of the mid-Forties was swimming star Esther Williams. The Norwegian ice-skater Sonja Henie had made money for Zanuck at Fox in the late Thirties and early Forties, but her act was really no more than a novelty and she never emerged as a great screen personality. Esther Williams was different. She came to the fore in 1944 in a movie called *Bathing Beauty* and she remained at the top for over a decade.

Fanny Brice summed her up with the phrase: 'Wet she's a star, dry she ain't,' which was just about right. The most unusual thing about her was that she was a reluctant star. A swimming champion at 15, she made a name for herself in Billy Rose's Aquacade and

*Above: Roddy McDowall and friend in* Lassie Come Home *(MGM, 1943).*

*Left: A beautiful young Elizabeth Taylor and Jackie 'Butch' Jenkins in* National Velvet *(MGM, 1944).*

*Overleaf: More Stars than There Were in Heaven? Not quite but a pretty good line-up none the less. MGM, headed by Louis B. Mayer (front centre) in the mid-1940s.*

would have been quite happy to have remained there if MGM hadn't intervened.

After the success of the *Bathing Beauty*, MGM scriptwriters suddenly found themselves having to concoct stories that, at various interludes, had to manoeuvre the cast into the vicinity of a swimming pool. Unfortunately the stories never amounted to very much, but once Esther Williams hit the water, just about anything could happen and usually did.

It didn't really matter whether she swam underwater, burst through coloured fountains on skis or dived into geometric shapes formed by other aquatic beauties and conjured up for her by her directors – Esther Williams made money whatever she did. She swam her way through a series of films that boasted titles such as *Fiesta* (1947), *On an Island with You* (1948) and *Neptune's Daughter* (1949). Not one of them was memorable and no one was ever quite able to define the exact appeal of the statuesque Miss Williams. She certainly had a magnificent figure, but her smile belonged to that of a photographer's model, her acting was limited and her singing voice

even more so. She said of her talents, or rather lack of them: 'I can't act. I can't sing. I can't dance. My pictures are put together out of scraps they find in the producer's wastebasket.' Perhaps, but she still managed to blend effortlessly into the musical scene at MGM, and she made her aquatic ballets look so easy that it seemed as though just about anyone could do them.

When he gazed at the rushes of the Esther Williams extravaganzas and the Pidgeon/Garson and Tracy/Hepburn movies – and, of course, the Freed musicals – Louis B. Mayer must almost certainly have felt an inner glow of contentment. MGM had never been stronger. The star line-up was superb, and the pictures themselves remained as glossy and well-crafted as any in Hollywood.

Yet for all that, the mid- and late Forties saw MGM at its peak: once the decade edged towards its close, so the once impregnable power of MGM began slowly to disintegrate. And for Louis B. Mayer, troubled waters, rather than the rippling, colourful, escapist waters of Esther Williams and her films, lay ahead.

*Esther Williams performs one of her memorable musical aquatic numbers in* Million Dollar Mermaid *(One-Piece Bathing Suit in UK, MGM, 1952).*

# 1945
## Paramount

Hope, Crosby and Lamour ...
and a *Lost Weekend*

By the mid-Forties, things had changed quite a bit on the famous Paramount lot on Marathon Street. There were still a few old faces around. Cecil B. DeMille, for instance, had been busy exploring American and Canadian history in the adventures *Union Pacific* (1939), *Northwest Mounted Police* (1940) and *Reap the Wild Wind* (1942). Preston Sturges had graduated to directing his own sharply satirical screenplays hitting out with deadly accuracy at such targets as crooked politics in *The Great McGinty* (*Down Went McGinty* in UK, 1940), hero worship in *Hail the Conquering Hero* (1944) and even Hollywood in the memorable *Sullivan's Travels* (1941).

However, it was primarily the newcomers who dominated – the vivacious Paulette Goddard, debonair Ray Milland, sarong girl Dorothy Lamour, the likeable 'dumb-ox' William Bendix and the raucous Betty Hutton, whose bouncy way with a song sent many an on-leave serviceman home happy and optimistic. In short, for Adolph Zukor and the top executives, it was a whole new ball game at Paramount.

There were two stars who stood out from all the rest – Bing Crosby and Bob Hope – throughout the entire decade. They weren't by any means newcomers. In fact, both had joined the studio in the Thirties – Hope in 1937 for the making of *The Big Broadcast of 1938* and Crosby as far back as 1932 in the first of the *Big Broadcast* series. But it was in the Forties that they really came into their own and in 1940, in particular, when Paramount, by a happy accident, teamed them with Dorothy Lamour in a zany comedy called *Road to Singapore*. The film was

originally intended as a one-off, but such was its popularity that it was followed by another 'Road' picture (*Road to Zanzibar*) the next year and another (*Road to Morocco*) in 1942. By 1945 the pair were on their fourth 'Road' escapade, this time in *Road to Utopia* as a couple of vaudevillians in search of gold in Alaska.

*Writer-director Preston Sturges directing Joel McCrea and Veronica Lake during the filming of his Hollywood satire* Sullivan's Travels *(Paramount 1941).*

*The first of the popular 'Road' pictures of the 1940s – Road to Singapore (Paramount, 1940). Eating their way through this scene: Bob Hope, Dorothy Lamour and Bing Crosby.*

*Ray Milland and Paulette Goddard, two of Paramount's brightest stars of the 1940s, in a scene from Cecil B. DeMille's Reap the Wild Wind (Paramount, 1942).*

The 'plots' of the 'Road' pictures differed very little from one another; in fact, according to Hope, many scenes were made up and improvised as they went along. Basically, Hope and Crosby found themselves on the run from both the villains and the law, and then met up with Lamour who was always in some kind of distress. It was only the settings that changed. Hope supplied the wisecracks, Crosby a song or two and Lamour, after tampering with the affections of the forever-eager Hope for most of the picture, finished up in the arms of Bing!

Paramount were as surprised as everyone else by the colossal success of the 'Road' pictures. They had expected to make money from the movies – the entertainment climate was too buoyant for them not to do so – and with both Crosby and Hope equally as popular on radio as they were on screen, they knew the chances were good. But there is no doubt that the scale of the success did surprise them. By accident, they had stumbled across what

was just about the perfect movie entertainment formula: slapstick, song and sex, all served up in just the right amounts.

Bing Crosby topped the list of moneymaking stars (from any studio) for five consecutive years from 1944 and when, in 1949, he was eventually toppled from the top spot, the guy who did the toppling was Bob Hope. All in all, Paramount weren't doing so badly, especially as both stars were big moneymakers in their own right. They didn't have to be in a 'Road' picture teamed with Dorothy Lamour to make money. They could do so on their own, in their own pictures. In 1941, for instance, Bing enjoyed a hit in *Birth of the Blues*, a tribute to the original Dixieland dance band. In 1942, he sang Irving Berlin's 'White Christmas' in *Holiday Inn* and in 1944 he even won an Oscar as the singing priest Father O'Malley in Leo McCarey's whimsical *Going My Way*.

Hope never reached the heights of winning an Academy Award, but he did come up with some funny moneymaking comedies. He

*Opposite:* This Gun for Hire *(Paramount, 1942), the film that made Alan Ladd a star as the cold-blooded killer Raven.*

*Barry Fitzgerald, Rise Stevens and an Oscar-winning Bing Crosby in Leo McCarey's* Going My Way *(Paramount, 1944), which also won an Academy Award as best picture of the year.*

featured in two, sometimes three a year, and Paramount hired an entire team of writers – Don Hartman, Frank Butler, Frank Tashlin, Norman Panama and Melvin Frank – to provide the long-nosed comedian with a permanent supply of wisecracks and one-liners. 'I'm a British agent,' whispers the lovely Madeleine Carroll to Hope in the 1942 spy comedy *My Favorite Blonde.* 'Too late, sister,' replies the dim-witted Hope. 'I've already got an agent.' Paulette Goddard received similar treatment in the earlier *The Cat and the Canary* (1939). 'Don't big, empty houses scare you?' she asks nervously. 'Not me,' says Hope. 'I used to be in vaudeville!'

It was this kind of humour, plus the hit Crosby songs – 'Moonlight Becomes You' in *Road to Morocco,* 'Swinging on a Star' in *Going My Way* – that made Hope and Crosby such valuable assets to the Paramount studio. In retrospect, they *were* Paramount in the Forties; they were the ones who consistently made the money. When they were teamed together, they were a box-office smash just as they were when they featured in their solo vehicles. At no other time, either before or since, has a major Hollywood studio managed to use two stars in such a profitable fashion.

However, Paramount in the Forties wasn't all comedy and songs. The studio did have its

VERONICA LAKE · ROBERT PRESTON

THIS GUN FOR HIRE

with
LAIRD CREGAR · ALAN LADD

Screen Play by Albert Maltz and W. R. Burnett          Based on the Novel by Graham Greene
DIRECTED BY FRANK TUTTLE · · · · · · A PARAMOUNT PICTURE

The Blue Dahlia
*(Paramount, 1946) starring
Alan Ladd and Veronica
Lake.*

darker side as well, and an actor by the name of Alan Ladd was very much part of that darker side. Ladd was as tough at Paramount as Cagney and Bogart were at Warners, perhaps tougher – hard, unfeeling, unsympathetic, 5 feet 6 inches of expressionless dynamite. A studio publicity slogan wrapped it up quite nicely when it claimed: 'When he smiles, it's not because he likes you . . . he likes what he's going to do to you!'

Ladd first made his mark at the studio in 1942 as the cold-blooded killer Raven in *This Gun for Hire*, a version of Graham Greene's novel *A Gun for Sale*. His co-star was the young Veronica Lake who featured as a blonde cabaret girl. Ladd's partnership with the slinky Miss Lake (whose 17-inch 'peek-a-boo' hair which hung down loosely over one eye was much copied all over the world) was second in popularity only to that of the Crosby/Hope/Lamour team. The Ladd/Lake pictures didn't tickle your ribs, however; they usually hit you in the solar plexus. All told,

the two stars made a quartet of films together, beginning with *This Gun for Hire* and continuing with *The Glass Key* (1942), *The Blue Dahlia* (1946) and *Saigon* (1948). The expertly-crafted *Blue Dahlia*, an original from the pen of Raymond Chandler, was their greatest success together and earned Ladd a place among the top ten moneymaking stars of 1947.

The Alan Ladd thrillers were tough, fast-moving melodramas that represented something of the real world to GIs – dingy streets, shabby apartments, faithless women – a world that, in 1945, many were already returning to in real life. However, the darkest world of all was brought alive on screen by writer-director Billy Wilder. He had written for Lubitsch at Paramount in the Thirties, when most of his screenplays had been endowed with wit and a satirical humour, but in the mid-Forties his mood became much blacker. In 1944, for instance, he filmed the classic *Double Indemnity*, which derived from a tough, no-nonsense novel by James M. Cain and starred Barbara

Stanwyck and Fred MacMurray. Together they became the most malevolent screen couple of the decade – he on the make from the word go, she cool, blonde and dangerous. They murder Miss Stanwyck's elderly husband for the insurance money and then find that life together, full of lies, deceit and double-cross, bears a close resemblance to hell on earth.

Billy Wilder's co-writer on *Double Indemnity* was Raymond Chandler. His next collaborator was Charles Brackett, and the subject this time was even more harrowing – alcoholism. *The Lost Weekend* (1945) told the story of three agonizing days in the life of a dipsomaniac novelist as he pours out his shattered dreams to a New York bartender and then drinks himself into a horrifying bout of the DTs. Hollywood film-makers had previously treated drunkenness as a subject for comedy. Not Mr. Wilder and, to drive

home the problems of alcoholism with as much force as possible, he chose an actor who, up until then, had been associated with only lightweight comedy roles – Ray Milland.

As it happened, Milland was not much of a drinker so he had to study those of his friends who did imbibe. Once he started to examine them at close quarters, he began to take his role very seriously indeed. 'I talked to some doctors,' he said. 'Then I had myself committed to Bellevue Hospital in New York. That's the general hospital where they have a psycho ward and where all the alcoholics and somnambulists and all the other rather oddball people they pick up off the streets of New York are put.

'I had myself committed there for three nights. After the middle of the second night, I couldn't stand it any longer. I got up and ran out of the hospital at three o'clock in the morning in my pajamas. I was arrested on the

*Dangerous territory! Insurance salesman Fred MacMurray gets the come-on from femme fatale Barbara Stanwyck in Billy Wilder's* Double Indemnity *(Paramount, 1944).*

street by a policeman and run right back in because he thought I was just another drunk. And strangely enough, that was the first scene we shot in the picture in New York. I really had to study the problem because it is a disease. In the end, I was supposed to be thin and drawn, having gone through a drying-out period. I actually was thin and drawn and very irritable at home. But it paid off.'

Indeed it did. For a role that he had been forced to accept, Milland won an Oscar as the best actor of 1945. The film was also named best of the year, and Wilder earned awards for his screenplay and direction.

*The Lost Weekend* began a trend. With the war almost over, audiences were no longer looking for the same kind of escapist fare they had enjoyed in the Thirties. The war had changed not only their opinions and outlook on life, but also their views as to what they wanted in the way of entertainment. They

didn't want films that pulled a discreet veil over unpleasant subjects and refused to look honestly at things. They wanted films that presented controversial subjects as forcibly as possible. *The Lost Weekend* was one of the first of these new-style pictures, treating alcoholism with an uncompromising realism. Billy Wilder spared his audience nothing, especially when he visualized Milland's attack of the DTs. An imaginary bat plunging its teeth into a mouse so that its victim's blood ran down the walls was just one image that stayed with moviegoers for many years afterwards.

In 1945, the American cinema came of age with *The Lost Weekend*. Paramount and Billy Wilder started the ball rolling, but it was another studio that was to develop realism to an even greater extent in the years that lay ahead – and that studio was Twentieth Century-Fox.

*Ray Milland goes through agonies as he begs for his next drink. Bartender Howard da Silva looks on. A scene from Billy Wilder's Oscar-winning* The Lost Weekend *(Paramount, 1945).*

# 1946
## Twentieth Century-Fox

### Postwar Realism and the 'Message' Pictures

Fox's 'new look' postwar realism came about partly because of the influence of the neo-realist movement in Italy, where directors such as Vittorio de Sica and Roberto Rossellini shot their films in the poverty and rubble of the war-ravaged streets and used non-professionals as their actors. Fox didn't go quite that far, and indeed, no commercial studio would have dared to and remain in business. None the less, Fox chief Darryl Zanuck *was* influenced by what he saw and was determined that his studio would be the first to reflect at least something of the new-look movies that were making such an impact in Europe.

In 1945, he put in motion a series of films that became well known for their realism and documentary-style accuracy. The series began with *The House on 92nd Street* (1945), a true account of how the FBI smashed an American-based spy ring trying to gain access to the secrets of the atomic bomb. It continued with *13 Rue Madeleine* (1946), *Boomerang* (1947) and *Call Northside 777* (1948).

The series didn't have a name as such, but each of the films was instantly recognizable as belonging to a group. Each had an opening scene that was accompanied by an off-screen narration and, on each occasion, the narrator informed the audience that what they were about to see was a true story and that the events had been filmed whenever possible (or in some cases in their entirety) in the actual locales in which they had occurred. They were primarily big-city crime stories. Most were fast-paced and tightly edited, few running to more than 100 minutes, many to just an hour-and-a-half. All were photographed in

black and white, and nearly all of them explored some flaw or injustice in the American way of life. In Elia Kazan's *Boomerang*, for instance, attorney Dana Andrews sets out to establish the innocence of a man arrested on circumstantial evidence for the murder of a priest; in *Call Northside 777* reporter James Stewart tries to secure the freedom of an innocent Chicago man convicted of murder years before; and in Henry Hathaway's *Fourteen Hours* (1951) New York cop Paul Douglas spends hours trying to persuade would-be suicide Richard Basehart not to jump from the ledge of a skyscraper.

The stories were filmed mostly in New York and Chicago (never in Los Angeles), and invariably opened with the familiar and melancholy sound of Alfred Newman's famous 'Street Scene' music. Once the brightly lit skyscrapers of New York or Chicago became visible, audiences knew exactly what was in store for them — a tough realism of a kind not experienced previously in American cinema.

One of the things that worked in Twentieth Century-Fox's favour during the immediate postwar years was the willingness of studio boss Darryl Zanuck to adapt to change. Most of the other moguls were not quite so amenable, especially Louis B. Mayer at MGM and Jack Warner over at Burbank. They were convinced that, with the war over, audiences would carry on as they had before, paying out their money two or three times a week. And for a while the audiences did return, but not for long. The boom was short-lived.

The main reason was that the ex-service-man, now back in civilian life, began to go out less. Instead of going twice a week to the movies, he and his family would go once. Audiences became more selective, and the reason why they became so was that something else was beginning to play an essential role in their leisure hours. What is more, that something was in their own homes and emitted a bright, flickering picture at the flick of a switch – *television!*

Zanuck was one of the few moguls who didn't appear to be frightened by TV, and he met its threat head-on. His semi-documentary thrillers were part of his answer to that threat, as were other pictures that were much more ambitious in scope. The press labelled these 'message' pictures, which was a fair enough description for they did indeed carry messages, but it was a little derogatory none the less and hardly did justice to the pictures, which were brave, courageous and pulled no punches.

In fact, nothing was safe from Zanuck's probing eye. In the Oscar-winning *Gentleman's Agreement* (1947), he dared to suggest that anti-Semitism was rife in the upper echelons of American society; in *The Snake Pit* (1948), he investigated the case history of a mentally disturbed woman novelist and, in doing so, exposed the conditions in some of the country's mental institutions; and in *Pinky* (1949) he tackled the most explosive issue of all, that of racial prejudice. The movie starred Jeanne Crain, who played a black girl who is so fair-skinned that she can pass for white.

*Crusading reporter James Stewart and editor Lee J. Cobb in Henry Hathaway's documentary-style thriller* Call Northside 777 *(Twentieth Century-Fox, 1948).*

*Gregory Peck in* Gentleman's Agreement *(Twentieth Century-Fox, 1947), Elia Kazan's Oscar-winning picture about anti-Semitism in the United States.*

*Olivia de Havilland in a scene from the harrowing* The Snake Pit *(Twentieth Century-Fox, 1948).*

Her emotional problems, stemming from this dilemma, formed the crux of a film that was daring for its time and proved to be a forerunner of many of a similar nature produced by other studios.

These adult movies were at the centre of Fox production in the late Forties and early Fifties, a period that saw the studio at its most authoritative. With a team of directors headed by Elia Kazan, Joseph L. Mankiewicz, Henry King and Henry Hathaway, Zanuck succeeded in coming to terms with a world very different from the one that had existed when he had first helped form the company back in the Thirties, in the days of Alice Faye and little Shirley Temple.

Although the 'message' pictures and the semi-documentary thrillers were the cornerstones of the Fox studio in the postwar era, they weren't by any means the only Fox pictures around. There were still plenty of Betty Grable musicals – *Mother Wore Tights* (1947), *When My Baby Smiles at Me* (1948) – to cheer up those who found that exposés of anti-Semitism and racial prejudice were not exactly what they were in need of on a Saturday night. There were also several new stars to enjoy: the handsome Gregory Peck who appeared in *Gentleman's Agreement* (1947) and the western *Yellow Sky* (1948); Richard Widmark of the maniacal giggle who made his debut in *Kiss of Death* (1947); and

Jeanne Crain who, as well as appearing in *Pinky*, became an American sweetheart with such films as *State Fair* (1945) and *Margie* (1946).

There was even the occasional, well-publicized flop, such as *Forever Amber* (1947), a version of Kathleen Winsor's bestseller about the amorous escapades of a trollop (played by Linda Darnell) in the reign of Charles II. It was a novel famous for its dirty bits, the kind of sexy book that parents used to hide away from their children in the top corner of a high cupboard. There were many who felt that Fox should have done the same with the film, for it was a fiasco. It was shot in 103 days with 318 major scenes at a cost of a massive (for those days) $3 million. It was left to the inimitable George Sanders as Charles II to speak the few good lines in Philip Dunne's script: 'Madam, your mind is like your wardrobe – many changes but no surprises.'

There were, on the other hand, many witty lines in the 'Mr. Belvedere' films of Clifton Webb. His acid-tongued babysitter Lynn Belvedere began his series of domestic adventures in the hilarious *Sitting Pretty* in 1948. This was the film in which he enjoyed a supreme moment of triumph (and one envied by many who had found themselves in a similar position) when he upturned a bowl of porridge on the head of a baby who had been flicking him with the goo throughout breakfast. Webb later remarked to one of the

*Above: Dan Dailey and Betty Grable in the 1948 musical* When My Baby Smiles at Me *(Twentieth Century-Fox).*

*Right: Racial prejudice – another controversial subject tackled by the Fox studio in the post-war years. Pictured here: Ethel Waters and Jeanne Crain in a scene from* Pinky *(1949).*

*Opposite: One of the Fox studio's loveliest stars of the late Forties: Linda Darnell in* Forever Amber *(Twentieth Century-Fox, 1947).*

*The most famous screen babysitter of them all – a yawning Clifton Webb as Lynn Belvedere in* Sitting Pretty *(Twentieth Century-Fox, 1948).*

charges in his care, '*Don't* call me "uncle". By no stretch of the imagination could I be any relation of yours!'

Bright amusing dialogue was also the key to the success of *A Letter to Three Wives*, a comedy written and directed by Joseph L. Mankiewicz. The film revealed something of the other side of the Fox studio – the witty, satirical side that demanded that an audience listened to as well as watched what was going on on the screen. It centred on a woman called Addie Ross (never seen) who sends a letter to three of her friends informing them that she has run off with one of their husbands. The trouble is that she fails to mention which one, and the rest of the film concentrates on each of the wives in turn as they cast their minds back and wonder if their husbands could be the guilty party. Still one of the wittiest films yet made about the subject of marriage, *A Letter to Three Wives* starred Linda Darnell and Paul Douglas, Jeanne Crain and Jeffrey Lynn and Kirk Douglas and Ann Sothern as the three couples. It earned writer/director Mankiewicz Oscars for both his script and his direction.

Mankiewicz did the 'double' again the following year when he won Academy Awards for writing and directing *All About Eve* (1950). This time, with Zanuck again personally at the helm as producer, he lined up a superlative cast for a tale of treachery

A Letter to Three Wives
(Twentieth Century-Fox,
1949). The wives in question:
Linda Darnell, Ann Sothern
and Jeanne Crain.

The Oscar-winning success of
1950: All About Eve
(Twentieth Century-Fox).
Pictured in this scene: Bette
Davis, Gary Merrill, Anne
Baxter and George Sanders.

among the theatre folk of Broadway. Bette Davis (in a part originally intended for Claudette Colbert) took the star role as the ageing Broadway actress, Margo Channing. Anne Baxter played her scheming understudy who does everything in her power to usurp Margo and replace her as the toast of Broadway. Close behind came Celeste Holm, George Sanders (superb as a New York drama critic), Gary Merrill, Hugh Marlowe and, of course, Thelma Ritter as Davis's sharp-tongued maid. A hugely enjoyable ride through the back corridors of New York's theatreland, *All About Eve* bristled with witty repartee, and proved to be the most polished Hollywood movie since the heyday of Lubitsch. It won six Oscars (including best picture) and still holds the record for the most nominations – 14!

It brought to an end a golden five-year period at the Fox studio, a period during which Fox had earned two Oscars for best picture – for *Gentleman's Agreement* and *All About Eve* – and another four best picture nominations: *The Razor's Edge* in 1946, *The Snake Pit* in 1948 and *A Letter to Three Wives* and *12 O'Clock High* in 1949. The late Forties proved to be the peak period for Twentieth Century-Fox, however, for the studio was never again to rise to such artistic heights. The arrival of the Fifties brought with it the chilling message that audiences were still dwindling rapidly and that something new would be needed if Hollywood were to recapture them.

That Zanuck, who had been in at the birth of the talkies and also helped establish the youngest of the Hollywood studios, should be the one to provide that 'something' in 1953 came as a surprise to no one.

*A battle-fatigued Gregory Peck in* Twelve O'Clock High *(Twentieth Century-Fox, 1949). Looking on: Lawrence Dobkin, Paul Stewart, Dean Jagger and Gary Merrill.*

# 1947
## Walt Disney

### A New Start and the Road to Disneyland

There was only one Hollywood studio that wasn't overly concerned with the television jitters of the late Forties: the Walt Disney studio in Burbank. There was one very good reason why it wasn't concerned. Those in charge at the studio had rather more important things on their minds; they were trying to keep Disney solvent. They had seen the studio stagger through the war years and survive (just) and were having to come to terms with the unpalatable fact that, in 1947, the Disney studio was still in a very precarious position and holding on by the skin of its teeth.

All of which was a great disappointment to Walt Disney himself, for he personally regarded the years between 1937 and 1942 as the first act of his ambitious programme of feature cartoon production. With the war over and the situation returning to normal, he was all set to go with what he regarded as Walt Disney Mark II, and that meant producing feature cartoons of some of the best-loved children's classics. Those he had in mind included *Alice in Wonderland* (which he had first considered filming back in the Thirties), *Cinderella* and *Peter Pan*.

For Disney, it was simply a matter of getting on with the job and putting his artists back to work behind those all-important drawing boards. But once again, as before, he was forced to come to terms with a harsh economic reality. His brother Roy informed him that, although the studio's wartime work on information films for the armed services had saved the studio from going under, that was just about all it had done. The Walt Disney studio was still in business, but it was

also still in hock to the bank to the tune of $4 million. The bankers informed both Walt and his brother that future plans for ambitious feature cartoons had to be shelved, at least temporarily. They also suggested that the studio find a new way of earning some quick cash; otherwise, the nagging debt problem could well last for years.

For Roy and the bank, the answer was simple. If the Disney studio could turn out seven-minute shorts quickly and efficiently, why couldn't it link a number of them together into a feature film and release it quickly to raise cash for the more important productions that lay ahead?

Walt's heart wasn't in it. For him, such a move smacked of a lowering of standards and a long retreat from the ambitions of the late Thirties and the brilliant animation of *Snow White*, *Pinocchio* and *Bambi*. It would, he argued, be going back on everything he'd worked for. However, when the alternatives were presented to him – either a possible closure of the studio or even a merger (something he would never countenance) – he realized he had no alternative.

The Disney studio made three 'package' cartoon features after the war: *Make Mine Music* (1946); *Fun and Fancy Free* (1947), which included appearances by Donald Duck, Mickey Mouse and Goofy; and *Melody Time* (1948). They were, at best, efficient bread-and-butter efforts, manufactured entertainments made to meet an immediate need. None of them was linked to any major theme; they were put together simply to make money. The best of them was the first, *Make Mine Music*. A kind of pop *Fantasia*, it

included animated sequences devoted to the Benny Goodman tunes 'All the Cats Join In' and 'After You've Gone', and a delightful character called Willie the Singing Whale (with a voice provided by Nelson Eddy) whose ambition was to sing opera at the Met.

However, the development of the package cartoon feature wasn't the only way in which Disney tried to solve his postwar financial problems. For some time, he had also been

toying with the idea of expanding the activities of the studio and entering into live-action feature production, thus challenging the other major studios on their home ground. And he felt that a suitable prelude to such a programme would be a picture that was part live-action and part animation.

He had already experimented with the technique of combining actors with cartoon characters in his 1945 *The Three Caballeros,*

photographed as an ordinary film, with actors such as James Baskett, Ruth Warrick, Bobby Driscoll and Luana Patten playing out a story of adolescence and marital break-up on a plantation in the American Deep South. The rest of the film was made up of richly detailed cartoon work devoted to three Brer Rabbit stories, all of them related by the philosophical Uncle Remus to cheer up the unhappy boy hero. The technique was applauded and the film was a success. It was helped considerably by the Oscar-winning song 'Zip-a-Dee-Doo-Dah', sung by James Baskett in an animated woodland with birds and butterflies fluttering down upon his shoulders.

Disney viewed *Song of the South* with a great deal more enthusiasm than he did the package cartoon features. The combination of live-action with animation was something that had rarely been done before (MGM had dabbled with it briefly a year earlier when Gene Kelly had danced with Jerry the cartoon mouse in *Anchors Aweigh*) and it offered possibilities for the future. It also offered him a new mountain to climb and Disney was always a man to need new challenges.

Someone once said of him: 'There were always two Walt Disneys, one the artist with a vivid imagination who produced *Snow White* and *Pinocchio*; the other the insatiable showman, builder of Disneyland, salesman of Mickey Mouse watches, whose genius doomed him to vulgarize his own creations in search of ever-wider audiences.' The remark has much truth to it, but it tends to overlook the fact that Disney's search for ever-wider audiences was almost entirely due to his wearying and seemingly never-ending battles to keep his head above water financially. This battle was never more intense than in the immediate postwar years.

However, to many, it did seem that when his first feature-length postwar cartoon, *Cinderella*, was eventually released in 1950, the 'artist' side of Disney had given way somewhat to the 'showman'. The film was capably produced and animated, excellently scored (it included the hit song 'Bibbidi-Bobbidi-Boo') and contained a number of intriguing animal characters, among them the mice Jacques and Gus and the cat Lucifer, all of which contributed imaginatively to the fairy tale. But although the draftsmanship, invention and enthusiasm were still in evidence, one vital ingredient was missing – style. A kind of postwar slickness had replaced the careful craftsmanship of the early Forties. The same criticism was levelled at *Alice in Wonderland* when it followed in 1951, and even more so at *Peter Pan* in 1953.

The criticism hurt Walt Disney. He had

*Overleaf: A glowering Captain Hook threatens a helpless Tinkerbell in Walt Disney's* Peter Pan *(© 1953 The Walt Disney Company).*

which he had made to try and earn money from the South American market. In one of the scenes, he had Donald Duck dance with Aurora Miranda in a big production number. In another, he had him prancing about on a Mexican beach with some gorgeous bathing beauties. The technique had looked so effective that he decided to pursue it further.

The result in 1947 was *Song of the South.* Almost three-quarters of the movie was

expected big things from the second phase of his animation policy, and although the films were successful financially, the fact that the critics felt them to be well below his own high standards (they often referred to them as 'vulgar') hit him hard and dampened his enthusiasm for the animated feature. Many of those who worked for him later recalled that it was at about this time, in the early Fifties, that they sensed Disney's ambitions moving in another direction – towards the more glorious wonders of Disneyland!

Even though *Cinderella* did not turn out to be quite the film Disney had hoped for, at least he had the satisfaction of seeing one of his feature cartoons actually make money again. The year of its release, 1950, was also to be all important as far as the future development of the studio was concerned, for it was the year in which Disney made his first all-live-action feature – a splendidly robust version of Robert Louis Stevenson's pirate tale, *Treasure Island*, with Robert Newton as an eyeball-rolling Long John Silver – and in which his documentary 'True-Life Adventure' series began to come into its own.

The documentaries had begun with *Seal Island* (1948), a one-off 27-minute colour film about the thousands of fur seals who migrate annually to raise their pups on the Pribilof Islands in the Bering Sea. So popular did the film become that Disney immediately commissioned several more in a similar vein, among them *Beaver Valley* (1950), *Nature's Half Acre* (1951) and *Water Birds* (1952). All were superbly filmed over many months by dedicated cameramen who spent long hours observing and photographing animal life across America. The shorts were eventually supplemented by feature documentaries, hour-long films devoted to *The Living Desert* (1953) and *The Vanishing Prairie* (1954).

All this meant that, by the early Fifties, Disney was at long last heading towards the financial prosperity that had eluded him for so long. Any disappointment he may have felt over the reception of his feature cartoons was offset by the fact that he was now operating in several different areas of film production: he had both cartoons and feature films on release, as well as documentaries and shorts. For the first time in his career, he was no longer putting all his eggs in one basket, and his diversification paid dividends, never more so than in 1954 when he diversified still further and went into television.

Disney was astute enough to realize that a television show made up of his backlog of old cartoons, sequences from his features, nature films, specially made adventure episodes combined with a special news bulletin hosted by himself, would be popular with audiences as a television show and also serve as an excellent way of advertising his own forthcoming cinema attractions. It was a master stroke that left the other studio heads openmouthed. As each and every one of them struggled to compete against television and its effects on the box office, Disney made the most of his opportunities, beating the threat by actually becoming the threat. His TV show, originally called *Disneyland*, was later retitled *Walt Disney Presents*, *Walt Disney's Wonderful World of Colour* and *The Wonderful World of Disney*. It ran for over 25 years.

In retrospect, Disney may well have wished that he had diversified much earlier in his career, for if he had, it would almost certainly have saved him a lot of financial worry. However, if he had concentrated on other things besides cartoons in the Forties, there may well have been no *Pinocchio*, *Bambi* or *Dumbo*. In the end, it was probably a good thing, and certainly so from an audience's point of view, that he left it so late in his career to discover other forms of film activity for the Disney studio.

In the early Fifties, Disney was distinguishable from the other movie tycoons not only because he was a master animator but also because he was a man who was looking forward. Most of the other moguls were looking back nostalgically to a time when box-office grosses used to be much healthier. Not Disney. He had not the slightest interest in the past – other than to discover to his delight that his old feature cartoons, when re-released every seven years, found a new audience and made more money when viewed by another generation of children. For him, the past held only heartache and worry and financial problems. It was the future that held out hope and a lasting financial reward.

*'Aha, Jim lad!' Robert Newton's immortal Long John Silver in Walt Disney's live-action version of* Treasure Island. *(© 1950 The Walt Disney Company).*

# 1948
## RKO

The only connection multi-millionaire Howard Hughes had with Walt Disney was that his studio – RKO – distributed the Disney films in the late Forties and for much of the Fifties. And by 1948, RKO had indeed become his studio for in May of that year, he had acquired a controlling interest in the company. No one quite knew why and Hughes' reasons remained a mystery, but

*The legendary Howard Hughes, the millionaire recluse who took control of RKO in 1948.*

most felt that he had acquired the studio so that he could promote the career of Jane Russell, a former model and chiropodist's receptionist whom he had discovered back in the early Forties and cast in the notorious western, *The Outlaw*.

Certainly it was Jane Russell who managed to get more out of the Hughes take-over than anyone else. He kept her name to the fore even though her movies were often no more than second rate. Together with Robert Mitchum, she was one of the two genuine superstars to emerge from the Hughes regime.

Before Hughes arrived on the scene, RKO, like other Hollywood studios, had come face to face with dwindling audiences. Like all the majors, they had done 'boffo' business in the first postwar year of 1946 and clocked up a huge profit of $12 million. Excellent pictures such as the Oscar-winning *The Best Years of Our Lives*, a Sam Goldwyn production about three returning war veterans, Frank Capra's *It's a Wonderful Life* and Hitchcock's Cary Grant/Ingrid Bergman thriller *Notorious* were largely responsible for the encouraging figures. But they flattered only to deceive. Just a year later that profit figure was halved, and by 1948, it was down to a catastrophic $500,000.

Dore Schary, a former writer at MGM, was called in to see if he could stem the tide and bring about an RKO recovery. His approach was similar to that of Zanuck at Fox; he wanted to produce quality films for a thinking audience. But whereas, at Fox, Zanuck had the glamorous musicals of Betty Grable and the pictures of other top stars as financial

*Mean, moody and magnificent and a few other things besides – Jane Russell in* The Outlaw *(1943), the notorious sex western that began her career.*

safeguards against his hit-or-miss semi-documentary experiments, RKO had none. They had to rely entirely on the brave policy of Schary. In fact, their well-crafted and often courageous little pictures were, in reality, their *big* pictures. They didn't cost much, but there wasn't a financial blockbuster among them.

Schary's reign at RKO lasted a mere 16 months. It was a period that produced more than its share of unusual and adult movies. *Crossfire* (1947), a savage account of anti-Semitism in the American postwar army proved to be one of the most successful and starred the three Roberts – Mitchum, Young and Ryan. Also high on the list of critical successes were the stylish *film noir, Out of the Past* (*Build My Gallows High* in UK, 1947) with Robert Mitchum and Kirk Douglas and Jane Greer as the deadliest of *femmes fatales*, and Joseph Losey's experimental little fantasy *The Boy with Green Hair* (1948), which starred Dean Stockwell and vividly illustrated the plight of the still-starving orphans of war-ravaged Europe.

However, when Hughes purchased the studio, the writing was on the wall for Schary.

It meant simply that he was 'out' and Hughes was 'in'. If ever there was a turning point in the fortunes of a major Hollywood studio, it was at that moment. If the fates (or, rather, Hughes) hadn't intervened and Schary had been allowed to continue for two or three more years, his films might well have formed the basis of a new-look RKO. As it was when he left the chances of RKO developing into a powerful, postwar studio disappeared for good.

In May 1948, most of the employees at RKO not unnaturally expected Hughes to pay the studio a visit immediately and thereafter begin to make changes. Many were uneasy about the possible outcome; others felt that their jobs might be under threat. However, they need not have worried. Hughes did not show up for quite a while. Director Fritz Lang, who was working at the studio at the time, later remembered how everyone became highly nervous: 'When the news got round that Hughes had bought RKO, all the big-shot producers who usually turned up for work at 11 o'clock or later were there at 9 a.m. awaiting the new boss who never appeared. This went on for about a fortnight until they said, "Oh, the hell with it," and lapsed back into their old ways.

'Then, after several weeks, Howard Hughes *did* finally appear. I'll never forget it. He had a large entourage and never spoke to anyone. He went through the whole studio, looked at every stage, at every shop, and after 2 hours and 20 minutes, all he said was "Paint it!" Then he walked out and was never seen again.'

Hughes' obsession with Jane Russell began in the early 1940s. The story goes that he first glimpsed Miss Russell's 38-inch bust when he was handed a photograph of her by a press agent. Thereafter her breasts remained a fixation of his for the rest off his career in movies, especially during the shooting of *The Outlaw*, when he had them photographed from every conceivable angle. It didn't matter whether she was wrestling in a haystack, leaning over a bed in a low-cut blouse, riding a horse or even simply moving round a fire, her breasts were always the highlights of the screen.

Jane Russell, in fact, was the first film star who underwent the super-hype treatment. She was labelled 'mean, moody and magnificent' and was a star before she ever hit the screen. Another label that was tied on to her was that she was 'the world's most exciting girl!' Hughes put it around that he was the one who had given her her first screen test but that was untrue. Other studios had tested her and weren't over-impressed: Fox regarded her as 'unphotogenic' and Warners thought she lacked 'energy and spark'. Hughes thought differently. Back in 1941 when he tested her

*Suspect Robert Ryan (centre) and cop Robert Young (right) in a scene from Edward Dmytryk's controversial thriller* Crossfire (RKO, 1947).

*Joseph Losey's fantasy* The Boy with Green Hair *(RKO, 1948) depicting the plight of starving orphans in a war-torn Europe. In this scene: Dean Stockwell, Pat O'Brien and Barbara Hale.*

for the role of Rio in *The Outlaw,* an unlikely variation on the relationship between Billy the Kid and Pat Garrett, she got the part out of no fewer than 700 applicants.

Renowned publicist Russell Birdwell immediately started the big build-up campaign. He stipulated that Jane always wore a low-cut blouse whenever she was photographed by the press, with the result that Jane found herself spending half of her days leaning forward. She later laughed about it all: 'They would tell me to pick up a pail of water or jump up and down on a bed in a nightgown while they shot from above and below. I

didn't realize what they were doing. I was as green as grass.'

One man who didn't laugh when the film finally premièred in February 1943 was censor Joseph Breen who wrote to his boss Will Hays: 'I have never seen anything quite so unacceptable as the shots of the breasts of the character of Rio. Throughout half the picture, the girl's breasts, which are quite large and prominent, are shockingly uncovered.' The Hays Office wrote back to Hughes with the order: 'Cut your movie. There's too much cleavage, too much sex, too much everything.' Hughes quickly replied

*Jane Russell, the star attraction at RKO in the 1940s and early 1950s.*

*Jane Russell and Robert Mitchum together in the torrid melodrama,* Macao *(RKO, 1952).*

with a firm 'No' and withdrew the film from circulation.

Hughes finally released *The Outlaw* in 1949 (he allowed it to go out on a restricted release without an official seal of approval in 1946), just a year after he had purchased the RKO studio. By that time, the atmosphere had changed quite a bit from the early Forties; people had begun to be more broadminded about such things, and when it was finally released *The Outlaw* came over as something of an anti-climax. Miss Russell looked as attractive as ever, however, and the film took big money – $5 million – which for RKO made a welcome change.

The films of Robert Mitchum also made money, not big money, but steady money for the actor had the happy knack of being able to

appear in any picture, good, bad or indifferent, and still turn that picture into a financial success.

The public took to Mitchum more or less immediately, and Hughes wasn't slow to realize his potential, or indeed to realize it in terms of cash. In 1948, Mitchum's contract was for $250,000 a year. Even Mitchum's run-in with the police the following year (he was arrested on a charge of possessing marijuana and served 60 days on a prison farm) didn't do anything to harm his image. In fact, if anything, the attendant publicity helped to enhance it.

Mitchum's languid, sleepy-eyed persona and Russell's sexy figure pushed RKO into producing a long line of sultry melodramas and thrillers. When the pair were teamed together, as they were in *Macao* (1952) and in the 1951 thriller *His Kind of Woman*, they provided a smouldering star-chemistry that was as torrid as it was sexy.

Mitchum, however, was of sufficient stature not to need Jane Russell in every movie. Indeed, he ran through a long line of attractive and sexy leading ladies during the Hughes regime at RKO. In Don Siegel's thriller *The Big Steal* (1949), a movie that was advertised with the slogan 'A Man of Ice! A Woman of Fire! A Guy with a Gun!' he came up against Jane Greer; in *Where Danger Lives* (1950), he had to be on his mettle to outwit the deadly Faith Domergue; in *My Forbidden Past* (1951), he played a Yankee doctor enamoured of 19th-century beauty Ava Gardner; and in Otto Preminger's much under-rated little thriller *Angel Face* (1953), he had to play it very rough even to stay in the same league as the psychopathic Jean Simmons.

Mitchum always turned in the same deceptively easy-going but professional performance. He and he alone was the one star on whom Hughes could rely in the late Forties and early Fifties. He was to RKO what Bogart and Cagney had been to Warners and Alan Ladd to Paramount – a tough guy who didn't say a lot but who managed to communicate with audiences through his laid-back, laconic manner and an immense physical presence.

It certainly wasn't through any fault of his that RKO hit crisis point in 1950 when the studio recorded a staggering loss of $6 million. Just how Howard Hughes viewed the matter isn't on record, but that overall massive deficit was accompanied by two more frightening statistics: in September of that year, the studio revealed that it was losing close to $100,000 a week; and when the books were examined more closely, it was discovered that there hadn't been a single RKO release to earn a profit of $100,000 or more.

There may have been a few in Hollywood who were aware that RKO was on a very slippery slope as the Fifties got under way, but it was probably only the accountants who realized that the number of years the studio had left as a major production company could be counted on the fingers of one hand.

*Mitchum waits! A scene from the 1949 thriller* The Big Steal *(RKO), directed by Don Siegel and co-starring Jane Greer and William Bendix.*

# 1950
# Universal-International

## A Return to the Big Time

Universal certainly wasn't a studio that had hit anything like crisis point in 1950. In fact, their financial situation was exactly the opposite to that of RKO. The year signalled not that their best days were over but that they were about to begin. It also proved to be the year in which the studio began concentrating once more on major feature production.

Universal had, of course, been producing films throughout the Forties – hundreds of them – so they still very much belonged in the major league of Hollywood studios. Where they differed from the other studios was in the fact that they specialized in the double-feature programme, pictures that ran for at most 80 minutes (and were sometimes even shorter) and, when combined into a double bill, made an attractive, undemanding three-hour show that provided what Universal believed to be (and the public accepted as) exceedingly good value for money.

Universal hadn't opted for the double feature by choice. The decision was forced upon them because, during the Forties, they did not have a stable of major stars and could not compete with the likes of MGM and Paramount and Fox. In fact, after the initial box-office impact of Karloff and Lugosi, they had only the musicals of the talented young Deanna Durbin to see them through the difficult years of the late Thirties. Her pictures – lightweight little soufflés in which she was always popping up as a pert Miss Fixit, a modern-day Pollyanna, and delivering her songs in a lovely soprano voice – included such titles as *Three Smart Girls* (1936), *100 Men and a Girl* (1937) and *Mad About Music* (1938). For several years, they were financial

blockbusters for the studio, but as in the case of Shirley Temple, the older Deanna Durbin became, the less popular were her films. She was still a force to be reckoned with in the early Forties, but once she passed the age of 20, her appeal began to fade rapidly.

All this left Universal in something of a spot. They had no big array of stars, no Bogart or Garland, no top producer like MGM's Arthur Freed, not even a regular major director on their books, and that left them with no alternative but to try and compete on a different level. They decided that, if they were to grab a slice of the box-office takings being enjoyed by all the other studios, they had to provide something a little different, and if that meant quantity rather than quality, then so be it.

During the Forties, Universal's films were, at best, cheap and cheerful. They rarely rated a mention in weekly film reviews, and when they were noticed, they were never rewarded with a 'best of the week' plaudit. Rather, they were described patronizingly as little more than mindless escapism for the masses. Universal, however, were not in the least worried about the critics. Their main aim was to make small profits with each and every one of their double features, and they quickly learned how to cut their cloth accordingly.

They aimed their sights at an audience that didn't want to think too hard about what it was seeing up on the screen. It was an audience that was perfectly happy to pay its money for a good belly laugh at Abbott & Costello or to catch a tantalizing glimpse of the beautiful Maria Montez's bosom, highlighted to perfection by the gaudy Tech-

*Sex, thighs and beefcake, Universal double-feature style! Jeff Chandler in* Yankee Pasha *(1954).*

*Horror and comedy, double-feature style! Bud Abbott and Lou Costello joined by monster Glenn Strange in* Abbott and Costello Meet Frankenstein *(Universal-International, 1948).*

nicolor of a piece of Arabian Nights hokum.

While the great films were being produced at MGM, Paramount and Fox, the 'little' pictures poured out of Universal. The studio was always very careful when matching up its movies into double bills. Generally, their programmes would consist of opposite entertainments. *House of Dracula* (1945), for instance, might be paired with a Maria Montez/Jon Hall opus such as *Sudan* (1945). Another combination would be Basil Rathbone and Nigel Bruce (as Sherlock Holmes and Dr. Watson) in *The Woman in Green* (1945) and Abbott & Costello in the comedy *Here Come the Co-Eds* (1945). Yet another would be a 'Ma and Pa Kettle' hillbilly comedy and a western such as *Calamity Jane and Sam Bass* (1949) or *The Gal Who Took the West* (1949).

The permutations were endless, but these permutations were always very carefully considered by the studio before it put its double-feature programmes on the market. There were never two 'strong' entertainments on the same bill; instead, there was always one certainty, such as an Abbott & Costello comedy or a 70-minute horror flick and one weaker movie. Universal made sure that they never wasted a picture, and their skill at marketing their films was second to none.

It was always the double-feature productions that kept the studio alive, especially those of Abbott & Costello. The mumbling little fat guy Lou Costello and his long-suffering stooge Bud Abbott were despised by the critics but loved by the public. Just how much was demonstrated by the top ten box-office star listings of the Forties: Abbott & Costello occupied the number two spot in 1941; they were top of the list in 1942; third in 1943; eighth in 1944; back in third place in

1948 and 1949; and still there in 1950. Their humour was simple and expertly timed and often depended on a large degree of verbal mix-up. The following example gives some idea of just how complicated things could become when Abbott started to discuss things with Costello:

ABBOTT: Lou, suppose you were 40 and you were engaged to a girl who was 10.
COSTELLO: Oh, boy, this is gonna be a pip.
ABBOTT: Never mind. Now you're four times older than that little girl. So you wait 20 more years. The little girl is 30 and you're 60. Now you're only twice as old as that girl. The question is: How long do you have to wait before you and the little girl are the same age?

All nonsense, of course – but for Universal, highly profitable nonsense, especially during the Forties.

However, in 1950 things changed dramatically for the studio. While Abbott & Costello remained an essential part of the Universal scene as did the long line of double-feature programmes, in that year a big star joined Universal. He had made a reputation for himself before the war in such pictures as Frank Capra's *Mr. Smith Goes to Washington* (1939) and *The Philadelphia Story* (1940), but after the war, he found it difficult to re-establish himself in Hollywood. His gangling gait and slow drawl didn't seem to appeal too much to postwar audiences, and he experienced difficulty in recapturing his former eminence. His name was James Stewart.

*Lou Costello as a private detective in another Universal double-feature moneymaker,* Abbott and Costello Meet the Invisible Man *(Universal-International, 1951).*

In 1950, he made a deal with Universal: he would be paid a salary for a series of Universal features which, if they grossed over a certain figure, would then earn him a percentage of the profits. If they didn't make the grade and turned out to be flops, then Stewart would be working for a salary alone. For Stewart, it was a gamble, not least because Universal-International (the studio had been renamed when it merged with International Pictures in 1946) had hardly become renowned for its major productions in the previous decade. For Universal, on the other hand, it was a splendid deal: it brought a big name to the backlot and allowed them to contemplate seriously returning regularly to top-feature production.

As it turned out, the deal proved to be beneficial to both star and studio. It also proved to be something of a turning point in movie history. The percentage clause was much publicized and made Stewart the first solo performer since the silent days to work on such a basis. Although Universal were happy, other studios viewed the deal with more than a little concern. For them it looked like the thin end of the wedge and as though it might possibly spell the end of studio power.

Many also felt that the gamble would not succeed. They were wrong: Stewart and Universal hit the jackpot immediately. In 1950, Stewart starred in two films for the studio – *Harvey*, in which he repeated his stage role of the eccentric Elwood P. Dowd

*James Stewart as the amiable eccentric, Elwood P. Dowd, in* Harvey *(Universal International, 1950).*

*James Stewart as the famous trombonist/bandleader Glenn Miller in Universal's smash hit of 1954 – The Glenn Miller Story (Universal-International, 1954).*

whose best friend is a 6-foot invisible rabbit, and the western *Winchester '73*, in which he co-starred with Shelley Winters and Dan Duryea. The fact that both films were photographed in black and white, thus reducing the costs, indicated just how carefully Universal were approaching their new arrangement, but with the success of both pictures, especially the western, they quickly realized that the Stewart/Universal deal was going to work out.

Stewart carried on at the studio in *Bend of the River* (*Where the River Bends* in UK, 1952), leading a wagon train of farmers to Oregon; in the contemporary oil-rig drama *Thunder Bay* (1953); and then, most successfully of all, in *The Glenn Miller Story* (1954), in which he co-starred with June Allyson. The latter recounted the early struggles and eventual success of the famous trombonist bandleader whose career was tragically cut short when he disappeared in a light aircraft carrying him from England to France for a Christmas concert in 1944. It grossed $7.5 million and became the studio's biggest-ever

moneymaker. It also, because of the percentage deal, made Stewart a rich man. His overall profit on the venture was close to $1 million!

The Stewart pictures encouraged Universal to bring other top stars to the studio lot. Gregory Peck arrived to appear in Raoul Walsh's vigorous sea epic *The World in His Arms* (1952); an ageing Errol Flynn made a swashbuckling appearance in *Against All Flags* (1952); Tyrone Power, on loan from Fox, played a *Mississippi Gambler* (1953); and Kirk Douglas and director King Vidor were hired for the western *Man Without a Star* (1955). Even Joan Crawford arrived on the scene for *Female on the Beach* (1955), in which she was described in the advertisements as being 'Too hungry for love . . . to care where she found it!'

The studio also decided to reactivate melodrama, remaking many of the movies they had filmed in the mid-Thirties but this time with the lushest of backgrounds and sets and all photographed in the most sumptuous Technicolor by ace cameraman Russell Metty. *Magnificent Obsession* (1954), *All That*

*James Stewart gets rough with gunslinger Dan Duryea in the 1950 western* Winchester 73 *(Universal-International).*

*Swashbuckler Tony Curtis as* The Prince Who Was a Thief (*Universal-International, 1951*).

*Yvonne de Carlo, dubbed 'the most beautiful girl in the world' and a regular performer in the glamorous double-feature line-up at Universal.*

Heaven Allows (1956), *Interlude* (1957) were just some of the films that came in for the lavish treatment, all of them directed by Douglas Sirk and produced by Ross Hunter, whose maxim was to spare no expense when it came to colour, sets and costumes. His pictures were intended to look as if they were set in a world far beyond the reach of the average moviegoer – and they invariably succeeded.

Universal's re-emergence as a major studio led it to groom, for the first time, a number of male stars for the years that lay ahead. Some didn't make it and quickly fell by the wayside, but there were four who did manage to stay the course even though their first forays into acting in the early Fifties were greeted with howls of laughter and derision by the critics.

The four stars in question were Jeff Chandler, Rock Hudson, Tony Curtis and America's most decorated soldier of the Second World War, the diminutive Texan, Audie Murphy. All attended acting lessons at the studio, and all were given rigorous courses in fencing and horse-riding. They certainly needed these skills, for their immediate reward at Universal was to be cast in either a series of westerns, as in Murphy's case – *The Cimarron Kid* (1951), *Gunsmoke* (1953), *Tumbleweed* (1953) – or in a series of 'easterns', swashbucklers that became affectionately known by those who worked on them as 'tits and sand' features.

Thus Tony Curtis of the famous curly haircut (10,000 letters arrived weekly at the studio asking for any spare locks that had been cut from the precious head) won Piper Laurie in *The Prince Who Was a Thief* (1951). Rock Hudson did the same two years later with the 'Magic Sword of Damascus' in *The Golden Blade* (1953). Jeff Chandler, just to ring the changes, tangled with Suzan Ball in *East of Sumatra* (1953) and Rhonda Fleming in *Yankee Pasha* (1954).

And if it wasn't Piper Laurie or Suzan Ball the three hunks were after, there were plenty of other attractive women stars who fitted the bill and who were prepared to display their not inconsiderable charms in films specially designed to show off their semi-naked limbs and swaying hips to good advantage. Yvonne De Carlo, who was once billed as 'The Most Beautiful Girl in the World', was one of the

most attractive. She became involved in not only sex and sand in *The Desert Hawk* (1950), but also in piracy in *Buccaneer's Girl* (1950) and adventure in New Orleans in *Scarlet Angel* (1952). However, perhaps the most delectable of all was the fiery redhead, Maureen O'Hara, who popped up as the *Flame of Araby* (1951), ran a western saloon in *Comanche Territory* (1950) and displayed her navel as an Arabian princess in *Baghdad* (1949). So much did she affect one New York critic that he wrote of her: 'Framed in Technicolor, Miss O'Hara somehow seems more significant than a setting sun!'

Such sentiments might well have been suitable when describing the female stars of Universal, but they were hardly appropriate when assessing the actual pictures produced by the studio. Significant they most certainly were not. Escapist? Yes. Corny? Yes. Colourful? Yes. Entertaining? Again, yes. But not significant.

In the early Fifties Universal simply revamped a series of old-fashioned entertainments, reworked some clichéd plots and gave them a new coat of paint. For good measure, they added a few rippling muscles and a bevy of beauties. The films didn't do much for the art of the cinema, but they did prove that old formulas, providing they were well enough presented, still held good, even in the changing Hollywood of the Fifties.

*The red-headed Maureen O'Hara, fiery, tempestuous and in a spot of bother with Macdonald Carey in a scene from the western* Comanche Territory *(Universal-International, 1950).*

# 1951
## Metro-Goldwyn-Mayer

### The Decline:
### More Stars Than There Were In Heaven

It was ironic that, just as Universal was beginning to head towards a new-found prosperity, the man who, for over a quarter of a century, had reigned supreme at the head of the most powerful studio in the world, should be on his way out. But in 1951 that was indeed what was happening. As Maureen O'Hara and Yvonne De Carlo were being framed in Technicolor and Rock Hudson and Tony Curtis were trying to perfect their lines, Louis B. Mayer was packing his bags and preparing to leave the once all-powerful Metro-Goldwyn-Mayer.

Mayer's exit had, in fact, been on the cards for some time – since 1948, when he had been joined at the studio by Dore Schary. Schary's arrival had been precipitated by Nicholas Schenck in the New York office. Schenck had not been entirely happy with the postwar performance of MGM and was determined that Mayer be made to hand over some of the responsibility that he had shouldered alone since Thalberg's death in 1936.

For more than a decade, Mayer's touch and his ability to discover and team stars had been invaluable to the studio, and Schenck and the others in New York had let him have his head. They could hardly argue with success. The problem was that Mayer's touch had been surest when the market was 'ready-made' and was there for the taking. Once that market began to shrink after the war, Mayer, unlike Zanuck at Fox, began to founder. A declining audience and rapidly changing times provided him with problems he couldn't handle satisfactorily, and his solution was the same as it had always been: bring out Gable, Tracy, Garson, Robert Taylor, Lana

Turner and all the rest. They'd done the trick before, he argued, and they would do it again. Only this time, they didn't, and that stopped L. B. Mayer in his tracks.

The public still liked Gable, of course. The difference was that they didn't like him quite as much. The same applied to Taylor and Garson and the rest. Part of the reason for the tailing off of the popularity of the MGM stars was that they had become a shade too familiar. Audiences knew in advance what they were going to get in an MGM film. On the other hand, they weren't quite so sure what to expect from a Gregory Peck film at Fox or a Richard Widmark thriller or a movie starring Kirk Douglas or the virile Burt Lancaster, and it was this uncertainty and the prospect of discovering stars who were new and exciting that turned them away from MGM and towards the other studios. All this meant that MGM had quite a fight on its hands in the very field in which it had dominated for so long – the world of stars!

On the surface, the public could see very little difference between the old-style MGM and the MGM of the postwar years. MGM's pictures were still glossy, the stars were still there in abundance and, when the studio celebrated its 25th anniversary in 1949, MGM made sure that the event was celebrated in typically lavish style, throwing a huge luncheon at Culver City in April of that year. Every one of the MGM contract stars attended, and 58 of the 80 were photographed together in what remains the most famous publicity shot of all time. Almost all of the stars were smiling, yet the smiles were deceptive and there were very few to be seen on the lot itself. In 1948, the studio's profits had amounted to just $5 million, the lowest figure since the early years of the Depression. Alarm bells began to ring through the studio, which had once boasted that it had 'more stars than there are in heaven' and the alarm bells summoned Dore Schary to the scene.

Schary was no stranger to MGM. He had worked there before the war as a writer and producer and had won an Oscar for his original story for *Boys' Town* in 1938. Thanks to Howard Hughes, his tenure at the RKO studio had been brief, but at MGM he was promised a fair crack of the whip, providing he could come up with a new style for the studio and something more in line with the demands of postwar audiences.

Politically he was a liberal, ambitious in his thinking and forward looking – the very opposite, in fact, to Mayer who was an arch-conservative, staunch Republican. For instance, Mayer's comment on the insidious witch-hunts instigated by the notorious Senator Joe McCarthy to investigate (and sometimes blacklist) any star, writer or director with left-wing views made clear where his sympathies lay: 'The more McCarthy yells, the better I like him. He's doing a great job getting rid of the termites eating away at our democracy. I hope he drives all the bums back

*The star who remained at Metro when all the greats began to leave the studio – Leo the MGM lion, pictured here on a plane ride with an MGM starlet.*

to Moscow! None of this made for a particularly harmonious relationship between the two men at the top at MGM, especially as several of the 'bums' (the blacklisted Hollywood Ten) had originally worked as writers, producers and directors for Schary at RKO.

Things came to a head at MGM in 1951. In the front office it was no longer a case of Mayer and Schary but Mayer *or* Schary. On the one hand there were the traditional MGM values of opulence and extravagance as typified by L. B. Mayer; on the other, there were the less expensive, more disciplined methods of Schary. Something, or rather somebody, had to give – and that somebody was L.B. Mayer.

When the crunch came, it came over John

Huston's version of the Civil War classic *The Red Badge of Courage*. The production of the film had been much troubled and the reactions of audiences at previews had been cool and unenthusiastic. Much cutting and pruning went on behind the scenes, but nothing could be done to make the movie (now regarded in some quarters as a classic) a commercial proposition, even though it starred Audie Murphy (on loan from Universal) in the leading role.

Mayer had opposed it from the first. Schary had backed Huston. The film cost a huge $1.6 million and, in the end, ran for just 69 minutes. Mayer appealed to Schenck, requesting that he stop Schary from making this kind of picture, saying that it would ruin

MGM. Schenck, who was secretly anxious for Mayer to leave, sided with Schary, and Mayer found himself boxed into a corner. He had no alternative but to resign, and his resignation became effective on 31 August 1951. Louis B. Mayer's reign at MGM had lasted for 27 years.

Mayer later reflected: 'I wanted to be associated with pictures which showed America in the right light – not as a nation of gangsters and drunkards.' He also commented: 'When a producer used to tell me that he had a prestige picture, I knew we were going to lose money.' Whether or not he was thinking of the films of Dore Schary when he made that remark is not known, but he might just as well have been, for by the time he left

*The MGM star line-up in 1949, photographed during the studio's 25th anniversary celebrations.*

*Audie Murphy in John Huston's* The Red Badge of Courage *(MGM, 1951), the picture that caused the split between Louis B. Mayer and Dore Schary.*

*Below:* Ivanhoe *(1952), one of MGM's most spectacular movies of the early Fifties, starring Robert Taylor, Elizabeth Taylor and Joan Fontaine, and featuring some of the biggest battle scenes ever staged.*

MGM in 1951, many of the pictures coming out of the studio no longer looked like MGM pictures, at least not in his eyes.

Schary adopted a two-pronged policy at MGM in the early Fifties. He didn't dispense entirely with the glittering entertainment side. He retained a degree of opulence by indulging in a series of spectacular epics that earned an ageing Robert Taylor a new lease of life in *Quo Vadis* (1951), *Ivanhoe* (1952) and *Knights of the Round Table* (1954), and also brought Hollywood stardom to British actor Stewart Granger, who began as Allan Quartermain in the 1950 version of H. Rider Haggard's *King Solomon's Mines* and then continued in elegant remakes of Rafael Sabatini's *Scaramouche* and Anthony's Hope's *The Prisoner of Zenda* (both 1952). British actresses Deborah Kerr and Jean Simmons were two other stars who did well out of the lavish period productions of the early Fifties. They were especially effective when they starred together (Simmons as the young Elizabeth I, Kerr as Catherine Parr) in George Sidney's *Young Bess* (1953), a film also notable for the brief reappearance of Charles Laughton as Henry VIII and for a magnificent score by Miklos Rozsa.

Schary's main thrust, however, was with the topical, thoughtful, intelligent pictures that he had tried to get under way at RKO and that Zanuck was already making with great success at Fox. In 1949, he made the bleak and realistic *Battleground*, a harrowing and much praised account of the 1944 defence of Bastogne, and investigated racial prejudice in the Deep South in Clarence Brown's version of the William Faulkner novel *Intruder in the Dust*. In 1950, he turned his back on Andy Hardy territory and instead probed into life on the sordid, cold streets of urban America in John Huston's crime thriller *The Asphalt Jungle*, and in 1951 he touched a nerve in many Americans when he backed Fred Zinnemann's film, *Teresa*. The picture

*Jean Simmons and Stewart Granger in the historical romance* Young Bess *(MGM, 1953).*

WHAT A JOY TO SEE MGM's TECHNICOLOR MUSICAL!

*An American in Paris*

Adventures of an ex-GI in the city of romance. Art Students' Ball biggest, most daring ever filmed. Screen's most spectacular musical!

to the Music of GEORGE GERSHWIN

Starring GENE KELLY

and Introducing LESLIE CARON

with OSCAR LEVANT / GEORGES GUETARY

NINA FOCH * Story and Screen Play by ALAN JAY LERNER * Lyrics by IRA GERSHWIN

Directed by VINCENTE MINNELLI * Produced by ARTHUR FREED

HEAR THE STARS SING THE HITS IN THE M-G-M RECORDS ALBUM

*The Arthur Freed/ Vincente Minnelli musical* An American in Paris *(MGM, 1951), named best film of the year at the Hollywood Oscar ceremony.*

starred Pier Angeli and centred on the problems facing many European GI brides when they were taken back to the States to start new lives in a new country.

One thing Schary left well alone was the musical. He knew that, whatever else had changed at MGM in the years since the war, the musical remained as fresh and as dazzling as ever. And in retrospect it was a good thing that he didn't meddle in Arthur Freed's territory, for in the early Fifties, Freed reached his peak with a trio of musicals that belong with the best ever made at any studio. Certainly no studio, before or since, ever produced three musical masterpieces in three consecutive years as did Freed in 1951, 1952 and 1953.

He won an Oscar for his first, *An American in Paris* (1951), a Vincente Minnelli feast set to the music of George Gershwin and starring Gene Kelly as a footloose painter in Paris. He also learned everlasting praise for his second, *Singin' in the Rain*, a brilliant musical satire of the early talkies, again starring Kelly, and he produced perhaps Fred Astaire's best-ever musical, *The Band Wagon*, as his third film in the series.

All in all, it was a remarkable hat-trick of musical classics that tended to overshadow, perhaps unfairly, many of the other fine musicals produced at the studio during that period. Among them were *The Great Caruso* (1951), in which MGM pushed heart-throb Mario Lanza through 27 arias; George Sidney's *Show Boat* (1951) and *Kiss Me Kate* (1953), both starring Howard Keel and Kathryn Grayson; the charming *Lili* (1953) with the young French actress Leslie Caron; and the studio's unexpected musical hit of the period, *Seven Brides for Seven Brothers* (1954), which starred Howard Keel and Jane Powell and, to everyone's surprise, earned the studio an unexpected fortune!

However, mixed in with all the success of the Freed musicals was an atmosphere of sadness at the studio. As the members of the Freed unit danced and sang their way across the sound stages, the non-musical stars who had become such permanent fixtures at the studio said goodbye. Schary had simply no more use for them. Whereas, in the Thirties and Forties, the studio had more than enough stories to go round to accommodate the huge roster of stars, by the early Fifties Schary was struggling to find projects that would enable performers to work out their contracts.

One by one, they left. Garland had already departed in 1950, a spent force physically and mentally, wrecked by the pressures of the MGM studio. In 1954, Greer Garson left after a routine production called *Her Twelve Men*. The same year Gable also made his exit after appearing in an equally routine espionage story called *Betrayed*. In 1955 the exodus continued. Jane Powell left, as did Howard Keel, and even Esther Williams called it a day after appearing in *Jupiter's Darling*, a film that had her mixed up with Hannibal and his elephants as they crossed the Alps. A brave

MGM publicity man released the statistic that Esther had performed in 50 spectacular water routines and had swum a total of 1,250 miles during her career, but by then no one really cared. The day of Esther Williams and all the other top MGM stars (Walter Pidgeon and Lana Turner also left in 1956) was past.

Only one established MGM performer managed actually to enhance his reputation under the Schary regime – Spencer Tracy. He managed to come to terms with middle age and white hair with not the slightest difficulties, and proved that he was not only the finest actor to emerge from MGM during the sound era but also, quite possibly the finest

*One of the most memorable dance solos ever filmed, Gene Kelly's splash-about in* Singin' in the Rain *(MGM, 1952).*

169

*An exhausted Spencer Tracy, at the peak of his comedy powers in Vincente Minnelli's* Father of the Bride *(MGM, 1950).*

actor ever to come out of Hollywood. He dazzled in comedies such as *Father of the Bride* (1950) in which he played the harassed father of bride-to-be Elizabeth Taylor; he excelled as another father, that of the stage-struck Jean Simmons, in *The Actress* (1953); and in *Bad Day at Black Rock* (1955), he was superb as the one-armed, black-suited war veteran who comes face to face with violence and death in a remote desert town. But, eventually, even Tracy decided that enough was enough and opted to quit the studio. In 1956, he walked out of his role as a ruthless cattle baron in *Tribute to a Bad Man* and drove through the gates of Culver City for the last time. He had been at MGM for 21 years.

In the end, Schary's regime at MGM did not turn out to be the success or miracle cure that everyone had hoped for. His appointment had been a gamble and the gamble simply didn't come off. After eight years at the studio, he was sacked in 1956.

By then MGM was neither one thing nor the other. The musicals and such hard-hitting pictures as Vincente Minnelli's Hollywood exposé *The Bad and the Beautiful* (1952),

Robert Wise's big-business drama *Executive Suite* (1954), and *The Blackboard Jungle* (1955) – Richard Brooks' searing look at teenage violence in a New York school – had helped the studio keep its feet on the ladder, but there was no disguising the fact that it had changed beyond all recognition.

In charge now was an independent producer named Sol C. Siegel and he didn't know which way to turn. From the very beginning, it had always been the stars who made MGM, and without them there was nothing left. Siegel was simply left to pick up the pieces, but the trouble was that they just wouldn't fit together any more.

Within the space of just ten years, MGM had descended to being just another Hollywood studio. If confirmation was needed of its loss of status, the fact that, in 1957, it recorded its first ever financial loss ($455,000) more than proved the point. In the league table of Hollywood studios, MGM no longer held pride of place, at best claiming fourth position a long way behind Fox, Columbia and Paramount. The proud roar of its trademark lion had been reduced almost to a whimper.

# 1952
## Paramount

### The Greatest Showman on Earth:
### Cecil B. DeMille

Paramount certainly didn't suffer from any drop in 'league status' in 1952 nor indeed at any time during the Fifties. If ever there was a consistently successful studio from an artistic point of view, it was Paramount. They may have suffered their financial ups and downs over the years, but there was always something of interest going on behind those gates on Marathon Street. It didn't matter which year or decade you chose; something of quality was always being made at Paramount.

As indeed it was in 1952. In fact, the old MGM slogan – 'Make It Good . . . Make It Big . . . Give It Class' – perfectly summed up the attitude of those in charge at Paramount as first one and then another distinguished production rolled off the studio assembly line. The old mountain peak ringed with stars and preceded by the stirring fanfare had lost none of its power. What is more, it heralded not only great movies but also plenty of new stars. The rugged Charlton Heston was one such newcomer; the elfin Audrey Hepburn was another. The prolific comedy team of Dean Martin and Jerry Lewis also joined the studio, as did Grace Kelly. If MGM suffered from star trouble in the Fifties, Paramount most certainly did not.

Neither did it have much director trouble. The great Billy Wilder was still working on the lot; so too were George Stevens, William Wyler and Alfred Hitchcock. And, of course, the veteran Cecil B. DeMille. By the time he came to make his circus extravaganza *The Greatest Show on Earth*, he had 68 films to his credit and was 71 years old. He had been in at the very beginnings of Paramount, back in 1913 when he had co-directed *The Squaw*

*Man* in just 18 days for a cost of $15,000. The star of *The Squaw Man* was Dustin Farnum, and the picture's eventual box-office gross was $244,700.

In 1952 there were rather more stars around for *The Greatest Show on Earth*, six in fact – Betty Hutton, James Stewart (hidden throughout the entire film behind a clown's make-up), Charlton Heston, Cornel Wilde, Dorothy Lamour and Gloria Grahame. The costs and profits of the film were also rather larger, and ran into not thousands but millions. However, the ratio between expenditure and profit remained the same. DeMille's films always made money, there was never any doubt about that, and that was why Paramount had relied on him for so long and why a new DeMille picture was always regarded as something of an event – as well as a profit-making venture.

DeMille's motto was 'Always give the public what it wants', which, in his view anyway, invariably meant sex, sin and spectacle, although not necessarily in that order. He filled the screen with spectacle, handled vast crowds with consummate skill and shrugged off the critics who said he was a vulgarian who cheapened his subjects (not least with exotic beauties in bathtubs), especially when he raided the Bible for his stories. He would gently smile at their comments and point a steady finger at the profit columns of every one of his films.

Even though spectacle, rather than great acting, was always the key factor in a DeMille movie, actors and actresses still queued up to be in his pictures. The dialogue they had to deliver was never of any great quality, but the exposure

*Overleaf: Cecil B. DeMille's* The Greatest Show on Earth *(Paramount, 1952). Charlton Heston is the man in agony, Betty Hutton the one offering sympathy and James Stewart is the clown about to save his life.*

they received in a DeMille production was enormous and worth the efforts of a dozen press agents working overtime.

Cornel Wilde discovered this to be the case when he came to be cast as the trapeze artist 'The Great Sebastian' in *The Greatest Show on Earth*. Despite suffering from vertigo, he agreed to appear in the film simply because it was a DeMille movie, and such was his determination to overcome his phobia that he did, eventually, conquer his fear of heights. But at a price, and a low price at that. When it came to negotiating his fee for the picture, the reply from DeMille's office was '$50,000!' Wilde couldn't believe it. '$50,000? I've been getting that many times over at other studios,' he protested. DeMille's reply was that being in one of his pictures was reward enough and, if Wilde cared to check around, he'd find that all the other stars in the film – Stewart, Hutton, Heston and the rest – were getting the same fee. DeMille also stated that the stars should really be appearing in his film for nothing, and that the $50,000 was a bonus. Wilde accepted.

So, too, did Charlton Heston, who had been in pictures only a couple of years when DeMille cast him as the circus manager in *The Greatest Show on Earth*. The big break made all the difference to Heston's career. He later remarked: 'I had been introduced to Mr. DeMille as a matter of form. Everyone who worked on the Paramount lot was introduced to him. It was a kind of ritual. He was an extremely courteous man and we exchanged a few pleasantries.

'A few weeks later, I was driving off the lot in a secondhand convertible when I passed the DeMille building. He was standing on the steps at the time with five or six of his staff, so I waved to him as I drove out. I was told later that he said to his secretary: "Who was that young man?" She flipped back immediately in the notepad she always carried and said: "His name is Charlton Heston. He just made a picture for Hal Wallis called *Dark City*. You ran it ten days ago. You didn't like it." And he said. "No, but I liked the way he waved. I think we better have him come in and talk about the circus picture." ' Heston has since stated that that was the moment when his film career really began: 'I often think about what opportunities might have been denied me if I had failed to wave to C. B. DeMille.'

As Heston and others before him were to discover, DeMille was not the greatest director of actors. He expected them to come to the set word perfect and, if they weren't, he wanted to know why. Any help he actually gave actors was minimal, his view being that they were actors so they should act. His job

was to take charge of the spectacular side of things, to control thousands of extras if need be and make sure that his many assistant directors (on the remake of *The Ten Commandments* they numbered 78) were on their toes.

DeMille himself was often inclined to give something of a performance on set. Certainly he dressed the part of a major Hollywood director: flannel shirt, well-tailored riding breeches and puttees, high-top boots, jewelled rings on his fingers and a megaphone in his

hands were all essential to his appearance. In the silent days, he even carried a revolver in order to shoot dangerous snakes when filming on location.

He was followed on all occasions by three assistants. Number 1 was a chairboy who never saw his master face to face but was ready at the rear with a chair for the great man to sit down in. Number 2 was the mikeboy who trailed a microphone around so that DeMille could seize it when necessary and pass on his orders. Number 3 was the

waterboy. He stood ready with a tray of iced water maintained at exactly the right temperature.

It wasn't perhaps surprising therefore that Billy Wilder, who had observed DeMille at work many times on the lot, approached the old master to play himself for a few minutes in a cameo role in Wilder's Hollywood film *Sunset Boulevard* (1950). DeMille found the prospect of playing himself an intriguing one and agreed, especially as Wilder suggested that he be shown directing scenes from

*DeMille's 1950 epic* Samson and Delilah *(Paramount) with Victor Mature as the blinded strong man and Hedy Lamarr as the beauty who gives him a haircut.*

*Samson and Delilah*. The two men made a tongue-in-cheek deal about DeMille's cameo: if DeMille would offer no suggestions as to how he should play his role, Wilder would offer no advice on how to direct *Samson and Delilah*!

Wilder's film, of course, was about as far removed from a DeMille movie as you could get – a scathing exposé of a Hollywood that, in 1950, very few audiences across the world were particularly familiar with. There was nothing glamorous about the world it portrayed nor was there anything appealing about its two central characters: a faded silent movie queen living in seclusion in an old decaying mansion, and a young hack writer who is hired to be her lover and to write her comeback movie. As adult entertainment, it was of the highest class, a cynical film of sharp wit that stripped Hollywood bare and revealed it to be a town where just about

anyone would do anything for a quick buck and a place at the top of the Hollywood heap.

The film brought new stature to the young William Holden and brought Gloria Swanson back to the screen as the ageing movie queen Norma Desmond, her performance going down in movie history as one of the most celebrated comebacks of all time. Her climactic scene as she walks half-crazed down the staircase of her old mansion and utters the words 'I'm ready for my close-up now, Mr. DeMille' belongs with the most dramatic endings of any film.

Comebacks turned out to be not infrequent at Paramount during the early and mid-Fifties. Alan Ladd, who for so long had been a top money-earner at the studio, was, in 1953, considered to be well past his best and no longer a box-office commodity. In fact, Paramount were offering him second-rate parts so that he could finish his contract quickly and

*One of the great screen comebacks: Gloria Swanson as Norma Desmond in Billy Wilder's* Sunset Boulevard *(Paramount, 1950).*

Alan Ladd in action. On the
receiving end: Ben Johnson.
The film? George Stevens'
classic western Shane
(Paramount, 1953).

leave the studio. However, when director George Stevens, who had earned the studio several Academy Awards for his brilliant *A Place in the Sun* (1951) with Montgomery Clift and Elizabeth Taylor, decided to make a western, Ladd's name – rather to Paramount's surprise – cropped up for the leading role. The picture was *Shane* (1953) and it extended Ladd's career by more than a decade. His buck-skinned stranger became one of the most heroic westerners of all time, a quiet-spoken man of few words who rides into a Wyoming valley to help the homesteaders in their fight against the cattlemen.

Stevens, who was known for his perfectionist methods, turned the film into a masterpiece, even capturing on film a distant thunderstorm. The distant rumblings and storm clouds that accompanied Jack Palance's gunning down of Elisha Cook, Jr. outside Grafton's saloon were caught on celluloid because Stevens carefully checked the weather report each day before shooting. A 4.30 a.m. phone call to the nearest weather station at Pocatello, Idaho, determined exactly which scenes he would shoot. His meticulous attention to detail paid dividends. *Shane* grossed a huge $9 million.

If Stevens was a perfectionist, so too was Alfred Hitchcock, and in the mid-Fifties he was yet another who enjoyed something of a comeback at Paramount. In the postwar years he had suffered a lean spell with a long run of inferior pictures, and it was only with the Warner Bros. thriller *Strangers on a Train* (1951) that he once again hit his stride. Shortly afterwards, he moved across to Paramount where he enjoyed perhaps the most lucrative period of his entire career, making six films in six years at the studio including three that are frequently regarded as masterpieces: *Rear Window* (1954), *Vertigo* (1958) and *Psycho* (1960).

However, despite the quality of his unique thrillers, Hitchcock's name remains as much associated with his promotion of the career of the lovely cool-blonde actress Grace Kelly as it does with his actual films of the period. He cast her in three films altogether. The first, *Dial M for Murder* (1954), was made at Warners, the other two at Paramount. In *Rear Window*, she played opposite James Stewart (restricted because of a broken leg encased in plaster), joining him in trying to prove whether a murder has been committed in the apartment opposite. Just as intriguing as the Crippen-like elements of the plot were Miss Kelly's superb gowns and equally tan-

talizing figure. 'Preview of forthcoming attractions,' she smiles at James Stewart as she holds up a slinky nightgown. In *To Catch a Thief* (1955), she was even more down to earth and this time the man struggling to resist her temptations was Cary Grant. 'Do you want a leg or a breast?' she asks as they picnic in a car overlooking the Riviera. 'You make the choice,' replies a wary Mr. Grant. For once the Paramount publicity department got things about right when it stated: 'Cary Grant as the jewel thief they called "The Cat"; Grace Kelly as a jewel anxious to get stolen!'

There were plenty of other jewels in the Paramount crown in the mid-Fifties, and plenty of Oscar winners, too. For instance, there was Audrey Hepburn, who captivated Gregory Peck as the runaway princess in *Roman Holiday* (1953). William Holden won a deserved best actor award the same year for his cynical P.O.W. Sefton in Billy Wilder's *Stalag 17*. Anna Magnani, in *The Rose Tattoo* (1955), was another winner for her portrayal of Tennessee Williams' neurotic seamstress Serafina Delle Rose, as was Shirley Booth for her slovenly but good-hearted housewife in *Come Back, Little Sheba* (1952). Producer George Pal also got in on the Oscar act by earning several best special effects awards for his science-fiction spectaculars *When Worlds Collide* (1951) and *The War of the Worlds* (1953), an updated version of the novel by

*Below: Grace Kelly with Cary Grant, in Hitchcock's Riviera thriller* To Catch a Thief *(Paramount, 1955).*

*Right: Peeping Toms James Stewart and Grace Kelly in Alfred Hitchcock's 1954 production* Rear Window *(Paramount).*

*Opposite: The lovely Audrey Hepburn, star of the 1957 musical* Funny Face *(Paramount).*

*Overleaf: The exodus from Egypt: a cast of thousands for DeMille's last movie,* The Ten Commandments *(Paramount, 1956).*

178

H. G. Wells. In terms of hard cash, the studio's big moneymaker was the syrupy (but seemingly everlasting) musical *White Christmas* (1954), which teamed Bing Crosby with Danny Kaye, popular songstress Rosemary Clooney and the lovely Vera-Ellen.

But the man who made both the money *and* won the Oscars was Cecil B. DeMille. Until 1952, he had been regarded simply as a moneymaking producer/director who catered for the public and was never once in the running for an Academy Award. But on 19 March 1953, the first time the awards were televised across the United States, that was put to rights when the Academy presented the grand old man of the cinema with the best picture award for *The Greatest Show on Earth*. It wasn't the best film in the world exactly, but it was a spectacular piece of entertainment and proved, if any proof were needed, that even at the age of 71, C. B. DeMille still knew how to make pictures . . . and, of course, money.

DeMille made only one more film before his death in 1959 – his huge 3-hour 40-minute remake of his own silent production *The Ten Commandments* (1956). It cost him a staggering $13.5 million to produce, included 10,000 props and 25,000 extras, and incorporated three months' location work in Egypt and 120 days on the Paramount lot. It didn't win him a second Oscar, but it didn't need to. It made a fortune.

It would be overstating things to say that DeMille carried Paramount in the Fifties, but without him and his films, the studio would have been only half of what it was. He was the figurehead. He was the man who dominated the entire studio. When he died, a great deal of Paramount died with him – technical brilliance coupled with vulgarity, epic vision combined with corn, flamboyance, style – all went with DeMille. And no one, no matter how hard they tried, was ever quite able to recapture that famous Cecil B. DeMille style again.

*Rosemary Clooney, Danny Kaye, Bing Crosby, Vera-Ellen plus juveniles in the musical* White Christmas *(Paramount, 1954).*

# 1953
## Twentieth Century-Fox

Marilyn Monroe and the CinemaScope Years

There wasn't a DeMille at Fox in 1953, but there was, of course, a Zanuck. And at just about the time that C. B. DeMille was making his acceptance speech at the Academy Awards ceremony, Zanuck had come to a fateful decision. He had called a halt to the production of a biblical epic called *The Robe* and told the cast and crew to stand by for an announcement.

The announcement didn't come immediately. Zanuck waited for a day. During that time, he paced the lawn of his Palm Springs home many times, weighing up all the pros and cons of a new wide-screen process called CinemaScope. What he had to decide was whether to shoot all his future films using the process or stick with the old square-shaped format that had served so reliably since the movies first began. If he decided on the new process, he knew it would be a gamble. Many of those close to him advised against it and suggested that he stick to the old screen and promote his sensational new blonde sex symbol, Marilyn Monroe. Zanuck, however, decided that, in 1953, no one star, no matter how talented, would do the trick. So he opted instead for both – CinemaScope and Marilyn Monroe. It was quite a combination.

The reasons for Zanuck's quandary were nothing new. They had to do with the same problem that had been nagging the studios for years – dwindling audiences. It was just that, in 1953, the problem had become more acute. Audiences were declining even faster, and many of Hollywood's top stars were now beginning to look towards TV as a means of extending their careers: Lucille Ball, for instance, and Fred MacMurray, Jack Benny and

Bob Hope. It was obvious that something dramatic was needed if Hollywood was to stop the rot.

The question was: Was there anything that *could* be done? Surely Hollywood had tried just about everything already, even the gimmicky 3-D movies that had begun with United Artists' *Bwana Devil* (1952) and had produced nothing more than the occasional thrill – Ann Miller swaying her hips in three dimensions in MGM's *Kiss Me Kate* and a disfigured Vincent Price skulking the darkened streets in Warners' horror piece, *House of Wax* (both 1953).

But 3-D, which required audiences to wear special glasses in order to appreciate the three-dimensional effect, was no more than a passing phase. Put another way, it was the *hors d'oeuvre* before the main meal. Early in 1953, Zanuck decided that the main meal would, in fact, be CinemaScope, a process that was projected on to a screen that was two-and-a-half times as wide as it was high. Zanuck reasoned that CinemaScope would yank people out of their armchairs and back into the seats of the cinema simply because it was big and would provide something they could not see at home on that small flickering screen in their living rooms. When he picked up the telephone at his Palm Springs home and issued the command: 'OK, we're going with CinemaScope,' it meant a complete change of image for the Fox studio.

Sophisticated films such as *All About Eve* were out. So, too, were message pictures. There would be no more of the type of film exemplified by *Gentleman's Agreement* and *Pinky*. Size and spectacle (and locations) were

*Overleaf: Richard Burton, Jay Robinson and Jean Simmons in the first CinemaScope feature,* The Robe *(Twentieth Century-Fox, 1953).*

the new order of the day. What is more, every Fox picture from *The Robe* onwards would be photographed in the new process, regardless of subject. It was a revolution not dissimilar to the advent of talkies a quarter of a century before. Zanuck had been around when that happened, and he was in the thick of things again when the new 'revolution' occurred.

Not surprisingly, the 'revolution' underwent plenty of teething troubles, mainly because Zanuck had plunged so quickly into CinemaScope and had not given much thought to the fact that there were plenty of imperfections still to be ironed out. The screen was indeed wide – enormous, in fact, in very large cinemas – and the stereophonic sound (an integral part of the CinemaScope

revolution) did boom out at you from all directions from speakers around the auditorium. However, in crowd scenes, people on the curved edges of the screen often looked skinny and squashed, and the new DeLuxe Color was light blue and sometimes mauve in tint, which did little for actors' faces. And if the stereo sound operated from only one side of a cinema because of a technical fault, the result was often a disaster.

None the less, the first CinemaScope film, *The Robe* (1953) was a financial success and a very big success at that. The public flocked to watch as Roman tribune Richard Burton, the man in command of the Crucifixion, went through torments of self-doubt before being converted to Christianity and walking off to a

*Richard Burton and Jeff Morrow battle it out in a sequence from* The Robe *(Twentieth Century-Fox, 1953).*

certain death with the lovely Jean Simmons, all to the accompaniment of a stereophonic heavenly choir!

The film was adapted from the novel by Lloyd C. Douglas, and its screenplay (although considerably revitalized by an uncredited Philip Dunne) was not its strongest point, but once CinemaScope arrived, that no longer bothered Zanuck. By 1953, the spoken word, so vital a part of Zanuck's postwar operations, was suddenly relegated in importance. So too were directors Elia Kazan and Joe Mankiewicz, whose departure from the studio coincided, perhaps not by accident, with the arrival of CinemaScope.

All Fox movies of the Fifties were photographed in CinemaScope, and they were photographed not just in Hollywood but all over the world. Location work was very much the order of the day. 'See the world in CinemaScope' was Zanuck's motto – Rome in

*Three Coins in the Fountain* (1954), Berlin with Gregory Peck in *Night People* (1954), Hong Kong with Clark Gable in *Soldier of Fortune* and with William Holden and Jennifer Jones in the tragic romance *Love Is a Many-Splendored Thing* (both 1955), and the Greek islands with Alan Ladd and Sophia Loren in *Boy on a Dolphin* (1957). Even the 19th-century kingdom of Siam was on view (although this time the 'locations' were restricted to the backlot) in the hit Yul Brynner/Deborah Kerr musical *The King and I* (1956).

Zanuck sent out invitations to many top stars who were not averse to seeing their features as large as the sculptures of Mount Rushmore on screen. Humphrey Bogart arrived in 1955 to play an American pilot who crashlands in China during the Second World War in *The Left Hand of God*; Gary Cooper accepted the lead in a Mexican western *Garden of Evil* (1954); and on the lighter side

*The musical goes CinemaScope – Yul Brynner and Deborah Kerr in* The King and I *(Twentieth Century-Fox, 1956).*

of things, Fred Astaire also visited Fox for the first (and only) time to appear opposite Leslie Caron in the musical *Daddy Long Legs* (1955).

On the face of it, the CinemaScope revolution had been a commercial if not a critical success, so much so that every one of the CinemaScope movies produced in the 12 months following the release of *The Robe* made money. Yet for all this, Zanuck must have entertained many private doubts about the way the Fox studio was going. Although the CinemaScope films were financially successful, the standard of much of the entertainment on offer was often no higher than the level of a comic strip, a far cry from the adult entertainments of the late Forties. CinemaScope was hailed as a new beginning, but more often than not it seemed, to many critics, to be more like the beginning of the end.

Once, when Zanuck asked comedian/pianist Oscar Levant what he thought of one of his

CinemaScope pictures, Levant replied bluntly: 'I think the picture stinks!' 'Who the hell are you to think the picture stinks?' Zanuck angrily retorted. To which Levant, in turn, replied: 'Who the hell do you have to *be* to think the picture stinks?' Certainly many of the top Hollywood directors thought Cinema-Scope stank. George Stevens, for instance: his reaction was 'It's fine if you want a system that shows a boa constrictor to better advantage than a man!'

Whatever people thought about the shape of CinemaScope, there was hardly a man or woman around in the Fifties who wasn't impressed by the shape of a young actress named Marilyn Monroe. She had shapely legs, an ample bust, blonde hair and an innocent smile. She shone like a beacon from the mediocrity of the films around her.

Born and raised in Hollywood, she had always wanted to be a movie star; she had no other ambition. Fox signed her to a seven-

*Joseph Cotten has had enough: exit Marilyn Monroe from her first starring movie,* Niagara *(Twentieth Century-Fox, 1953).*

Marilyn Monroe and Jane
Russell, stars of the 1953
musical Gentlemen Prefer
Blondes (Twentieth Century-
Fox).

year contract in October 1950, having not
renewed, a few years earlier, a former contract
hiring her at $125 a week. They made it just
in time. MGM had been showing interest
(and how they could have done with her!) but,
not wishing to offend Lana Turner, had
hesitated for just that moment too long and
Fox snapped her up.

'I'm not interested in money,' said Marilyn
later. 'I just want to be wonderful.' And for
most of the people who watched her on
screen, she was indeed just that – vulnerable,
sexy, innocent, magical. On screen, she
danced and sang and showed a talent for
comedy that combined well with her sexy
image. As an actress she was hardly of top
stature but she didn't really need to be.
When, in *Niagara* (1953), she wiggled across
the screen in a clinging red satin dress that
was two sizes too small and someone remarked, 'To wear a dress like that, you've got
to start laying plans at 13,' it said it all.

As the wide-eyed innocent of *Gentlemen
Prefer Blondes, How to Marry a Millionaire*
(both 1953) and Billy Wilder's *The Seven-
Year Itch* (1955), Marilyn was superb. Off-
screen, she dealt with stardom with a flashing
smile, a curvacious pose and a ready wit.

What did she have on when posing for the famous nude photograph? 'The radio!' Why did she do it? 'Hunger!' On being a sex symbol: 'I always thought that symbols were things that clashed.' On whether or not she wore falsies: 'People who know me better, know better.'

Later, of course, she suffered a tragic decline, not dissimilar to that of Judy Garland at MGM, and found it difficult to cope with both her public and private turmoil over her marriages and her career. But in the mid-Fifties at least, during her early years at Fox, she was happy. Between 1953 and 1956, she and Zanuck enjoyed a success that temporarily revived the sagging image of Hollywood: big screens and stereophonic sound; Marilyn Monroe and comedy and song. It wasn't a bad formula whichever way you looked at it.

Despite all its teething troubles Cinema-Scope was, in the end, a revolution of sorts. Without it and the massive Cinerama (a process that originally utilized three cameras and three projectors), there might not have been the huge Panavision screens of the Seventies and Eighties on to which were projected such science-fiction epics as *Star Wars, Close Encounters of the Third Kind* and the *Superman* films with Christopher Reeve.

Zanuck pioneered the big screen. Of the other top Hollywood studios, only Paramount, which adopted its own high-fidelity system, VistaVision, didn't follow Fox's example and jump on the CinemaScope bandwagon. MGM's first film in Cinema-Scope was *Knights of the Round Table* (1954) with Robert Taylor and Ava Gardner. Warners' first movie using the process was the Guy Madison western *The Command* (1954). Universal opted for a Tony Curtis costume spectacular *The Black Shield of Falworth* (1954) for its CinemaScope debut; Disney for the James Mason/Kirk Douglas adventure *20,000 Leagues under the Sea* (1954); and Columbia for a Betty Grable musical *Three for the Show* (1955).

And Zanuck? In 1956, he decided at last that enough was enough. He had been in charge at Fox for over 21 years and wanted to concentrate fulltime on producing his own films. He left for Europe to make pictures independently, which were released under the Fox banner. Many felt that that would be the last that Fox would see of him, that he would remain an independent for the rest of his career. As usual, the pundits were wrong. In the Sixties, Zanuck did return – to become the last tycoon and to deal with catastrophe.

# 1954
# Columbia

## The Last Hurrah:
## The Final Years of Harry Cohn

Something unusual happened at the Oscar ceremonies between the years 1949 and 1954. Columbia Studios, once of Poverty Row on Gower Street, won three Academy Awards for best picture in five years. Previously only MGM had achieved such a feat, and that was back in the Thirties. Since then, no one had come close.

That it should be Columbia that pulled off such a coup came as something of a surprise, especially as the studio had been without a single best picture Oscar since the days of Capra. But then the Fifties were the time when Harry Cohn decided to get serious. He didn't have much use for Zanuck's Cinema-Scope (even though he eventually adopted the system for his more expensive productions), but he did have time for writers and directors who came to him with slightly off-beat ideas that could be turned, reasonably quickly and without too much expense, into interesting movies.

The Oscar-winning trio comprised *All the King's Men* (1949), Robert Rossen's drama of corruption in American politics; *From Here to Eternity* (1953), Fred Zinnemann's account of life in the American army just prior to the Second World War; and Elia Kazan's *On the Waterfront* (1954), a vivid exposé of racketeering on the cold and cheerless waterfront of New York.

Of the three, *All the King's Men*, which was based on the career of the Louisiana governor and senator, Huey 'Kingfish' Long, was the least successful financially. It was based on the bestselling novel by Robert Penn Warren and made a star out of Broderick Crawford, but it didn't make a dime for Harry Cohn – it

brought him only prestige. *On the Waterfront* was the sleeper and it *did* make money – $8 million worth! It also starred Marlon Brando in perhaps his best-ever role, as the broken-down ex-boxer Terry Malloy. Yet every studio in Hollywood had turned it down (even Zanuck at Fox) before Harry Cohn said 'yes' to director Kazan and writer Budd Schulberg. Without Harry Cohn, *On the Waterfront* would never have been made.

It was, however, *From Here to Eternity* that caught the public's imagination the most. It was based on the bestselling novel by James Jones, which dealt with the lives of a group of soldiers serving in Hawaii just prior to the bombing of Pearl Harbor. Its sex scenes were explicit, its pages liberally sprinkled with four-letter words and it was tough and uncompromising in its attitude towards the U.S. Army. In the eyes of most Hollywood moguls, it was thought to be unfilmable. In fact, when it was discovered that Harry Cohn had purchased the book for $82,000 and then immediately began to have problems with the script, it became known as 'Cohn's Folly'. A joke also went the rounds of Hollywood at the time: 'Why would Harry Cohn buy a dirty book like *From Here to Eternity*?' 'He thinks everyone talks that way!'

Harry Cohn hadn't changed one jot since the early days of his career. Stars and directors still feared his bullying tactics, and to enter his huge office, for whatever reason, was still a terrifying ordeal. Glenn Ford, who was under contract to him for 14 years, remembers not so much the office as the outer door leading to it: 'All the paint had been worn off where you pushed it, the result of years of sweating

*Karl Malden and Eva Marie Saint give aid to a battered Marlon Brando in the famous climax from* On the Waterfront *(Columbia/ Horizon, 1954).*

*Love on the beach: Burt Lancaster and Deborah Kerr in the famous love scene from the 1953 production* From Here to Eternity *(Columbia).*

palms. People – big stars and directors – were terrified when they went in there. I told Harry he should get the door painted. He shouted to his secretary: "Don't let anybody ever paint that door. It's the escutcheon of Columbia!"'

Ford wasn't one of the stars of *From Here to Eternity*, but he almost certainly came under Cohn's consideration for one of the key roles, as did many others. Once producer Buddy Adler and director Fred Zinnemann had shaken hands on the deal, Cohn came up with his cast list: Burt Lancaster for the role of the tough Sergeant Warden (Zinnemann nodded in complete agreement); Joan Crawford for the part of the company commander's sleep-around wife, Karen Holmes (puzzled looks from Zinnemann); Columbia contract star Aldo Ray for the younger bugler Prewitt (silence); and Donna Reed for his girl-friend (OK, Zinnemann had wanted Julie Harris, but Harry had looked and sounded threatening so he gave way).

Cohn also demanded Frank Sinatra, who was then going through a lean patch, both as a vocalist and as a movie star, for the tragic little Private Maggio. Again, Zinnemann, who had asked for Eli Wallach, gave in. But he fought Cohn all the way on two of the roles. For Prewitt, he insisted on Montgomery Clift, whom he considered one of the finest actors in America, and he created a sensation when he asked for Deborah Kerr for the role of Karen Holmes.

Zinnemann later remembered: 'Joan Crawford was more or less set for the part. Then Deborah's agent rang up and said to me, "What about Deborah?" Now Deborah, up until that point, had played only very cool parts, the virgin queen of England types. It was impossible to believe that she could do a part of a nymphomaniac. But then I realized that it was a brilliant suggestion because of that very reason. If you heard the soldiers on the barracks saying that she sleeps with everybody on the post, then the audiences wouldn't at first believe it, but they would be curious to see what was going to happen. Whereas, with Joan Crawford, you more or less accepted it. You know, so what else is new?'

Deborah Kerr couldn't believe her luck. She bleached her hair blonde, wore tight-fitting sweaters, changed the way she walked and, in a then-sensational love scene on the beach with Burt Lancaster, exuded a feeling of raw, unrestrained sex. 'It was sort of Burt's idea that the water should wash over us on the beach,' she said. 'He has a lot of power and a lot of strength. And that helped me enormously. I must have seen the scene over a dozen times, and everytime they show it on American TV, I groan. But funnily enough, the audience doesn't. Most of them were aged about five when the scene was filmed, but for some reason, it still seems extraordinarily erotic. Far more erotic than all the stuff that one has seen where everybody is absolutely naked.'

That scene helped make *From Here to Eternity* the hit picture of 1953. It was shot in just 42 days, and was premièred at New York's Capitol Theater five months after the camera had turned on the first scene!

On the night of 25 March 1954, Harry Cohn's Columbia picked up eight Oscars for *From Here to Eternity*, including awards for Zinnemann, Sinatra and Donna Reed. A year later, the studio picked up another eight when *On the Waterfront* similarly swept the board. Taken with the three that had been earned by *All the King's Men*, it added up to a grand total of 19 Oscars for just three films – a round 20 if the best actress award won by Judy Holliday for her dumb blonde in *Born Yesterday* (1950) is taken into account.

Judy Holliday's part in Columbia's affairs was all-important, her films being the perfect antidote to the more dramatic movies of the studio. In many ways, she was a unique comedienne, superb when playing a squeaky-voiced blonde and equally adept when playing a more down-to-earth woman who, despite her innocent appearance, knew exactly what was going on around her and how to handle herself in any situation.

In the early Fifties, she appeared with another fast-rising comedy star, Jack Lemmon, in the Columbia comedies *It Should Happen to You* and *Phffft!* (both 1954) – the latter a title that indicated the sound of a dying marriage. She also starred in the Capra-esque *The Solid Gold Cadillac* (1956), in which she played a small stockholder who exposes the board of directors of a large company as a bunch of crooks. One of her best lines occurred in the George Cukor comedy *The Marrying Kind* (1952), in which she appeared as a woman struggling to save her marriage. When a woman judge asks her sincerely: 'What is it that makes you incompatible?', she answers: 'Being married to each other!'

There was nothing incompatible about Harry Cohn and success during the Fifties. Profits and quality went hand in glove, just as they had in previous decades when first Capra and then Hayworth had helped turn Columbia from a minor to a major studio. The only difference was that, in the Fifties, things weren't quite so clear cut. There was no one all-dominating star or director, and success was spread over very many different kinds of film.

Judy Holliday, the gal who provided most of the comedy in the Columbia pictures of the early and mid-1950s.

*Right: Jose Ferrer about to break down the defences of Humphrey Bogart's neurotic Captain Queeg in* The Caine Mutiny *(Columbia, 1954). An anxious Van Johnson looks on.*

*Opposite: William Holden, one of the stars of David Lean's* The Bridge on the River Kwai *(Columbia/ Horizon, 1957).*

*Below: Fritz Lang's* The Big Heat *(Columbia, 1953). Getting rough with Gloria Grahame is Lee Marvin.*

There was *The Caine Mutiny* (1954), for instance, with Humphrey Bogart playing the neurotic Captain Queeg and Joshua Logan's version of William Inge's stage play *Picnic* (1955), in which William Holden and Kim Novak danced to 'Moonglow' and raised the temperature almost as high as when Lancaster and Kerr had rolled on the beach in *From Here to Eternity*. Then there were the popular musicals *The Eddy Duchin Story* (1956) and *Pal Joey* (1957); Bogey's last movie, the boxing drama *The Harder They Fall* (1956); and the tough Fritz Lang thrillers *The Big Heat* (1953) and *Human Desire* (1954). Only the comeback pictures of Rita Hayworth – *Affair in Trinidad* (1952), *Salome* and *Miss Sadie Thompson* (both 1953) – whom Cohn tried to restore as one of Hollywood's leading stars – failed to hit the mark.

When Harry Cohn died suddenly from a heart attack in 1958, Columbia were on the crest of another wave. David Lean's anti-war epic *The Bridge on the River Kwai* (1957) was cleaning up at the box office and on its way to becoming the biggest financial hit in the studio's history. It was also on its way to seven Academy Awards, due to be presented in the spring of 1958, but that was one Oscar ceremony that Harry Cohn was destined

never to attend. He died in February, and Columbia seemed to sag under the loss.

When the news of his death came through, people were stunned. John Ford, who was working on *The Last Hurrah* at the studio, closed his set for the day, something that had never been done before at Columbia. There were tales of secretaries weeping and executives walking the studio corridors in a daze. It seemed for all the world as though a great and popular star had died, not a ruthless ogre. Suddenly, it seemed as though everyone had liked Harry Cohn.

The tributes poured in from every quarter. Most people – writers, directors, stars – admitted he had been a bastard, but then added, a little coyly, that even allowing for the never-ending obscenities, they had also rather enjoyed his company. Glenn Ford perhaps summed him up best of all when he said that 'he could be cruel, kind, giving, taking, despicable, benevolent, compassionate and malevolent, all at the same time.'

Cohn supposedly formed the basis of many screen characters: Willie Stark in *All the King's Men*, the tough junk tycoon in *Born Yesterday* and the movie mogul in Clifford Odets' *The Big Knife* (1955), directed by Robert Aldrich, to name but three. Yet the first two films were produced at Columbia, and Odets wrote the eulogy for Cohn's funeral.

Two thousand people turned out for the event, cramming into two of Columbia's sound stages. It was all strictly against Cohn's wishes. He had wanted a quiet funeral with no fuss of any kind. Red Skelton, when seeing the size of the crowd, quipped: 'Well, it only proves what they always say – give the public what they want to see, and they'll come out for it.' It was a joke in the poorest of taste, but it was undoubtedly one that Harry Cohn himself would have enjoyed.

*Face to face: Japanese commandant Sessue Hayakawa and British colonel Alec Guinness in David Lean's Oscar-winning* The Bridge on the River Kwai *(Columbia/Horizon, 1957).*

# 1955
# Warner Bros.

## The All-American Gal and the All-American Guy:
## Doris Day and John Wayne

Jack Warner was one Hollywood mogul who didn't have too much to joke about in 1955, mainly because the position of his studio was, unhappily, closer to that of MGM than it was to that of Fox, Paramount and Columbia. In other words, he had parted company with the stars who had made the money for his studio in the Thirties and Forties. Davis had gone, as had Crawford. Bogart had formed his own independent company, Santana Productions, and branched out to work at other studios. Cagney had left that very year after making his last Warner film, *Mister Roberts*, with Henry Fonda. Flynn, a sick man by the Fifties, was nearing the end of his career, and the screen's most memorable fat man, Sydney Greenstreet, had died just a year before after a ten-year screen career in which he had made 20 films for the studio.

Although Jack Warner had lost (or got rid of) most of his established stars, he had also made a couple of notable acquisitions, and at least that was something that neither Mayer nor Schary had been able to do at MGM. He had also made a third signing, but any long-term hopes he had in that direction were shattered when James Dean, the young rebel actor who many predicted would become the biggest star of the postwar American cinema, was killed in a car crash in September 1955. So Warner was left with just the two major stars – Doris Day and John Wayne.

The vibrant, bouncy Doris Day was Warner's golden girl. Between 1948 and 1955, she made 17 films for the studio, proving that Warner hadn't forgotten how to get the most out of his stars and their seven-year contracts. Performing in more than two films a year,

especially when most of them were musicals, was hard going, but in 1948 Doris Day was young (24), she had energy and vitality and her break into the movies was just what she needed, for her career as a dance-band singer had fizzled out and she had gone to Hollywood to pick up the pieces after an unhappy marriage.

She was 'discovered' at a party held at the Beverly Hills home of composer Jule Styne. Doris was asked to sing, and she delivered 'Embraceable You' perched on Styne's piano. Styne and his partner Sammy Cahn then informed her that they had just written the songs for a new Warner picture called *Romance on the High Seas* (*It's Magic* in UK) and that the leading part – that of a young nightclub singer who travels by ship to Rio – had become vacant because Warner had not been able to borrow Judy Garland from MGM and that her replacement, Betty Hutton, had become pregnant. They suggested that Doris try for the role, which she did, sailing through her screen test without the slightest difficulty.

One critic who wasn't over-impressed with Doris Day was *New York Times* critic Bosley Crowther, who was quite scathing about her first screen performance: 'As much as we all like to welcome new faces and talents to the screen, it is hard to work up enthusiasm for Warner's new starlet Doris Day. Maybe this bouncy young lady has ability and personality. But as shown in this picture, she has no more than a vigorous disposition which hits the screen with a thud!'

Crowther's reservations didn't seem to carry much weight, however. Doris Day, who

*The girl next door. Warner's pert and bouncy musical star Doris Day.*

*Doris Day and Gene Nelson in Warner's spectacular musical* Lullaby of Broadway *(Warner Bros., 1951).*

was already famous as a dance-band and radio songstress, turned out to be a success in whatever she appeared. In many ways, her Warner vehicles were not dissimilar to the films that Fox had prepared for Betty Grable during the war years: they didn't amount to much but they were enjoyable, fluffy bits of nonsense that pleasantly passed an hour and a half. They were designed to promote Doris's ever-smiling, cheery personality and to allow her to sing at least six songs during a film.

Doris Day's appeal lay in the fact that she was the All-American girl, the honest, wholesome one that the guys could always trust and take home to Mom without the slightest embarrassment. She was the epitome of the girl next door, the type men would marry and who would raise their kids in a little house surrounded by a white picket fence, like the ones so often portrayed in her Warner films.

Sometimes she was tomboyish, sometimes she was a shade too abrasive, but she was as American as blueberry pie and she was everyone's sweetheart.

Her best musicals at Warners were *Tea for Two* (1950), *Lullaby of Broadway* (1951), *Calamity Jane* (1953) (in which she sang the year's Oscar-winning song 'Secret Love'), and the film she made in 1955, the romantic *Young at Heart*, a remake of the 1938 Warners' hit *Four Daughters* in which she co-starred with Frank Sinatra.

If Doris Day was the all-American girl, then John Wayne was, without question, the all-American guy. In the early Fifties, when he embarked on some vicious anti-communist thrillers for his newly formed independent company, Wayne/Fellows, he was much *too* American. Pictures such as *Big Jim McLain* (1952) and *Blood Alley* (1955) were as crude

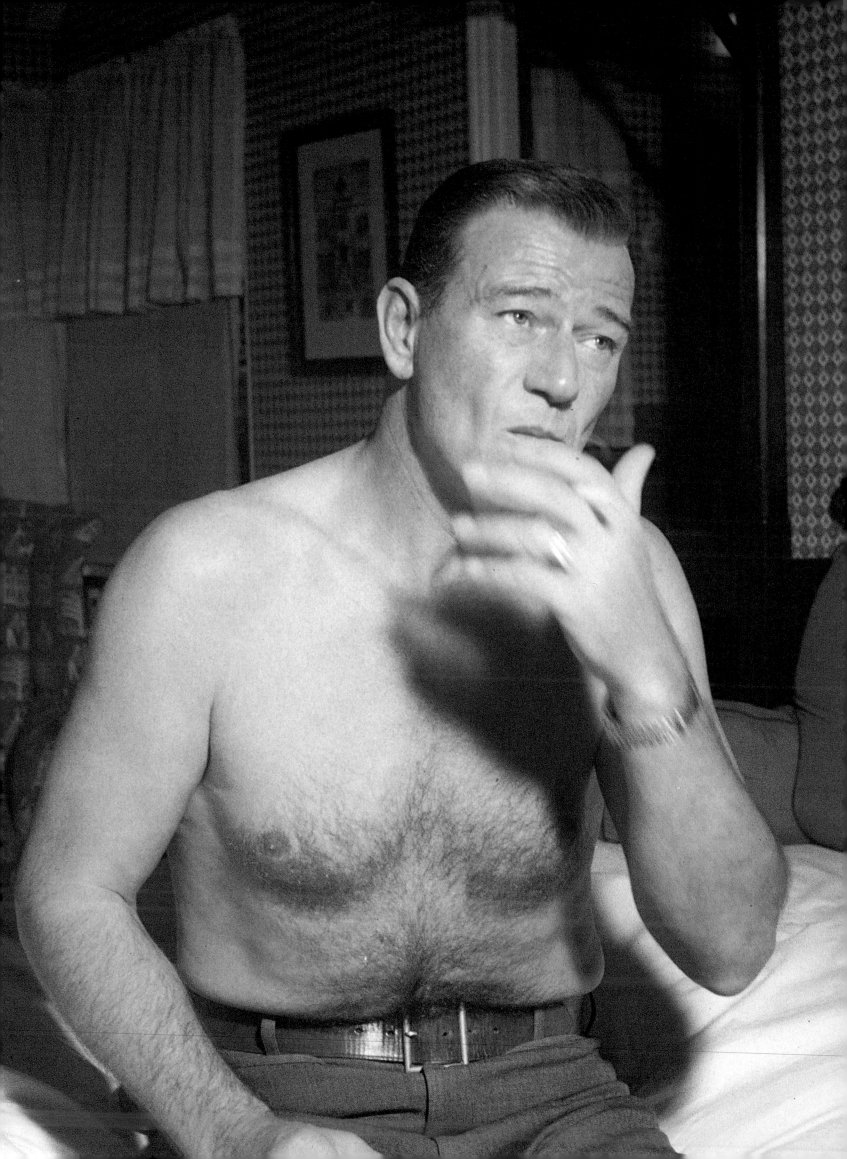

as any propaganda pictures ever put out by a Hollywood studio. Yet there was something about Wayne that caught the public imagination. He was tough, he was plain-speaking, he stood no nonsense and he was a man of action. He had, at most, two expressions – a glare that he used most of the time and a disarming smile that he didn't use enough – but those were enough for most people. They knew that, whenever he was in a scene, things would never stay quiet for very long.

He made nine movies at Warners in the Fifties. Some of them were produced by the Warner studio itself; others by his own company (subsequently renamed Batjac Productions) and released through the studio. Most of them were no more than routine actioners or dramas such as *Island in the Sky* (1953) and *The High and the Mighty* (1954), but occasionally, when Wayne was working with a top-flight director, a memorable movie would emerge. For instance, in *The Searchers* (1956), he worked for John Ford, playing a Confederate veteran who spends years searching for a baby girl kidnapped by Indians. Later, in the Howard Hawks' western *Rio Bravo* (1959), he staved off the villains against all odds for 141 exhilarating minutes, helped by drunken deputy Dean Martin, grizzled old-timer Walter Brennan and the glamorous Angie Dickinson.

It was during the Warner years that Wayne became a permanent fixture in the top ten list of world-ranking stars – in fact, he was only out of the top ten once throughout the decade. From the Sixties onwards, he became steadily more popular until he ranked as the number one star in the world, a position he held for many years. That wasn't bad going for an actor who had made nearly 100 movies

*John Wayne rides out for revenge in John Ford's classic 1956 western* The Searchers *(C. V. Whitney/Warner Bros.).*

*Opposite:*
*John Wayne, one of Warner's most successful stars.*

before he earned his first Oscar nomination, for *Sands of Iwo Jima* (1949). His only real successes before he became a box-office star at Warners had been when he went west with director John Ford – *Stagecoach* (1939), *She Wore A Yellow Ribbon* (1949) and Howard Hawks' *Red River* (1948). Before that it had been a bit of an uphill struggle at the unfashionable (and usually hard up) Republic Studio and in 60-minute westerns at Monogram and Universal. He was 44 when he reached the top at Warners in 1951, and he was to stay there for the rest of his career.

James Dean's career at Warners in the mid-Fifties couldn't have been more different. It lasted for just 18 months and comprised only three feature films – Elia Kazan's *East of Eden* (1955), Nicholas Ray's *Rebel Without a Cause* (1955) and the posthumously released *Giant* (1956), directed by George Stevens and co-starring Elizabeth Taylor and Rock Hudson.

Dean was killed in the late afternoon of 30 September 1955, shortly after completing his final scenes in *Giant*. He was driving his new $6,900 Porsche Spyder along a highway near Cholame, California, when he hit an oncoming black-and-white Ford sedan, the driver of which escaped with minor injuries. Police later estimated that Dean was travelling at 86 miles an hour. He was just 24 when he died.

Whether, if he had lived, he would have endured as long as John Wayne, is doubtful, but his death stunned the movie world and also the youth of America, who had come to regard him as their symbol of rebellion and protest, especially because of his film *Rebel Without a Cause*, which had examined with some insight the problems of adolescent children in the upper middle-class society of America.

Dean's death robbed Warners of a star of the future. With him as a major attraction,

*James Mason and Judy Garland share a tender moment in a scene cut from, but eventually restored to, George Cukor's memorable* A Star Is Born *(Warner Bros., 1954).*

*James Dean and Natalie Wood in Nicholas Ray's perceptive study of juvenile delinquency,* Rebel Without a Cause *(Warner Bros., 1955).*

the late Fifties and early Sixties might well have turned out to be boom years for the studio. As it was, only the occasional class film came out of the Burbank lot: the bright Doris Day musical *The Pajama Game* (1957); *Auntie Mame* (1958) starring Rosalind Russell; and Fred Zinnemann's lovingly made *The Nun's Story* (1959) with Audrey Hepburn. Even these didn't rival the superb 1954 remake of *A Star Is Born* with Judy Garland and James Mason, a film that encountered plenty of production problems while it was being made, but which quickly came to be regarded as one of the classic tales of Hollywood.

What Jack Warner failed to realize was that, in 1955, a star *had* been 'born', not so much in the make-believe world of Garland and Mason but actually on the lot at Warners. The trouble was that everyone at the studio was so immersed in the publicity resulting from James Dean's premature death – rumours that he was still alive and badly disfigured went on for years, culminating in the ghoulish release *The James Dean Story* (1957) featuring a cast of people 'Who knew,

*One of the worst films of the 1950s, but the one that began the career of superstar Paul Newman, pictured here with Virginia Mayo. The movie? The Silver Chalice (Warner Bros., 1954).*

knew of or were related to James Dean' – that they didn't really bother to pay too much attention to a young actor who was slowly beginning to climb the ladder.

At first, many people said he looked too much like Marlon Brando to achieve success in his own right (and it was true that, in the Fifties at least, he did closely resemble Brando), and also that he seemed to be no more than another addition to the mumble-grunt-grumble brigade. But Jack Warner, who was by then on his own at the studio (Hal Wallis had left to form his own production company in 1944), seemed unable to recognize talent even when it stared him in the face. Shrewd and ruthless (and mean) he might have been as a studio boss, but he didn't have the knack of a Cohn or Zanuck for talent-spotting.

He signed the actor to a five-year contract at $1000 a week and then starred him in a series of forgettable pictures, including *The Silver Chalice* (1954, a $4.5 million flop about which the actor later said: 'I had the privilege of being in the worst motion picture filmed during the Fifties'), *The Helen Morgan Story* (*Both Ends of the Candle* in UK, 1957) and *The Young Philadelphians* (*The City Jungle* in UK, 1959). The result was that Warner missed out. In 1959, the young actor, who by then had established himself as a top star in pictures at other studios, i.e. *Somebody Up There Likes Me* (1956) and *Cat on A Hot Tin Roof* (1958), bought himself out of his contract for $500,000 and went on to become one of the first true superstars of the Sixties. Jack L. Warner was one man who never forgot the actor's name – Paul Newman.

# 1956

# United Artists

## Controversy, Realism and a New Independence

As Hollywood began to head out of the Fifties and towards the next decade, it became more and more obvious that the great days of men such as Jack Warner and Harry Cohn (and even the far-seeing Zanuck at Fox) no longer lay in the future nor even in the present. They lay in the past, back in the Thirties and Forties. It wasn't only the dwindling audiences and the threat of television that bore this out. It was also seen in a company that, in the Fifties, suddenly found its teeth again.

That company was United Artists. In the Forties, it had become, at best, an 'also-ran' studio. Sam Goldwyn's failure to take control of the company in his celebrated attempted coup of 1937 had proved to be very nearly fatal for the company and, without him it stumbled along from one year to the next with product that was second- and sometimes even third-rate. Chaplin's only ventures into production were *The Great Dictator* (1940) and *Monsieur Verdoux* (1947), which proved to be a box-office disaster, and the films of David Selznick – the schmaltzy romance *I'll Be Seeing You* (1944), the sentimental *Since You Went Away* (1944) and the spectacular but lurid western *Duel in the Sun* (1946) – proved that the once-infallible producer of *Gone with the Wind* and *Rebecca* was past his best.

As 1949 became 1950, it looked like the end of the road for United Artists. By the end of the year, the company was facing bankruptcy and losing in the region of $100,000 a week, but it was then that two men arrived on the scene. Their names are never bandied about as much as those of Zanuck, Cohn or Mayer, but in terms of the story of Hollywood

they are every bit as important. Arthur B. Krim and Robert S. Benjamin were the men who put United Artists back on its feet again, and what is more in doing so they pioneered the way for the modern cinema of the Seventies and Eighties.

Both were partners in one of the ablest law firms in the film industry. Well versed in all aspects of the movie business, they were brought in as a managerial team to change the company's image, but they changed much more than that. They approached Charlie Chaplin and Mary Pickford (the two surviving members of the original founders of 1919) with the suggestion that they be made trustees for 100 per cent of United Artists' stock, which would, in effect, give them operating control of the company for ten years. Chaplin and Pickford agreed.

Within five years, Krim and Benjamin had rejuvenated United Artists to such an extent that the company was once again thriving, and 1956 proved to be the key year of the 'new-look' United Artists for it marked the occasion when the old guard finally succumbed and bowed out of the scene altogether. Mary Pickford, like Chaplin a year before, sold her UA stock for $3 million and Krim and Benjamin found themselves in complete charge – outright owners of the company. In 1956, United Artists' worldwide gross was $64 million, an increase of $45 million over that of 1950. Figures don't always reflect the true story, but in the case of United Artists they more than demonstrated the success of Krim and Benjamin.

By 1956, United Artists had, to all intents and purposes, become a 'new' company, yet it

*David Niven and William Holden in a scene from the Otto Preminger 'naughty' comedy* The Moon Is Blue *(Preminger/Herbert/United Artists, 1953).*

still thrived on the principle expressed by the four founders back in 1919 – independence. Krim and Benjamin made 'independence' seem suddenly exciting again. At United Artists, they provided a home for every independent worth his salt. They encouraged stars and directors to form their own companies and come to them with projects that they would partly or sometimes wholly finance and then also distribute.

It was the kind of set-up that Hollywood stars and directors had been dreaming about for years. Previously, only the select few had been able to embark on independent careers –

Selznick and Goldwyn, a handful of top stars. Now everyone had the chance, providing they had the subject, a good script and an independent company, no matter how small. Stars in particular found that United Artists was just the kind of company they needed. They could star in, write or direct their own pictures (Burt Lancaster directed himself in the Hecht-Hill-Lancaster production *The Kentuckian* in 1955), something they would never have been allowed to do at other studios.

Producer-director Otto Preminger who, in the Fifties, was one of those who benefited most from the set-up at United Artists, summed up the company when he said: 'Only United Artists had a system of true independent production. They recognized that the independent had his own personality. After they agreed on the basic property and were consulted on the cast, they left everything to the producer's discrimination.'

What is more, United Artists (who as a general rule took 25 per cent of the profits for providing the up-front money and distribution) were never content to play safe. They thrived on controversy, and Preminger was one who was always stirring the pot. In 1953, he turned a lightweight little Broadway comedy called *The Moon Is Blue* into a top box-office success. On the face of it, it shouldn't have been a success at all, for its story was little more than the experiences of a young American girl (Maggie McNamara)

with a couple of New York wolves (William Holden and David Niven). A pleasant but strictly minor vehicle, it created something of a sensation by using for the first time on screen such words as 'virgin', 'seduction' and 'mistress'. The censor was shocked and refused it the Production Code Seal of Approval, the Church also made its objections known, but the public, eager to find out what all the fuss was about, flocked to see it and theatre managers booked it despite the fact that it didn't carry the censor's seal of approval. Strange though it may now seem, the modern cinema began with the innocuous little 1953 comedy *The Moon Is Blue*.

This beginning was continued two years later when Preminger tackled the much more serious problem of drug addiction, the director stating categorically that it was better to

*The horrors of drug addiction portrayed in Otto Preminger's* The Man with the Golden Arm *(Carlyle/United Artists, 1955). Frank Sinatra was nominated for an Academy Award for his performance as the addicted Frankie Machine.*

The Magnificent Seven
(Mirisch-Alpha/United
Artists, 1960): Steve
McQueen, James Coburn,
Horst Buchholz, Yul Brynner,
Brad Dexter, Robert Vaughn
and Charles Bronson

face and expose a problem than to pretend it wasn't there. His film was entitled *The Man with the Golden Arm* (1955), and it starred Frank Sinatra as a dope-addicted poker dealer struggling to kick the habit ('the monkey on his back') in a sleazy Chicago world inhabited by drunks, cardsharps and dope peddlars. The picture's harrowing final sequences, showing Sinatra, locked alone in a room, going through agonies in an attempt to conquer his addiction, shocked many, but this time the picture went out with a Production Code Seal, the Code having been liberalized because of such movies. The film was yet another success for Preminger, earning him the reputation of being one of the most controversial directors of the Fifties.

It would be wrong to assume that everything was grim and harrowing under Krim and Benjamin at United Artists during the Fifties. The company's films were as wide-ranging (or even more so) than those produced by the other Hollywood majors. In 1956, for instance, spectacle and entertainment on the grand scale were very much the order of the day when the company released the ebullient Mike Todd's *Around the World in 80 Days*. The film was ostensibly a version of Jules Verne's 19th-century tale about an Englishman who accepts a wager that he can circle the globe in 80 days, but more often than not, it bore a close resemblance to a three-ring circus on a huge screen. The stars were David Niven (as the intrepid traveller

Phileas Fogg), the Mexican comedian Cantinflas (as his servant Passpartout) and in an early role, Shirley MacLaine (as Princess Aouda). To make sure that the audience did not fall asleep during the three-hour journey, Todd added some 50 other top stars in cameo roles. The result was five Oscars and a huge box-office gross of $23 million.

Westerns, too, were frequently in evidence. In 1952, Gary Cooper found himself left alone to face a vengeful killer and his gang of outlaws in Fred Zinnemann's classic *High Noon*, and won himself an Oscar. In 1954, the same actor joined forces with the wide-smiling Burt Lancaster in the much more exuberant *Vera Cruz*, and in 1960 action director John Sturges also ventured west for *The Magnificent Seven* (1960). Even the all-star war epic cropped up occasionally, notably John Sturges' *The Great Escape* (1963), featuring Steve McQueen and James Garner.

Comedy was invariably best handled by Billy Wilder (late of Paramount), who in 1959 made the best of all drag comedies when he cast Marilyn Monroe, Tony Curtis and Jack Lemmon in *Some Like It Hot*. Then, a year later, he repeated his success with *The Apartment* (1960), in which insurance clerk Jack Lemmon discovers that the quickest way to career advancement is to hire out his apartment to executives for their extra-marital activities. Wilder won the Oscar for his direction, and *The Apartment* was named best picture.

*Cantinflas and David Niven celebrate their journey by balloon across the Alps. A scene from* Around the World in Eighty Days *(London Films/Mike Todd/ United Artists, 1956).*

*Overleaf: the end of Steve McQueen's heroic motorcycle dash for freedom, in* The Great Escape *(Mirisch-Alpha/United Artists, 1963).*

*Tony Curtis on sax, Jack Lemmon on bass and Marilyn Monroe on ukulele. A scene from Billy Wilder's comedy classic* Some Like It Hot *(Mirisch/United Artists, 1959).*

However, by and large, United Artists was best known during the period for the films that probed into the more realistic side of things. The net was cast wide – the indictment of capital punishment in Robert Wise's *I Want To Live* (1958), the corruption of Hollywood in Robert Aldrich's *The Big Knife* (1955), the corruption of the New York Press in *Sweet Smell of Success* (1957) and the corruption of the French High Command in

Stanley Kubrick's brilliant First World War movie *Paths of Glory* (1957). On the other side of the coin there was the loneliness of the unattractive New York butcher *Marty* (1955) – the Oscar-winning film which made a star of Ernest Borgnine – and the honesty of juror Henry Fonda who, in Sidney Lumet's first film *Twelve Angry Men* (1957), eventually convinces the other 11 members of the jury that an 18-year-old youth accused of murder might just possibly be innocent.

By 1957, no fewer than 50 independents were working at United Artists and by the end of the decade that number had increased still further. Actor-producers John Wayne, Frank Sinatra, Gregory Peck, Bob Hope and Robert Mitchum; producer-directors William Wyler, Joe Mankiewicz, Stanley Kramer, Billy Wilder and Otto Preminger; and production units such as the Figaro Company, Bryna Productions, the Mirisch Corporation and the Hecht-Hill-Lancaster Group were all operating at the company.

The re-emergence of United Artists proved as potent a threat to the big studios and their bosses as did television. Not only was the company making interesting and controversial new-look films, it was also siphoning off the talent from the other studios. No longer did stars or directors need to be bound by contracts and seven-year 'sentences'. They could make their own movies, share in the profits and say 'no thanks' to a major studio whenever they felt like it. For the studios, it was the beginning of the beginning of the end. And by some strange quirk of fate, by the end of the decade, United Artists had at last become what its original founders had always intended it to be – 'The Tiffany's of the Industry'.

*Jack Lemmon, Shirley Maclaine and Edie Adams in Billy Wilder's Oscar-winning* The Apartment *(Mirisch/United Artists, 1960).*

# 1960s
## The Studios

### The End of the Golden Age

Set against the exciting developments taking place at United Artists, the scene at RKO bore a close resemblance to that of a morgue. By 1955, there were no more than 14 movies (most of them double features) being shot on the lot, and what had been promising to happen for almost a decade did eventually happen in 1957: the studio closed its gates for good. Once the Mitchell Leisen musical *The Girl Most Likely* finished shooting, the sound stages that had once witnessed the making of *Citizen Kane* and the Astaire/Rogers musicals darkened for ever. Howard Hughes, no longer interested in the studio, had washed his hands of it in 1955 and concentrated on other ways of making money. Although the studio attempted to carry on for some 18 months under the guidance of William Dozier, the end result was always inevitable.

For many, the collapse of RKO meant the end of the 'Golden Age of Hollywood'. If one top Hollywood studio could go under, they argued, so could others. However, things didn't turn out quite like that. RKO had been something of a special case for nearly a decade and its demise had been predictable, especially when Howard Hughes had become involved.

The other Hollywood studios did not go under in RKO's wake. They carried on into and through the Sixties, still trying to keep ahead of the game and most operating in exactly the same way as they had done since the beginning of sound. That was their big mistake. In the Sixties, the studios, many of them no longer distinguishable from one another either in style or in personnel, began to look like dinosaurs, huge combines that

were hopelessly old-fashioned and ill-equipped to meet new and constantly changing situations.

The studios that kept a steady course and continued with 'safe' entertainments were the ones that managed best. Universal (it dropped its Universal-International tag in 1963) was the luckiest. Producer Ross Hunter was still in full swing with his expensive-looking thrillers and tearjerkers – for example, *Midnight Lace*, *Portrait in Black* (both 1960) and *Back Street* (1961) – and Doris Day, to everyone's amazement and surprise, began a second career for herself as a talented and often very witty screen comedienne. Her lush Universal comedies included *Pillow Talk* (1959), *Lover Come Back* (1961) and *Send Me No Flowers* (1964) – all with Rock Hudson – *That Touch of Mink* (1962) with Cary Grant, and *The Thrill of It All* (1963) with James Garner. All dealt in a fresh and lively way with the age-old 'battle of the sexes' theme and, to Universal's delight, helped make her the most popular star in the world during the early Sixties.

Universal were also lucky to have at their studio the most popular director in the world, Alfred Hitchcock. After the terrifying *Psycho* (1960), which he had shot on the Universal lot but which had been released by Paramount, he plunged into a new Universal career with relish, scaring the daylights out of audiences with his spectacular version of Daphne du Maurier's *The Birds* (1963), a tale of a small coastal town in California invaded by enormous flocks of vicious birds; '3,200 birds were used in the picture, all of them specially trained,' claimed a solemn Hitch. He also teamed 007 star Sean Connery with his new

blonde discovery Tippi Hedren, in the psychological thriller *Marnie* (1964).

It was when the studios began searching for the really big profits that things started to go wrong. And the three that suffered the most were Paramount, MGM and Twentieth Century-Fox.

The film that started all the trouble was *Ben-Hur*, which MGM had decided to remake at great expense at the Cinecittà studios in Rome in 1959. Basically, the movie was little more than a variation on the familiar theme of Christianity chipping away at the edges of a pagan Roman society, a theme that

had been explored many times in the past. When MGM first announced that *Ben-Hur* was going to be refilmed and by the great William Wyler (who at first had wanted to film only the famous 11-minute chariot race), the executives of other studios shook their heads doubtfully. Somehow, the 'epic', which even *Ben-Hur*'s star Charlton Heston admitted was 'the easiest kind of picture to make badly', didn't seem like the answer to their prayers, which by the early Sixties had become frequent and most heartfelt. But *Ben-Hur*, to their surprise, *was* a success and a very big one at that. In the United States and

*Doris Day and Rock Hudson in* Lover Come Back *(7 Pictures/Nob Hill Productions/Arwin/Universal International, 1962) – one of the three highly popular comedies they made together.*

*Overleaf: Cary Grant in a spot of bother in the Doris Day comedy* That Touch of Mink *(Granley/Arwin/Nob Hill/Universal International, 1962).*

217

Canada alone it took over $36 million, despite the fact that it ran for 3 hours 37 minutes, thus cutting down the number of times it could be shown each day on cinema screens. And on top of that, it won a record 11 Academy Awards.

Those in charge at other studios, convinced at last, jumped on the epic bandwagon. Large budgets and spectacle became the order of the day. A formula was devised: all epics should run to a minimum of three hours; they should be filmed in a wide-screen process and be projected on to the largest screens possible; their casts should run into thousands; a lush four-minute overture would precede each film; there should be an interval halfway through the film during which patrons could stretch their legs and search earnestly for high-priced popcorn and soft drinks; all movies would be shown at separate performances and all seats would be bookable in advance.

Most of the studios involved in the production of large-scale spectaculars felt that they were more or less in charge, until two stars came along and, between them, with just three films, more or less wrecked their plans completely. One of the stars was Marlon Brando. The other was Elizabeth Taylor.

The first big crisis arose not over the production of an epic but, of all things, over the making of a western. It was just that the crisis grew to epic proportions and made the headlines. The western was called *One-Eyed Jacks* (1961), and it related a Billy the Kid/Pat Garrett-type story, hinging on the revenge of one outlaw against another and containing more than the usual degree of sadism. Brando had bought the rights to the original novel (*The Authentic Death of Hendry Jones* by

Charles Neider) back in 1957, and for three years had tried to set up a film through his own Pennybaker Productions. When, at last, a package was agreed with Paramount, the film had Brando as its main star, Karl Malden as his co-star and the young Stanley Kubrick as director. Brando forfeited his salary in lieu of a substantial slice of the film's profits and also the rights to the negative after a certain period of time.

The Brando/Kubrick partnership lasted for no more than a few weeks. The top star and rising young director didn't hit if off, and Kubrick left. The sensible thing for Paramount to have done was to insist on Brando hiring a new director, but they let the star have his way and allowed him to direct the picture himself, even though he had no previous experience.

It was a fatal decision and one that Paramount was to rue for many a long day, for instead of making the film quickly and efficiently, Brando spent months on the project.

The result was a financial disaster. Brando exposed more than a million feet of film during the six-month shooting schedule. A quarter of this was printed, resulting in the rough cut running to over 4 hours and the final cut to 2 hours 21 minutes. The original budget was set at $1.8 million, but the final cost was nearly $6 million. At the box office, the film flopped.

At least Paramount had the profits of the Audrey Hepburn/George Peppard comedy *Breakfast at Tiffany's* (1961) to cheer them up, which is rather more than MGM had when they found themselves next in line for the Brando treatment. They must have regarded the *One-Eyed Jacks* fiasco as an isolated case of self-indulgence, for in 1962 they cast Brando as Fletcher Christian (opposite Trevor Howard as Bligh) in a lavish and spectacular remake of their 1935 hit *Mutiny on the Bounty*.

The result was disaster yet again. The three-hour film, with Brando as a foppish Fletcher Christian, cost a huge $19 million

*Tippi Hedren rests in bed, Diane Baker and Sean Connery look on and Hitchcock directs:* Marnie *(Geoffrey Stanley Inc/ Universal, 1964).*

and grossed just $10 million – fatal economics whichever way one looked at it. Worse still, no one even liked the film; indeed, most were bored by it. MGM reeled from the effects of the *Bounty* disaster, and at one stage during 1962 they had not a single movie in production on the Culver City lot, the first time this had happened in their long impressive history.

That the situation was out of control was blatantly obvious to all those in charge of the Hollywood studios. Unfortunately, there was no longer a Louis B. Mayer or a Harry Cohn around to shout 'Stop, enough!' The budgets just went on escalating and the stars became more and more powerful. Compared to the well-oiled, well-run studios of the Thirties and Forties, Hollywood was now close to chaos!

The worst blow was yet to come, and this time it was Twentieth Century-Fox who were on the receiving end. The film that almost sank them (it certainly brought them to their knees) was *Cleopatra* (1963). When it had originally been considered back in 1959 as a vehicle for Joan Collins, it was budgeted at just over $1 million. But like Topsy it just grew and grew, and it grew because producer

*Stephen Boyd and Charlton Heston clash during the celebrated 11-minute chariot race in William Wyler's epic* Ben-Hur *(MGM, 1959).*

Walter Wanger insisted on Elizabeth Taylor for the role of the beautiful Egyptian queen. No one else would do. It was a case of no Taylor, no *Cleopatra*. Studio boss Buddy Adler put forward other possibilities, including Audrey Hepburn and Susan Hayward (even Marilyn Monroe and Shirley Maclaine!), but to no avail.

Walter Wanger got his way and, by the time the film was ready to roll in the autumn of 1960, Taylor was firmly set as Cleopatra, with Peter Finch (as Caesar) and Stephen Boyd (as Mark Antony) joining her in the co-starring roles. The director was Rouben

Mamoulian and the cost had already reached $6 million without a single scene having been shot.

The initial decision to shoot the film on large outdoor sets at Pinewood Studios outside London during a chilly September and October had about it a craziness that only Hollywood logic could justify. From the moment the cameras started to turn (and they didn't turn very often), disaster either threatened, loomed or struck. For example, one story has it that, one morning, Mamoulian arrived on the set at Pinewood ready to shoot a large scene, but found that he had just one problem: the scene was an outdoor one and, because of the thick fog, he couldn't see the hundreds of extras who were an integral part of the set-up. The extras were on the lot all right, but they were in another part of Pinewood searching desperately for the set!

Apocryphal the story may be, but there was nothing fanciful about what was to follow. Elizabeth Taylor's health, never good at the best of times, declined rapidly and she was rushed into a London hospital where she nearly died of pneumonia. Production was brought to a halt with just ten minutes of

*Audrey Hepburn as Holly Golightly, plus 'Cat', in* Breakfast at Tiffany's *(Jurow-Shepherd/Paramount, 1961).*

*The death of Julius Caesar: Rex Harrison perishes in Fox's 1963 spectacular* Cleopatra.

*Elizabeth Taylor and Richard Burton in* Cleopatra *(1963), the film that nearly brought the Fox studio to its knees.*

footage shot, and Mamoulian resigned as director.

When the film restarted in Rome in the summer of the following year with a new cast (Richard Burton was now Mark Antony and Rex Harrison Julius Caesar), director Joseph Mankiewicz had taken over, although he had entertained plenty of doubts as to whether he should get involved with the production. When he met up with the outgoing Mamoulian, he asked him: 'Now you're a director and I'm a director. What do you *really* think of the picture?' Mamoulian replied; 'Well, I resigned, didn't I?' to which Mankiewicz came back with. 'Let me rephrase the question.

What would you do if you were me?' Mamoulian replied: 'I'd resign!'

Mankiewicz didn't resign, although there must have been many occasions when he wished he had, for when the film restarted in Rome, he had an unfinished screenplay and was literally writing by night and directing by day. Worse, he had the sudden all-consuming Taylor/Burton love affair to contend with, and that was the last thing he needed.

In the end, *Cleopatra* was finished, but at a cost: $37 million was its final budget figure. Mankiewicz had originally wanted to make it two films, one that would deal with Cleopatra's relationship with Caesar, the other with

her love affair with Mark Antony, but due to studio pressure he finished up with one film that, when released in June 1963, ran for four hours. (It was eventually reduced to three-and-a-half.) The critical reception was lukewarm, and needless to say, the picture never got close to recouping its cost. Mankiewicz's reaction to the nightmare of being in charge of *Cleopatra* was: 'It was the toughest three pictures I ever made. *Cleopatra* was conceived in a state of emergency, shot in confusion and wound up in blind panic!'

And panic was definitely what the executives at Fox were feeling when they totted up the bill for *Cleopatra*. No wonder the cry went up: 'Call for Zanuck!' And as always, Zanuck responded to the call. His years as an independent producer in Europe had not been particularly successful, but in 1962, when *Cleopatra* was struggling towards completion, he had hit the jackpot with his huge black-and-white epic of D-Day, *The Longest Day* (1962). The picture had grossed a massive $18 million and had made Zanuck the golden boy once again. By the time he drove once more through the studio gates of Twentieth Century-Fox (this time as president of the company), he was both a successful independent producer and an all-powerful mogul in complete command.

The problems facing him were enormous. Because of *Cleopatra* Fox was in grave danger. The studio's losses amounted to over $40 million. The situation was aggravated by the fact that an additional $2 million had been written off against the proposed Marilyn Monroe picture, *Something's Gotta Give*. During the making of the film, Marilyn had been unwell and unreliable, and had turned up for work on just 12 of the 32 days of shooting. At the end of that time, director George Cukor had just 7½ minutes of usable film in the can. The result was that Fox fired her and scrapped the film. A few weeks later, on 5 August 1962, her body was found by her housekeeper; she was nude on her bed, one hand clutching a sheet to her throat, the other touching a telephone, with an empty bottle of sedatives by her side. She was just 36. She had been in pictures for 14 years and had made 29 films, 11 of them as a star and 20 at Fox. It had been thought that she was worth $1 million, but in fact, she died broke, owing $917,000 in back taxes. It took until 1969, with income from the reruns of her pictures, to pay if off.

The *Cleopatra* disaster and the Monroe tragedy caused many in Hollywood to ask a question that, just three years before, they would never have thought to ask: Would Fox close down for good? After all, RKO had already gone. MGM was only half the studio it once was. Would Fox be next?

Zanuck entertained no such thoughts. His first act was to close down all films in production at the studio and install his son, Richard Zanuck, as the head of all forthcoming productions. The lot had already been reduced from its once-massive 280 acres to a new 76-acre facility (with 21 sound stages) after a land sale to Alcoa (the Aluminium Company of America) and Webb Knapp, Inc. back in 1958. For nine months, it remained empty; not one single film was shot on the 76 acres.

Economies were made and staff were cut back. It was 1935 all over again, although this time, the cutbacks had about them a hint of desperation, not a touch of optimism. When production started again, Zanuck proceeded with caution. The budgets were smaller, as were most of the pictures, but history was to repeat itself. Just as little Shirley Temple had come to Zanuck's rescue in 1935, so another songstress, more mature but no less charming, came to his assistance in 1965. Her name was Julie Andrews, and the film she starred in was *The Sound of Music*. Its success took literally everyone by surprise, even Zanuck.

Zanuck had, of course, expected to make money with the film. It had been a long-running hit show on Broadway and boasted one of Rodgers' and Hammerstein's most tuneful scores, but never in his wildest dreams did he expect it to become the biggest moneymaker in the history of movies. But after just a few months out on release, that is indeed what it became, ending the 26-year reign of the previous box-office champion *Gone with the Wind*.

People went to see *The Sound of Music* not once but several times. For most males in the audience, it was too sugary, too sweet and altogether too much, but for many women and children, it was the perfect screen entertainment. A film about an Egyptian queen had nearly sunk Fox with all hands; a film about a singing governess, formerly a nun, in pre-war Austria helped to keep it afloat and bring it to life again. As someone later remarked: 'Perhaps they should have scrapped *Cleopatra* halfway through and remade it as a musical!'

The success of *The Sound of Music* vindicated those Hollywood producers who, since the beginning of the Sixties, had preferred to opt for expensive large-scale versions of Broadway musicals than to concentrate on epics. And, overall, the musicals came out rather better than the spectaculars. In the epic field, only *Spartacus* (1960) directed by Stanley Kubrick, *El Cid* (1961) with Charlton

*A beautiful Marilyn Monroe, pictured in the film she never completed: Something's Got to Give (Twentieth Century-Fox).*

*Overleaf:
Stanley Kubrick behind the camera filming the hand-to-hand combat between Kirk Douglas and Woody Strode in Spartacus (Bryna/Universal-International, 1960).*

Heston and Sophia Loren, and the international films of David Lean – *Lawrence of Arabia* (1962) and *Doctor Zhivago* (1965) – emerged as truly profitable ventures. The rest came nowhere: *Barabbas* (1962) with Anthony Quinn, *The Fall of the Roman Empire* (1964), *King of Kings* (1961) and *55 Days at Peking* (1963). All flopped as did John Huston's *The Bible . . . In the Beginning* (1966) and George Stevens' huge failure about the life of Christ, *The Greatest Story Ever Told* (1965).

The musicals, on the other hand, were continually profitable, at least during the first half of the decade. *My Fair Lady* (1964) with Audrey Hepburn as Eliza Doolittle earned a nice profit for Jack Warner, even though he had paid a then-record $5.5 million for the screen rights of the Lerner and Loewe musi-

cal. *The Music Man* (1962) with Robert Preston was another Warner success, and *Mary Poppins* (1964) starring Julie Andrews earned enormous profits for Disney. *Bye Bye Birdie* (1963) was a moneymaker at Columbia, and United Artists received enormous profits from the Oscar-winning *West Side Story* (1961).

However, despite all his early success during his second term at Fox, Zanuck made the same mistake that all the other studio heads had been making for the previous ten years. He believed that a star (in his case, Julie Andrews) would automatically be a success in whatever he or she appeared in. It was a way of thinking that had been ingrained in the minds of movie moguls for nearly half a century, and even Zanuck was unable to come

*Julie Andrews operates the marionettes in* The Sound of Music *(Argyle/Twentieth Century-Fox, 1965).*

to terms with the fact that a top star no longer *ensured* money at the box office. Just because Julie Andrews had earned large grosses in a couple of movies, once at Fox and once at Disney, it didn't mean that she was a permanent and infallible moneymaking superstar. And so it proved.

When her large-scale *Star!* (1968), an expensive version of the life of Gertrude Lawrence, nose-dived and became almost as big a flop as *The Sound of Music* had been a success, Zanuck couldn't believe it. When his two other family musicals – *Doctor Dolittle* (1967) with Rex Harrison, and *Hello, Dolly!* (1969) in which he had cast (as box-office insurance!) Barbra Streisand, the young Oscar-winning star of *Funny Girl* (1968) – also flopped, he realized that he had at last completely lost his touch.

By then, of course, Zanuck was 67 years old and no longer a young man. The movie audience had changed beyond all recognition since the late Thirties and early Forties, and the new stars of the Sixties were no longer as easy to pigeon-hole as in the days when Tyrone Power could be labelled as a swashbuckler and Alice Faye as a blonde singing star.

Warren Beatty, star of Arthur Penn's cult gangster film *Bonnie and Clyde* (1967), was one such actor who was difficult to classify. So too was Dustin Hoffman, who seemed to appear from nowhere as *The Graduate* (1967). Jane Fonda, who had returned to Hollywood after a period in France (with her then-husband Roger Vadim), surprised everyone by becoming one of America's major actresses, notably as the self-destructive all-time loser Gloria Beatty in *They Shoot Horses, Don't They?* (1969).

Then there were Clint Eastwood and Charles Bronson, previously regarded by the moguls as just so much Hollywood deadwood, who had gone to Europe to find work in westerns and emerged triumphant as huge moneymaking stars. And, perhaps, most interestingly of all, Jack Nicholson made his mark as a drunken small-town lawyer in the film *Easy Rider* (1969).

And it was *Easy Rider* that really threw Zanuck off course – and for the last time. Starring Peter Fonda and Dennis Hopper as a couple of motorcyclists who make an odyssey across the States in search of the real America of the Sixties, it was made on a shoestring and, for much of the time, seemed as though

*Live action combined with animation at its best. Dick Van Dyke and Julie Andrews stroll through a cartoon wonderland in* Mary Poppins *(© 1964 The Walt Disney Company).*

*Faye Dunaway and Warren Beatty as the Thirties' gangsters* Bonnie and Clyde *(Tatira-Hiller/Warner Bros.-Seven Arts, 1967).*

it was improvised as the actors went along. It was a kind of amateur do-it-yourself youth protest movie that, through its content and its method of presentation, struck a chord with younger audiences who were tired of seeing the same old faces and welcomed the freshness of Beatty, Hoffman, Nicholson and others. The new stars promised a Hollywood of the future, not of the past.

Zanuck eventually resigned from Fox in June 1971 (his son Richard had left in 1970) when he was in his 70th year. By then Disney had gone (he had died just before Christmas in 1966), Jack L. Warner had retired and Sam Goldwyn too was living out his final years.

Zanuck lived for another eight and achieved one final ambition: he had become the very last Hollywood tycoon.

By the late Sixties and early Seventies, the Hollywood studios had become pale shadows of their former selves. No longer did they boast on their credits the names of the familiar stars, cameramen and art directors that one used to associate so readily with them. Most had been swallowed up by conglomerates, many of which had little interest in movies and made more money out of insurance and financial services, parking lots, electronic toys and computers. In 1962, the Music Corporation of America (MCA) bought Decca Records and, with it, Universal, for the studio had been acquired by Decca back in 1951. In 1966, Gulf & Western took over Paramount; in 1967 Seven Arts absorbed Warners and shortly afterwards became Warner Communications, Inc. In 1968, Las Vegas financier Kirk Kerkorian purchased control of MGM for $80 million and, a year later, the Transamerica Corporation took over United Artists.

The people who ran the conglomerates knew little if anything about producing movies and, in some cases, couldn't have cared less about the industry. In one year at Gulf & Western, the movies produced by Paramount amounted to just 14 per cent of the company's total profits. Within a decade movie-making had changed beyond all recog-

nition. All the moguls had gone – suddenly making movies wasn't fun anymore. To quote Frank Capra, it was all 'Money, money, money!' Only the Disney studio, safe with its family image, kept on the same way as it had before.

As things turned out, the faceless men of the conglomerates were themselves to encounter star power and financial problems in the Seventies and Eighties. *Cleopatra* had been a key film in many ways. It had almost brought down a studio and it had almost killed its star during the filming, but that star survived and became the first performer to be paid $1 million for a film role. Things were never quite the same again; the floodgates had been opened. Now the stars ruled, not the studios.

They Shoot Horses, Don't They? *(Palomar/Cinerama, 1969). Bonnie Bedelia and Bruce Dern, and Jane Fonda and Red Buttons endure the agonies of one of the notorious dance marathons of the Thirties.*

233

# Today
## The New Hollywood

### Star Power and the Movie Brats

The symbolic event that finally marked 'the end' to studio power occurred in May 1970. Between 3 and 20 May, MGM held a public auction on Stage 27 at Culver City. Over 20,000 items were catalogued and the net receipts amounted to $1.5 million. Several former MGM stars attended, returning to the studio for the first time in many years. However, the great majority stayed away, saying that the event was a melancholy one, that too many memories of the great days would come flooding back if they put in an appearance.

It was all a bit like the opening scene in MGM's famous 1953 musical *The Band Wagon* when auctioneer Douglas Fowley begins the bidding for the personal property of has-been Hollywood star Fred Astaire. 'What am I bid?' he asks. 'Shall we start at a thousand dollars?' and then finishes with a plaintive and croaky, 'Anything?'

But if that scene can evoke something of the atmosphere of Stage 27 in May 1970, it certainly wasn't a reflection of the financial side of things, for bidding for the MGM items was fierce: $62,500 was paid for the 1870 locomotive (called Reno) that had been used in 35 MGM movies, including *How the West Was Won*, *Raintree County* and *Annie Get Your Gun*; Judy Garland's ruby slippers, which led her down the yellow brick road to Oz went for $15,000 dollars; other items included Clark Gable's trenchcoat ($1,250); Elizabeth Taylor's wedding dress from *Father of the Bride* ($625), Charles Laughton's hat from *Mutiny on the Bounty* ($300), Tarzan's loincloth ($200) and even an Esther Williams swimsuit ($50).

That the old had finally succumbed to the new was plain for all to see, for the money raised from the auction was not to be ploughed back into film production but to help finance the world's largest hotel, the $120 million, 2,084-room MGM Grand Hotel in Las Vegas. Movie-making was thus relegated to a secondary activity. In 1973, MGM announced its complete withdrawal from distribution, and that any future product (the number of which throughout the Seventies and Eighties was to be minimal) would be handled by United Artists.

Even though the studios had now become little more than anonymous combines, their job was still to make movies. The only difference in the Seventies was that the films being produced were no longer instantly recognizable as belonging to any one particular studio, but to the public at large and certainly to the Hollywood financiers that no longer mattered. What did matter was that the movies made money, and many of those made during the Seventies did just that, achieving higher grosses than ever before. Steeper admission prices certainly helped to boost the revenue, but there was no question that, when a studio did hit the jackpot with a blockbuster, it could count on enormous profits.

Paramount, for instance, revived the romantic film with *Love Story* (1970) and to everyone's surprise earned $50 million from a genre that most people believed was long since dead. Columbia did the same three years later, when it successfully teamed Barbra Streisand and Robert Redford in the nostalgic and bittersweet *The Way We Were* (1973).

*Demons in Georgetown, Washington D.C! The terrifying climax to William Friedkin's* The Exorcist *(Hoya/Warner Bros., 1973).*

On the other side of the coin, Warners' sexually as well as horrifically explicit *The Exorcist* (1973) soared up the box-office charts to become the most profitable horror film of all time. *Butch Cassidy and the Sundance Kid* (1969) and *The Sting* (1973), the two films that Paul Newman and Robert Redford made together, earned over $124 million between them. In addition, when director Francis Ford Coppola turned his attention to the inner workings of the Mafia in *The Godfather* (1972), the result was that a violent three-hour film about organized crime took over from a musical about a singing governess as the most popular movie up until that time.

That the situation was in a constant state of flux was demonstrated by the fact that in just ten years (between 1972 and 1982), the film occupying the number one spot as the top moneymaking movie changed on four occasions. In 1972, the box-office champ was *The Godfather*; three years later, Steven Spielberg's *Jaws* (the first film to break the $100 million barrier) took over; in 1977, it was George Lucas's *Star Wars* that wore the crown; and in 1982, Steven Spielberg (the only director ever to make two number one box-office hits) regained the lead with another excursion into science fiction and fantasy, *ET: The Extra-Terrestrial* (1982), this time chalking up another record by breaking through the $200 million barrier. In the 33 years preceding Coppola's *Godfather*, there had been only two films that filled the number one box-office spot – *Gone With the Wind* and *The Sound of Music*.

The reason why the situation was so uncertain (at least until Spielberg came along) was that no one really knew what the public wanted anymore. And that meant that the Seventies became the era of the 'deal'. Between them, the financiers, agents and stars tried to manufacture success, and on occasion even tried to develop formulas supposedly guaranteeing it.

Basically, a 'deal' meant that, if a top star such as Paul Newman, Robert Redford or Steve McQueen liked the outline of a project, he would tentatively agree to appear in the picture provided the final script was to his satisfaction. Salary and a percentage of the profits were other factors that had to be settled, as well as a distribution deal with a major studio. A star also had the right to approve or veto a director. If, by the time the final script came along, it was not satisfactory or the star had gone cold on the idea (and opted for something more attractive that had come along since), the whole thing could fall through. All this meant that writers and directors, in particular, could waste as much as two years of their time preparing productions that got nowhere. They would then either have to start all over again or search for new properties. Little wonder then that, in the Seventies, more projects fell by the wayside than actually appeared on screen. Little wonder, too, that director Billy Wilder suggested a new category for the annual Academy Awards presentation: 'best deal of the year'.

It was left to a talented group of young film-makers to bring home the fact that it was a film's subject rather than its star or stars that

*The last desperate rush for freedom. Paul Newman and Robert Redford as* Butch Cassidy and the Sundance Kid *(Campanile/Twentieth Century-Fox, 1969).*

*Opposite: Marlon Brando and heir-apparent Al Pacino in the Mafia epic* The Godfather *(Alfran/ Paramount, 1972).*

*Left: The Movie Brats: George Lucas and Steven Spielberg, young masters of the modern cinema.*

the younger audiences were most interested in. These directors, nicknamed the 'Movie Brats' didn't work for any one studio in particular, but in their way they became the new movie moguls, only this time they were *film-making* moguls. They themselves sought out what they wanted to film. Many were in their twenties or early thirties and were only just above the age of the audiences they were trying to please. The result was a certain amount of empathy with those audiences, which was duly reflected in their films.

They also made films to please themselves. They backed hunches, they earned the profits

and they reaped the rewards. Said George Lucas: 'We are the pigs. We are the ones who sniff out the truffles. You can put us on a leash, keep us under control. But we are the guys who dig out the gold. The man in the executive tower cannot do that.'

Ironically, several of the new breed of younger directors emerged from a studio background, but it wasn't a studio the size of Fox or MGM or any of the others. It was a little studio called American International Pictures, which had been formed by Samuel Z. Arkoff and James H. Nicholson back in 1955. During the Sixties, it had very shrewdly

*Shark attack! A scene from Spielberg's record-breaking blockbuster* Jaws *(Zanuck – Brown/Universal, 1975).*

marketed its films to appeal to a teenage audience, a market that the top studios had overlooked or disregarded.

The studio averaged close to 20 films a year, none of them amounting to very much. All were cheaply made, shot in a matter of weeks (sometimes even days) and concentrated on such subjects as beach parties and drag racing. Occasionally, director Roger Corman would raise the tone slightly with one of his Vincent Price horror spoofs – for instance, *The House of Usher* (1960) and *The*

*Pit and the Pendulum* (1961) – but generally there was no question of producing a film for any other reason than to make quick money and feed the market.

AIP, however, did provide a valuable training ground for young film-makers who wanted to break into movies but found that the major studios, who were then in the process of shedding their staff rather than hiring them, could no longer afford them the opportunities. Out of American International (and, later, Roger Corman's New World

Pictures) came such directors as Francis Ford Coppola, Martin Scorsese, Peter Bogdanovich, John Milius and Walter Hill.

In the Seventies, they were joined by George Lucas, horror-expert Brian De Palma, Michael Cimino and, most notably of all, Steven Spielberg. Of the entire group, only Spielberg received his professional baptism at one of the major studios – Universal – which gave him a contract in the late Sixties. His first job for them (at the incredibly early age of 22) was to co-direct a pilot for a TV mini-series. The project was called *Night Gallery* (1969) and was made up of three segments, of which Spielberg got to direct only one, but he made the most of the opportunity. He was

offered other work at the studio, including the brilliant chase film *Duel* (1971) – originally shot in an unbelievable 16 days and later expanded into a cinema format – and ultimately, at the grand old age of 27, the film of *Jaws* (1975). Through brilliant editing skills (plus, it should be said, the talents of the late veteran film editor Verna Fields) he turned a 'B'-movie yarn about a big fish eating up American holidaymakers into one of the most profitable movies of all time!

One of his biggest assets, apart from his undoubted technical skills, was his passion for science fiction and fantasy, a passion he had had since childhood, when he had been weaned on such Universal science-fiction

*Overleaf:* ET: The Extra-Terrestrial *(Universal, 1982) directed by Steven Spielberg and the top moneymaking film of all time!*

*Ben Kenobi (Alec Guinness) and Darth Vader (Dave Prowse) clash with laser swords in* Star Wars *(Lucas/ Twentieth Century-Fox, 1977).*

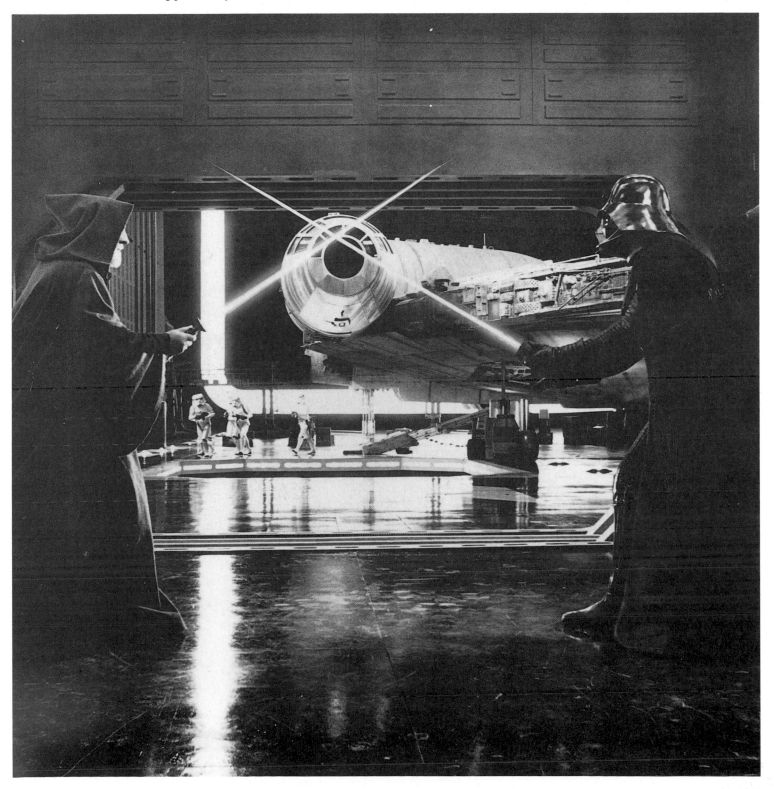

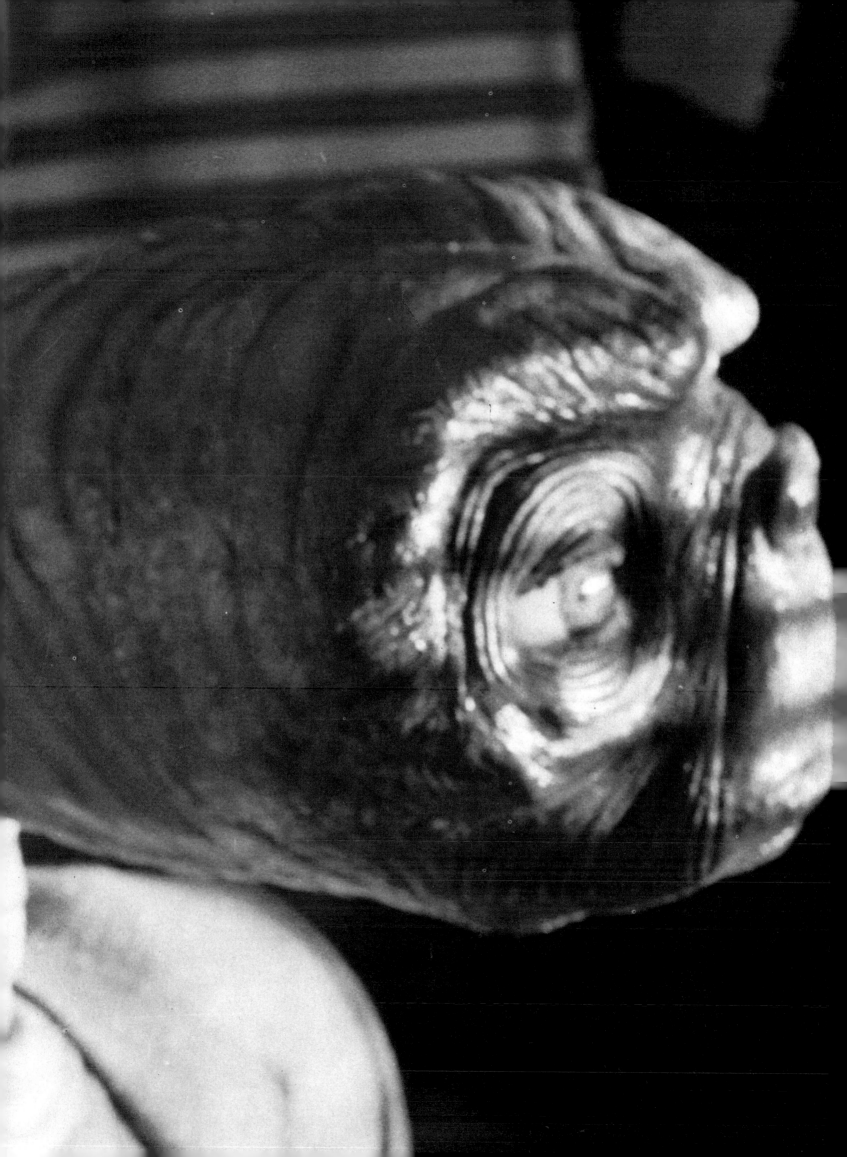

*'Fings Ain't What They Used to Be.' A wary Harrison Ford in* Raiders of the Lost Ark *(Lucas/Paramount, 1981).*

double features as *It Came from Outer Space* (1953), *Tarantula* (1955) and *The Incredible Shrinking Man* (1957). Many of these Fifties science-fiction programmes had been directed by veteran film-maker Jack Arnold, and considering the meagre facilities at his command, he did a more than creditable job on the pictures.

When Spielberg, Lucas and the others arrived on the scene in the mid-seventies, however, they found to their delight that they had a huge armoury of special effects at their disposal. Stanley Kubrick's *2001: A Space Odyssey* (1968) had proved a few years earlier just what could be achieved in the field of special effects, and Spielberg and Lucas, in particular, grasped the technical opportunities with relish, just as Orson Welles had grasped the intellectual possibilities offered by the medium some 30 years before. For them, the cinema offered the chance to realize their wildest dreams, and they were lucky; the audiences were ready and eager to share in those dreams.

The result of all their subsequent endeavours were large-scale fantasy movies such as Lucas's *Star Wars* (1977) and its two successors *The Empire Strikes Back* (1980) and *Return of the Jedi* (1983), and Spielberg's awesome *Close Encounters of the Third Kind*

(1977) and *ET: The Extra-Terrestrial*. In theme and content, many of the pictures were as old as the hills, in some cases no more than remakes of the Universal films of the Fifties simply dressed up in new clothes and enhanced by dazzling effects. But to the young, 'under-25s' audiences, they were 'new', and even adult audiences hadn't experienced such wondrous and colourful effects before.

Perhaps the most interesting thing about the Spielberg and Lucas films was that none of them needed or in fact boasted any top stars. Admittedly, Harrison Ford, who later went on to star for Spielberg in the adventure epics *Raiders of the Lost Ark* (1981) and *Indiana Jones and the Temple of Doom* (1984), and for Lucas in the *Star Wars* trilogy, eventually became a top star through these movies, but, initially at least, his presence only contributed to the success of the films – it was not responsible for it. He was just part of the machinery, an essential part, but in no way the dominating factor. The films belonged in every way to the directors, Spielberg and Lucas.

The dominating factor as far as many top stars were concerned was money. During the late Seventies, Charles Bronson had said, 'Us legends tend to get picky in our twilight years.' He was very close to the truth. For 12

Dustin Hoffman as Michael Dorsey (in the guise of TV soap-opera star Dorothy Michaels) in Sydney Pollack's Tootsie (Delphi/Mirage – Punch/Columbia, 1982).

Overleaf: Sylvester Stallone in Rocky (Chartoff-Winkler/United Artists, 1976), the first of his successful films about the fighter Rocky Balboa. The film was the sleeper of its year and was made for under $1 million in just 28 days!

days' work as the father of *Superman* (1979), Marlon Brando was paid $3.5 million – more than $290,000 a day. Dustin Hoffman is supposed to have earned close to $4 million for *Tootsie* (1982), a fee he was able to command because of his Oscar-winning success in *Kramer vs. Kramer* (1979); Burt Reynolds was offered $5 million plus a percentage of the profits for *The Cannonball Run* (1981); Sean Connery was paid the same for his 007 comeback role in *Never Say Never*

*Again* (1983); and Sylvester Stallone, whose personal success story closely resembles that of his fictional boxing hero *Rocky* (1976), continually earns vast sums for his *Rocky* movies, which show no sign of abating.

In some ways, it could be said that, of all the top male stars, only Clint Eastwood, who has worked through his own company, Malpaso Productions, since 1971, has been true value for money as far as the public is concerned. Unlike Redford, Hoffman and

*Clint Eastwood, superstar of the 1970s, as Dirty Harry (Warner Bros./Malpaso, 1971).*

Beatty, who tend to disappear for some three years after a making a hit movie, Eastwood is always around. He is not afraid of over-exposure; in fact, he seems to welcome it.

He carries on working as an actor, director or both. He has had his flops, but he has simply ignored those and gone straight on to his next project. As the tough cop *Dirty Harry* (1971), a figure he has played on several occasions, and the lone westerner *The Outlaw Josey Wales* (1976), he created two of the most

famous screen characters of the Seventies. He is the modern-day equivalent of the old-time studio star, a kind of latter-day John Wayne. Since he returned from Italy in the late Sixties and left behind him the famous 'Man with No Name' spaghetti westerns, he has, on average, made something like two films a year, an abnormally high rate for a superstar. And for some 15 years, he has released most of his films through Warners, a star-studio associ-ation that is a rarity in modern-day cinema.

*Woody Allen, writer, director and star of the Oscar-winning* Annie Hall *(United Artists, 1977).*

Reds *(Paramount, 1981);*
*Warren Beatty's epic story of*
*American journalist John*
*Reed.*

The fact that Eastwood, like so many of today's top stars, directs many of his own projects indicates, perhaps more than anything else, just how much power the stars now hold. In the Fifties and Sixties the occasional star would make a name for himself by going behind the camera for a spell – for example, Charles Laughton and Paul Newman – but mostly they were content to let the professionals do the work. Not any more. Nowadays, just about every major star has a crack at directing – Mel Brooks, Burt Reynolds, Sylvester Stallone, Barbra Streisand with *Yentl* (1983). Many of them have proved that they are more than adept at film-making. Woody Allen, for instance, has directed the great majority of his films, including *Annie Hall* (1977) for which he won two personal Academy Awards (for best director and best screenplay). Robert Redford also won an Oscar for his *Ordinary People* (1980), and Warren Beatty was the Oscar-winning director of 1981 for his massive epic *Reds.*

The Hollywood of the Eighties seems to have divided itself into two camps. On the one hand, there are the stars such as Hoffman, Redford and Eastwood. On the other, there are the directors such as Spielberg, Lucas, Coppola and Scorsese. Only the latter, among modern film-makers, seems to have

struck up a lasting working relationship with an actor similar to those that prospered during the golden days. Scorsese's partnership with Robert De Niro has so far resulted in *Mean Streets* (1973), *Taxi Driver* (1976), *New York, New York* (1977), *Raging Bull* (1980) and *King of Comedy* (1982).

Sandwiched a little unluckily between these two power-based groups are the actresses, but although they don't have quite the financial clout of the actors or the directors, they do have one thing going for them. It is they who are making many of the most interesting and adventurous films to come out of Hollywood. Meryl Streep, for instance, is always fascinating and never afraid to appear in an unsympathetic role. She has become the foremost actress of the last decade in such films as *The Deer Hunter* (1978), *Kramer vs. Kramer* (1979), *Sophie's Choice* (1983), and *Out of Africa* (1985). There is also the politically committed Jessica Lange who was outstanding in *Frances* (1983), *Country* (1984) and *Sweet Dreams* (1985), Sissy Spaceck in *The Coal Miner's Daughter* (1980) and *The River* (1984), and Sally Field in *Norma Rae* (1978) and *Places in the Heart* (1984).

If Hollywood is now ruled by its directors and stars, what of the studios themselves? Where do they fit into the scheme of things nowadays? Comedian Milton Berle once said: 'I don't know what's happened to motion pictures, but I know what's happened to TV – it's become motion pictures!' And in many ways that is indeed what has happened. The great studios still exist, but their huge sound stages, many of which were made redundant back in the Sixties when crews began to shoot more and more on location, are now used to shoot TV series such as *Dallas* and *Dynasty*. Often the amount of space taken up by the sets of these series is miniscule. They are often buried away in one corner of a sound stage that was once filled with hundreds of extras and echoed to the shouts of 'Lights! Action! Camera!' from directors such as DeMille and John Ford.

Although this change is sad in many ways, by and large the studios still make profits. The films they finance or distribute are sold, sometimes before they are even released, for huge sums for showing on TV, so that many of them have covered their costs before they even reach the movie theatres. And on top of

*Out of Africa starring Robert Redford and Meryl Streep and winner of seven Academy Awards including best picture (Universal, 1985).*

*Jack Nicholson, Kathleen Turner, veteran director John Huston and his daughter the Oscar-winning Anjelica on the set of* Prizzi's Honour *(ABC, 1985).*

that, there is now the additional revenue to be gained from video rights.

However, the continued success of a particular Hollywood studio does beg one all-important question. Universal is today stronger and more secure than any other studio in Hollywood. It was the first of the majors to be formed back in the silent days and it remains tremendously powerful in a Hollywood now dominated by TV and the music business.

The reason why it is all-powerful is that it was quick to spot the advantages of diversification. In the Sixties and Seventies, it was one of the first studios to concentrate seriously on superior TV production and enjoyed considerable success with such series as *Kojak* with Telly Savalas, *McCloud* with Dennis

Weaver and *Columbo* with Peter Falk. It also went into the 'Disneyland business' by opening up its studio to the public for day tours that include a glimpse of the famous *Psycho* house and a chance to brave the shark-infested waters of *Jaws*. And it continued to make movies.

All the other studios have long since lost their dominance. Perhaps their unwillingness to adapt to change brought about their demise. Perhaps, if they had followed Universal's example, they might still be as large as they once were. Who knows? And who can tell? One thing is certain, however: Hollywood still exists. It may be a different Hollywood now than it was when the pioneers first arrived back in 1913. But it's still Hollywood. And the Hollywood story still continues.

255